Psychological aspects of
physical education and sport

Psychological aspects of physical education and sport

Edited by

J E Kane

Physical Education Department, St Mary's College
Institute of Education, University of London

Routledge & Kegan Paul

London and Boston

First published 1972
by Routledge & Kegan Paul Ltd
Broadway House, 68–74 Carter Lane,
London EC4V 5EL
and 9 Park Street, Boston,
Mass. 02108, U.S.A.
Printed in Great Britain by
Western Printing Services Ltd, Bristol
© Routledge & Kegan Paul 1972

ISBN 0 7100 7207 4

Contents

Contents

Acknowledgments

The editor and publishers would like to thank the following for permission to reproduce copyright material:
Psychometrika, E. Fleishman, W. E. Hempel; Taylor and Francis Ltd; Figures and data from 'Differences in age of walking in five European longitudinal samples', C. B. Hindley et al., from *Human Biology*, 38, No. 4, 1966, reprinted by permission of the Wayne State University Press; The Journal Press and E. Pikler for material from 'Some contributions to the study of the gross motor development of children', *Journal of Genetic Psychology*, 1968; figure from E. Fleishman and S. Rich, 'Role of kinesthetic and spatial-visual abilities in perceptual-motor learning', *Journal of Experimental Psychology*, 66, 1963, 6–11. Copyright 1963 by the American Psychological Association and reproduced by permission.

Preface

The behavioural sciences have long been of interest and importance to those working in the area of physical education and sport. The psychology of learning and performance in particular, has been an area of study in which the teacher and coach have continually sought guidance as to the nature of the psychomotor abilities and skills with which they were concerned, and to the ways in which most effective performance might be achieved. The recent intensification of academic study in physical education, particularly with respect to a wide range of psychological interpretations, has been both exciting and bewildering. The excitement has come about by the possibilities and implications that open up as each new aspect of psychology is studied. The bewilderment has occurred when confusing arrays of new ideas and concepts have had to be rationally organized into coherent summaries and workable rules for the teachers and coaches.

We are apparently only at the encouraging beginnings of our understandings of the ways in which psychological knowledge may be applied in physical education and sport. At last, thanks to Fleishman and others, attempts to describe the psychomotor domains are being rigorously pursued and are beginning to provide a taxonomy of human motor abilities which will serve as a sound frame of reference. The use of models, adapted from the more recent theories of learning and performance, to explain skills acquisition, seems also to be promising. In this area, the conceptual and experimental leads provided by Welford have been invaluable. Notions emanating from the work of Fitts and Poulton have even prompted some (e.g. Cratty) to propose comprehensive theories of performance based on abilities, perception and behavioural supports. However, the implications for performance, learning and teaching in physical education and sport of the recent psychological writing with respect to development (including concept development), instruction, perception, personality, aspiration and motivation have hardly been attempted. The possibilities, for instance, of the extensive work and recommendations of Piaget, Bruner and Skinner have not, as yet, been seriously considered.

It is timely, therefore, that the present book should have been prepared in order that authoritative reviews and statements should be assembled concerning psychological interpretations relevant to physical education and sport. The fundamental and contentious issues concerning the nature of the relationship between motor aptitude and intellectual performance which have been disputed since the earliest days of physical education are revisited (Chapter 1) by A. H. Ismail in the light of his own substantial and thorough researches in this area. Five other chapters are given over to relevant reviews and implications from five major areas of psychology: perception, learning, personality, motivation and emotion. In these chapters, the authors, in their different ways, have tried to focus attention on important current research in the field, to emphasize developments that seem to be important to physical education and sport and above all they have attempted to open up these areas of psychology and give general directions for the serious student.

The chapter by Douglas Sandle presents a very welcome detailed interpretation of the psychology of qualitative movement, an area of central importance in current physical education. A critical review of researches demonstrating the psychological importance of motor skills and activities in the rehabilitation of handicapped children is given by James N. Oliver in a chapter which emphasizes the increasing recognition being given to physical education in this special area of therapy.

The book was initially planned to answer the particular needs of undergraduate and graduate students in physical education, for whom psychological interpretations of psychomotor activities and sport have become essential. No doubt many other students in education and psychology will find something here that will appeal to them.

J. E. KANE

1

Integrated development

A H Ismail

Ancient civilizations stressed the development of human qualities through the cultivation of the body and mind. Socrates stated that 'even in the process of thinking, in which the use of the body seems to be reduced to a minimum, it is a matter of common knowledge that grave mistakes can often be traced to bad health' (Van Dalen, 1953). Plato spoke of healthy bodies for healthy minds. During the seventeenth century Descartes, although he treated the individual as having two parts, namely, body and mind, yet he recognized the interaction between them. Rousseau considered the relationship between body and mind and stressed that they should be treated accordingly. He believed that in the education process if we want to cultivate the mind we must cultivate the parts which the mind governs, namely, physique.

In the nineteenth century, Wundt atomized the mind by reducing it to the elementary parts of sensations, feelings and images (Hall and Lindsay, 1957). Since then there have been continuous attempts to investigate the relationship between body and mind. Sherrington (1940) shared and elaborated on treating human organism as a unified entity by stating: 'The muscle is the cradle of recognizable mind.' On the relationship between body and mind he went on to say, 'recognizable mind seems to have arisen in connection with the motor act. Where motor integration progressed and where motor behavior progressively evolved, mind progressively evolved.'

Accordingly, body and mind are never independent; such subdivision is entirely arbitrary and unfounded. Although much remains to be learned about the brain and central nervous system, neurologists in general agree that the idea of two lives, somatic and psychic, has

1

outlived its usefulness. Thus, the psychosomatic concept of medicine recognizes this fact of biological integration and acknowledges its significance.

Theories in perspectives

A survey of some related theories is of prime importance. One is the organismic age theory by Olson (1959) which proposes that the performance of a child is associated with certain factors closely related to his total motor, emotional, social and intellectual development. He advocates that the average of a number of developmental ages such as height age, mental age, carpal age and reading age can be used to estimate the child's organismic age. It has been postulated that any available developmental measure may be used in computing the organismic age, the best components of which, according to Olson, are not yet known. Olson finds the organismic age concept useful in predicting intellectual performance, particularly during the growing years. However, Olson points out the limitations of such predictions by stating:

> While we can secure some firm generalizations about the growth of children on the average, we find that individuals may not fit these generalizations. Size, shape, strength, appearance and the timing of growth help to determine the situations in which children find themselves. They have pervasive effects that do not show up in correlation coefficients since the pattern for an individual has meanings which are different than meanings running through a group of individuals.

Along this line the Gestalt psychology has seen the necessity of considering the individual as a 'whole' within the framework of his environment. Hall and Lindsey (1957) express the feeling of the Gestaltists when they say: 'The organism always behaves as a unified whole and not as a series of differential parts. Mind and body are not separate entities, nor does the mind consist of independent faculties or elements, and the body of independent organs and processes. The organism is a single unity. What happens in a part affects the whole.' Hence educators, as well as psychologists, should recognize that development is the result of a complex interaction between hereditary, maturational and environmental domains. Educators who attempt to separate these elements are overlooking a fundamental principle of developmental psychology.

Woodworth and Sheehan (1964) acknowledge the inseparable nature of those domains when they say: 'Untangling the influences of nature and nurture is a delicate operation that is never completely successful, and on the question of their relative contributions to perceptual development, research findings can be offered in support of either position.'

Another theory is that proposed by Delacato (1959, 1963). This emphasizes the need for 'neurological organization' which, in normal children, is the result of uninterrupted ontogenetic development. Therefore, they advocate that neural patterns omitted during the neurological development of the child be introduced in order to compensate for these missing links.

A third theory, the perceptual-motor concept of Kephart (1960, 1966) stresses the complete perceptual-motor development which explains learning difficulties as a result of a 'breakdown' in the perceptual-motor development of the child.

Recently, Denny (1966) proposed a theory labeled as elicitation theory which involves stimulus (S) and response (R) in terms of the relationship between them, called response tendency (S-R). By and large, the approach adopted in developing the theory borrows heavily from Hull, Guthrie, Tolman and Skinner and hopefully represents an integration of the neobehavioristic schools.

It is a fact recognized by neurologists that in order for the organism to perceive a complex motor task correctly, all structures in the central nervous system must be fully developed and physiologically 'ready' to integrate stimulus and response patterns. Hence, all theories are built on the basic assumption that perceptual-motor training which takes advantage of the relationship between sensory processes and motor responses acts through the cortex and lower brain centers to improve perceptual and motor functions.

Motor performance provides stimulation of the central nervous system to such an extent that the underdeveloped, dead or dying cells will either be rehabilitated or their function assumed by other or newly generated cells. Joseph Altman (1968) is among those who support the possibility of neurons undergoing mitosis when he states: 'new neurons might nevertheless arise from undifferentiated precursors, embryonic cells that might differentiate, becoming neurons after multiplication.' Doman (1966) let the child rebreathe much of the air he exhaled because he claimed that 'this method of increasing carbon dioxide content at the cortical level is a well known chemophysiological aid to the cortex's making better use of the oxygen which is supplied.'

3

Steinhaus (1964) calls our attention to the fact that the most important sense organ in the body is muscle tissue, since some 40 per cent of the axons in the motor nerve to a muscle are actually sensory fibres which carry impulses to the brain. Thus, over half of our body weight, namely, muscles, serve as 'neural information' because information from the outside world is transmitted from the muscles to the central nervous system in different forms such as memory, concept formation, thinking and reasoning.

In the complexity of the relationship between body and mind, the domain of personality is often included. Sheldon (1942) has contended that there is a parallel between his somato-types and personality 'types' or there are two closely related temperaments, namely, body and personality. Cratty (1964) points out that personality theories include physical activity as a part contributing to one's personality. In addition, each theory also includes some aspect of intellect as an integral part of personality.

In summary, all propositions rest on the basic assumption that the human organism is more than the total sum of its parts. Breckenridge and Vincent (1955) provide an acceptable explanation of the 'integrated development' concept when they say:

> The individual consists of many parts which act in an integrated fashion. His intellect is related to his physical well-being; his physical health is sharply affected by his emotions; his emotions are influenced by school success or failure, by his physical health and by his intellectual adequacy. His growth—physical, intellectual and social—is product of his family history, his personal history, his current satisfactions and strains. His daily schedule affects all phases of his growth and, in turn, the pattern and speed of his growth affect his reaction to his daily schedule. What he accomplishes in school, in play or in any other part of his living is deeply and continuously affected by his physical health, by his intellectual adequacy, by his interest in his work or play, and by his emotional freedom to attend to school demands.

One important goal of science is the development of theory. The examination of any theory is an essential part in the growth of the scientific aspect of any area or field. No theory can stand indefinitely on conjecture alone; eventually it must be supported or refuted by scientific evidence. Thus, it is the intent of this chapter to examine the 'integrated development' proposition (Ismail and Gruber, 1967) for validity or falsity utilizing scientific evidence obtained through survey of related literature.

It is a recognized fact that different developmental processes, whether physical, mental or emotional are dependent on heredity and innate properties which are affected and conditioned by environmental factors. In treating the topic 'integrated development', I shall attempt to avoid discussing the effect of social or environmental conditions, rich or poor, on the motor, intellectual and personality domains. Such discussion was based on two obvious reasons which are, firstly, that very little pertinent research is available where the effects of environmental conditions on physical, mental and emotional development are studied using human subjects; and secondly, that most of the respectable research (Altman, 1966, 1968; Hebb, 1949) along this line was conducted on animals, and the inference space or generalization from animals to human beings must be treated with utmost care. Hence the interrelationships among the various domains of development presented in this chapter are dealt with under the assumption that the environmental conditions were held constant or at best desirable.

Motor and/or physical attributes usually employed

Before presenting the literature dealing with the concept under consideration, it is important to discuss the status of motor and/or physical attributes which are usually employed. The reason for such an action is that the motor and/or physical domains are often misunderstood by those who used them most frequently in their research activities.

Items geared to measure motor and/or physical fitness are frequently used. On the other hand, measurements of gross and fine perceptual-motor performance are also employed. Regardless of the usefulness of these measures, conflicting results have been achieved when correlating such measures with intellectual variables. Thus, there is an apparent need to analyze and define motor measures precisely before relating them to intellectual tasks. Furthermore, adequate description should be given pertaining to the administration of these items, including the testing situation. In addition, full description of subjects involved should yield important information in terms of both interpreting the results and making proper generalizations. More information concerning the problem associated with the assessment of motor performance measures is discussed by J. F.

5

Keogh (1964). Examples of studies devoted to either defining or clarifying motor attributes are nothing but a humble effort in the right direction. In 1927 Farmer found that the term 'motor' was too wide and suggested that a narrower view be taken and tests should be divided according to particular types of motor performance they seem to test. Along this line Seashore (1942) investigated the relationship between fine and gross motor abilities, and no overall positive relationship was found between them.

In order to define the term 'motor aptitude' Ismail and Cowell (1961) conducted a study to identify the factors which could explain twenty-five selected items that authorities claim to measure such motor aptitude. Utilizing factor analytic procedures, five independent factors were extracted and named. These factors are speed, growth and maturity, kinesthetic memory of the arms, body balance on objects, and body balance on the floor.

Bass (1939) made an analysis of balance items for the purpose of determining the different factors affecting balance. She extracted nine factors of which five were given names. These factors are general eye-motor, general kinesthetic response, general ambulatory sensitivity, function of the two vertical semicircular canals and tension-giving reinforcement. Also studying balance, Travis (1945) reported the following findings: (1) the dynamic component of equilibration is quite unrelated to static component; (2) no relation is found between balancing skill on the stabilometer and ability to maintain manually orientation of the rotation chair; (3) low correlations were found between perceptual and motor components of body orientation on the rotation chair; (4) weight is more important than height in dynamic stabilometer performance; (5) weight and height have no importance on sway scores, rotation scores, steadiness and manual pursuit; and (6) visual cues are of help in both dynamic and static equilibrium.

Using the multiple-group method of factoring, Cumbee, Meyer and Peterson (1957) investigated motor co-ordination items. They extracted nine factors and four were given names. These factors are balancing objects, speed of change of direction of arms and hands, total body quick change of direction, and body balance. As a result, it was concluded that a different definition of motor co-ordination for different age levels should be considered.

Cratty (1964) recently suggested a two-level model to explain perceptual-motor functioning. He distinguishes between constructs which are specific to the task and those of a more general nature such as ability to analyze an activity. He has further proposed the inversion of 'Vernon's Pyramid' assuming that factors at three levels influence final performance and learning output (1966a). 'General behavioral supports' which influence several kinds of human behavior, including intellectual as well as perceptual-motor abilities, are located at the base level of the pyramid. At the second level are various perceptual-motor factors spawned by factor analytic studies. At the apex of the pyramid, specific factors are situated. Thus, the conflict between specificity and generality of perceptual-motor behavior could be explained by such constructs. The work of Frank (1941) supports the concept of generality as related to the influence of level of aspiration on performance. Further, Ryan (1963) explains that the feelings of an individual about his performance potential and strivings may influence his performance and learning in a diversity of tasks. Other investigators who support the existence and importance of generality of behavior are Elizabeth Duffy (1962), Magoun (1958), Fleishman and Hempel (1954) and Cratty (1962a, b). Evidence that skilled output is also governed by factors specific to the tasks and the situation is abundant. Examples of studies supporting specificity are being conducted by Strong (1963), Henry (1960) and Namikas (1960).

In conclusion, additional research is needed to clarify the generality and specificity concepts in perceptual-motor skills, level of aspiration and other factors which might influence motor performance. For the time being, the researcher should describe the variables of interest in detail and provide evidence as to the logical relevance of each variable.

Related literature on integrated development

A great deal of literature has been accumulated on the relationship between motor, intellectual and emotional development. The literature reviewed in this chapter is selected with a view toward illustrating the status of such relationship.

According to Gates et al. (1949) the development of behavior is influenced particularly by two factors: the factor of growth and that of learning, and these are often so closely interrelated that it is impossible to separate the two. If we are to truly educate or modify any part of a child, however, it is necessary to have a clear understanding of him as a whole and this entails a clear knowledge of how each aspect of growth depends on, and interacts with every other aspect of growth. The interrelatedness of development is well described by Breckenridge and Vincent (1955).

Relationship between intellectual and motor performance

Studies dealing with retarded population

Comparing the motor proficiency of feeble-minded children with that of the normal, Sloan (1951) used the Lincoln Adaptation of Ozeretski Tests. He found that the retarded children were significantly poorer than the normal children in all the proficiency tests. The abilities tested were general static co-ordination, general dynamic co-ordination, dynamic manual co-ordination, speed and simultaneous voluntary movement. These findings were confirmed by Malpass (1960).

Turnquist and Marzolf (1954) compared two matched groups of retarded and normal children using the Lincoln-Ozeretski Motor Development Scale (L.-O.M.D.S.). At no time did the mentally retarded have an advantage over the normal groups. Significant results were obtained on synkinesia, simultaneous movement and general static components.

Rabin (1957) investigated the relationship between age, intelligence and motor proficiency in endogenous and institutionalized mental defective boys and girls. He found that age rather than intelligence or sex was related to motor proficiency of institutionalized mental defectives. Double or higher interactions among the variables of interest were found insignificant. As to the relationship between I.Q. and motor proficiency it approached significance; and he maintained that such relationship could very well be, as reported in other studies.

Kugel and Mohr (1963) studied the relationship between mental retardation and physical growth in a wide range of age (2 days to 16 years). They made the following conclusions: (1) they confirmed the existence of the relationship between mental and physical development; (2) the degree of physical impairment is related to the severity of mental retardation; further, the greater the retardation, the greater the physical growth deficiency; (3) the cause and effect relationship between mental retardation and physical growth is not clearly confirmed.

Comparing physical fitness of mentally retarded and normal boys, Sengstock (1966) used the AAHPER Youth Fitness Test. He found that the mentally retarded group was inferior to the normal children of the same age.

Recently, Verduzco (1969) investigated the relationships between motor and intellectual performance of forty-two educable mentally retarded children using factor analytic technique. In addition, he attempted to identify the motor items which have high predictive power in estimating intellectual achievement. He was able to extract and name six independent factors of which two are of interest. In the first factor labeled as 'bilateral coordination of the limbs', the Wide Range Achievement Test (WRAT) had appreciable loading with co-ordination of the lower and upper limbs. Furthermore, the second factor given the name 'growth and development', the WRAT arithmetic and reading tests had moderate loadings along with certain co-ordination and athletic performance items. In estimating intellectual performance using the motor items as independent variables, he developed five regression equations with significant correlation coefficients ranging between 0·75 and 0·85. He concluded that there was a significant relationship between motor and intellectual performance. In general, the important motor variables in predicting intellectual performance were motor co-ordination items and Ellis Visual Design Test.

Reynolds and Chalmers (1955) compared the learning ability of subnormal and normal children using the motor task of mirror drawing. They found that the normal children were superior to the subnormal. This finding was supported by Rarick and McKee (1949) when they used two extreme groups of third-grade children. The two groups were selected using a battery of physical performance tests. When the two groups were compared they found that the superior group in physical performance was also superior in scholastic ability. In another study, Francis and Rarick (1959) used 284 mentally retarded boys and girls whose ages ranged from 7·5 to 14·5 years and with I.Q. scores between 50 and 90. The retardants were compared with normal children of the same age using a battery of eleven motor performance tests designed to measure strength, power, balance and agility. The following findings were reported: (1) the trend in strength for each sex followed approximately the same pattern as those for the normal children, although at a lower level at every age; (2) the means of both boys and girls on most measures were two to four years behind the published norms of normal children; furthermore, the discrepancy between the normal and the mentally retarded tended to increase with each advancing age level; (3) intelligence was positively correlated with most of the motor performance tests. Similar results were reported by Blatt (1958).

Thurstone (1959) compared the gross motor achievement on eight motor items between mentally retarded and normal children. It was

9

found that there were significant differences between the two groups in favor of the normal children on the ball throw for distance, ball punt for distance, ball throw for accuracy, standing broad jump, side slipping, 40-yard run, right-grip strength and left-grip strength.

Using 170 mentally retarded boys, Heath (1942) found a correlation coefficient of 0·66 between mental age and beam-walking scores of endogenous (hereditary) mentally retarded children. Meanwhile, no relationship was found between motor and mental scores for the exogenous (non-hereditary) retardants. Thus he suggested the possibility of supporting etiological classification through test performance.

Relatively high correlations between I.Q. scores and motor ability traits were found by Howe (1959) and Oliver (1958). Guyette et al. (1964) reported that positive medium correlation coefficients are generally obtained between I.Q. and motor ability scores of retarded children. Further, they indicated that balance items tend to discriminate highly between normal and retarded children. Similarly, Cratty (1966b) reported a correlation coefficient of 0·63 between I.Q. and a test battery of gross motor attributes for retarded children. The test consists of the following sub-tests: body perception, gross agility, balance, locomotion agility, throwing and tackling. Furthermore, he advocated that the magnitude of this coefficient reflects the extent to which 'movement accuracy and cognition are inseparable in the retarded'.

Keogh and Keogh (1970) compared a group of educationally subnormal (E.S.N.) boys ages 9 and 10 with a group of normal school boys ages 6 through 9 on the ability to copy four simple line patterns by drawing and walking. The E.S.N. were similar to the normal 6-year-olds on both tasks and significantly worse than all other normal groups. No differences were found between walking and drawing patterns for the normal boys. However, the E.S.N. were significantly poorer in the ability to walk than to draw patterns. Both objective scores and subjective evaluation of performance suggest that the E.S.N. boys had extreme difficulty in organizing their gross movements to re-execute patterns in a larger spatial field. Thus, the gross movement patterns performed by the E.S.N. apparently is related to age, intelligence and varying conditions of disturbance or delay in development. Similar results were obtained using paper and pencil tests which were reported by Bender (1938), Frostig et al. (1961) and Koppitz (1964).

Keogh and Oliver (1966) pointed out some of the crucial problems pertaining to the relationship between intellectual and motor performance of the mentally retarded children. Their clinical observations led them to believe that the traditional method for assessing motor performance lacks accuracy due to several difficulties which are present when the child performs the motor task. The difficulties may be summarized as follows: (1) hesitating and halting movements —also difficulty in initiating movements; (2) consistent failure on one side of the body; (3) movement in one set of limbs interferes with movement in another set of limbs; (4) difficulty in initiating and maintaining movements requiring alteration of rhythm or count such as alternate foot hopping; (5) inability to control force or speed of movement; (6) inability to perform in a limited area or space; (7) inability to control extraneous or superfluous movements; (8) timid behavior and lack of effort. Consequently, they proposed that accurate description of performance should be adopted rather than scoring the events on pass or fail procedures.

In summary, it could be concluded that there is a positive relationship between intellectual (mental) and non-intellectual (motor) abilities of the retarded children, and such a relationship increases when departing from normality toward retardedness.

Studies dealing with normal population

Several studies were conducted to compare athletes with non-athletes in terms of intellectual performance. Examples of these studies are those by Snoddy and Shannon (1939) and by Reals and Rees (1959). No significant differences in intelligence were found between the two groups. In addition, neither Keeler (1938) nor Johnson (1942) were able to find a significant relationship between physical performance as measured by the Johnson Test and intelligence scores. However, reviewing several investigations dealing with relationship between athletic participation and intellectual ability in high schools, Jacobson (1931) concluded that athletes are higher than non-athletes in terms of academic achievement as measured by the school marks. Along this line similar results were obtained by McIntosh (1966) on British boys and girls. Furthermore, their academic achievement did not suffer during participation. It was pointed out by Jenny (1959) that McCloy's Motor Quotient was closely correlated with intelligence. Jenny maintained that one reason athletes sometimes make poor grades is that too much attention is given to sports and not enough is given to the classroom work.

11

The relationship between physical fitness and intellectual performance was investigated by many researchers. Weber (1953) found a significant correlation of 0·41 between physical fitness scores and grade point averages using college freshmen. Using 207 boys and 202 girls in the first grade, Kagerer (1958) found significant relationships between the Metropolitan Readiness Test scores and the two items of the Kraus-Weber Test. The two items purport to measure strength of the upper and lower back muscles. Barry (1961) examined the related patterns in freshmen students in four domains, namely, academic achievement, motivation, cardiovascular and motor fitness. Twelve factors were extracted and named, two of which are of interest. Two factors of interest were labeled 'self-inflicted-discomfort' and 'assertion-by-power' factors. In the self-inflicted-discomfort factor, grade point average has a high factor loading with other motor and cardiovascular fitness items. In the assertion-by-power factor, grade point average has a high factor loading along with assertion, self-sentiment, pre- and post-exercise systolic blood pressure, mile run and standing broad jump.

Arnett (1968) investigated the relationships between selected physical fitness items and academic achievement of college women. The physical fitness domain was measured by standing broad jump, flexed-arm hang, curl-ups and 3-minute step test, and the academic achievement was measured by the grade point average (G.P.A.). The 827 college women were classified into three fitness groups, and the grade point averages were determined for each fitness classification. Analysis of variance revealed that significant differences were observed among high, fair and poor fitness classifications in terms of G.P.A. Those who achieved higher G.P.A. also were high on the physical fitness scores. However, the magnitude of the relationship between physical fitness variables and G.P.A. was not high enough for prediction purposes.

Several studies, however, reported non-significant relationships between physical fitness and intellectual performance. Jarmon (1965) found that the multiple correlations between twenty-one physical variables and intellectual performance were too low to justify the prediction of scholastic success from physical tests. Thus, these investigators concluded that measures of height, weight, grip strength, physique type, dental age and carpal age contribute little to the prediction of academic performance. Several other investigators (Bloomers et al., 1955; Goetzinger, 1961; Klausmeier, 1958; Miller, 1962; Ray, 1940) reported low correlations between growth in terms of chronological age, height, weight, grip strength, speed, power, etc., and intellectual performance. An absence of relationship between intellectual performance and these variables was reported by Burley and Anderson (1955) and Day (1965).

For a time it appeared as though there was little relationship between mental and motor performance. Perhaps the conflict stems from the fact that researchers have erroneously put into their design those variables which would not permit an association to evidence itself. In general, studies along this line seem to indicate that the relationship between physical fitness and intellectual performance is far from being firmly established.

The relationship between physical growth and intellectual performance was investigated by several researchers. Bayley (1956) studied 61 babies in terms of growth and intelligence, and it was found that no relationship existed between the scores in the first few months of life and scores earned at the end of the first year. Consequently, it is well established that later intelligence cannot be predicted from the scores on tests made in infancy. Bloomers, Knief and Strand (1955) studied 120 pre-adolescent children using the organismic age concept. They found that measures of growth items are not related to academic achievement. Furthermore, they concluded that growth tends to proceed at the rate at which it starts out. Sontag, Baker and Nelson (1958) reported a longitudinal study and concluded that there was no relationship between physical growth rate and mental growth rate during late pre-school and early school years, from about 4 to 8 years of age. Klausmeier, Beeman and Lehmann (1958) found that height, weight, grip strength, dental age and carpal age contributed little to the prediction of arithmetic and language scores. Also, Klausmeier and Check (1959) reported that a low level of physical growth within the child does not accompany low achievement in arithmetic and reading. Furthermore, uneven physical growth does not accompany low achievement in arithmetic and reading. In addition, the children of low intelligence do not differ significantly from average and high intelligence children in terms of physical growth measures. Gleason and Klausmeier (1958) found consistent negative correlations between uneven physical growth and achievement in reading, arithmetic and language in pre-adolescent children.

Due to the insignificant relationships which appear consistently between physical growth and intellectual performance, it seems conclusive that physical growth items are poor predictors of intellectual items.

Numerous studies were conducted on the relationships between non-intellectual domain including physical growth, physical and/or motor attributes and intellectual domain including I.Q. and academic achievement scores. Again the purpose of those studies was to determine the best non-intellectual items for predicting intellectual performance. Brown and his associates (1962, 1963, 1964) embarked on a longitudinal study which started during 1960. They found that physical performance followed by emotional development make the largest non-intellectual contribution in predicting intellectual performance (arithmetic achievement and battery median). Based on his experience along this line of research, Brown (1964) concluded that the relationships between intellectual development and physical and motor performance have been greatly oversimplified. This has been largely due to the use of correlation technique where the correlation coefficients are usually inflated due to contamination by several factors. Furthermore, he believes that physical performance is a discrete developmental characteristic of children, and that there is some concomitance in the growth and maturation of the nervous system which affects both physical and intellectual performance. In addition, he maintains that longitudinal studies should be conducted involving populations of different kinds of children, and including many other physical and/or motor items, social and emotional variables in order to understand the individual as a whole. Utilizing such an approach the contribution of physical activity to the concept of integrated development could be adequately studied.

Bengston (1966) studied the interrelationships among perceptual-motor development, motor performance, school achievement and intelligence of 9-year-old boys. She found significant relationships between school achievement sub-items, word knowledge and reading, and perceptual-motor survey. The relationships between school achievement sub-items and motor performance tasks were low except for the throw for accuracy and shuttle run items. She concluded that the observed interrelationships among the motor tasks supported the theories dealing with specificity of complex movements.

From the above review of literature dealing with normal population, one might infer that the relationship between intellectual and motor performance is not definitely conclusive unlike that of the relationship between physical growth and intellectual performance. Such results motivated the writer to study this relationship in a systematic manner. Since the motor domain includes different motor items of various functions, it was deemed necessary to define such a domain operationally in a scientific manner. Undertaking this definition, the writer employed the factor analysis technique to identify the factors which different authorities claim to measure motor aptitude. As a result, Ismail and Cowell (1961) were able to define motor aptitude by the factors isolated. Five factors were extracted and named: speed and strength, growth and maturity, kinesthetic memory of the arms, body balance on objects and body balance on the floor. However, one definite shortcoming in this study was the absence of motor co-ordination items. Hence, in the follow-up studies, the writer included motor co-ordination items which were identified as an independent factor. Finally it was possible to define motor aptitude operationally by the five independent factors extracted in addition to the motor co-ordination factor. Recently, Kirkendall and Gruber (1969) established reliability and objectivity coefficients for the co-ordination items which range between 0·42 and 0·91 for reliabilities and 0·92 to 0·97 for objectivity.

After defining motor aptitude by the factor analytic technique, Ismail, Kephart and Cowell (1963) studied the relationship between motor aptitude and intellectual achievement. Using the factor analytic approach, the investigators isolated a factor called 'development'. In this factor only the Otis I.Q. Test, the Stanford Academic Achievement Test, co-ordination items and some balance items have high factor loadings. It was concluded that these items have much in common, as witnessed by the factor loadings, and they present scientific evidence supporting the theory of the individual as a 'whole' even though the motor and intellectual domains only were considered. In addition, the authors were able to predict intellectual performance utilizing motor aptitude test items. However, the degrees of freedom associated with predictions were limited, which affected the reliability of such a prediction. Consequently, the study was repeated utilizing a large number of different subjects of the same age in order to obtain better reliability.

Ismail and Gruber (1965a, b, 1967) undertook an extensive series of sequential studies on fifth- and sixth-grade children. Forty-two items gleaned from the literature were used for measuring motor and intellectual abilities. Correlation coefficients were computed between these variables for the total group, for boys and girls, and for high, medium and low achievers. The following is a summary of the matrices of intercorrelations: (1) growth (height, weight) is not significantly related to intelligence and academic achievement—except for age, which is obvious, because I.Q. is confounded with age; (2) strength, speed, power and accuracy are virtually unrelated to intelligence; however, they have some relationship with academic achievement; (3) co-ordination[1] is significantly and positively related to intelligence and academic achievement; (4) balance and kinesthetic skill are positively related to intelligence and to academic achievement in girls more than in boys; these coefficients are generally lower than those relationships between co-ordination and academic performance; (5) the coefficients for boys and girls just mentioned tend to point in the same positive direction, and the coefficients for girls are generally higher than for boys.

All correlation matrices were submitted to factor analysis in order to identify those basic factors which are present in the forty-two items selected.

The tables of factor structure for the total group, boys and girls, reveal that one factor is present in all three of these groups, namely, 'academic development', whose name is derived from those items having the highest loadings—Otis I.Q. and Stanford Academic Achievement scores. Other items which load on this factor are some co-ordination and balance items. It is also interesting to note that one of the factors identified for girls was 'co-ordination of lower limbs' on which intellectual achievement was found to load on this factor. Regardless of sex, a 'mental and motor aptitude' factor was identified in high achievers and in which I.Q., co-ordination, balance and a shuttle run were all a part of the same statistical cluster. In medium-achievers an 'academic development' factor was similarly indicated as a result of the clustering of I.Q., co-ordination and academic achievement. In general, the same factor structure was found in the low academic achievers.

The next state of this study involved computing thirty-six multiple regression equations to predict I.Q. and academic achievement in the total group, boys, girls, high, medium and low achievers. The multiple correlations ranged from 0·62 to 0·92. Hence, it is possible to predict I.Q. and academic achievement scores from a motor aptitude test battery for certain groups; whereas other groups' motor performance can be used for classification purposes based on the regression equations. The motor aptitude tests met one important criterion: they appear to be 'culture fair' tests in that they are not associated to a certain degree with undesirable emotional upset which is often present with paper and pencil testing; they do not depend on the ability to use paper, pencil or draw designs; and they promote a 'natural'

[1] Co-ordination refers to various hopping patterns utilizing one or both feet simultaneously.

testing atmosphere since the tests are administered in a play situation. The next stage of the study dealt with the determination of the relative contribution or importance of growth, strength, balance and co-ordination as predictors of intellectual achievement (see Tables 1, 2, 3). In order to attain the above objective, the total amount of variance accounted for by each regression equation was computed. The items associated with co-ordination and balance were sequentially eliminated—i.e. one group of items at a time, and then the amount of variance accounted for by the new sub-set of items was computed. Next, both balance and co-ordination items were eliminated leaving only growth, motor fitness and kinesthetic data in the prediction scheme. From the amount of variance lost or reduced by eliminating a set of items, the relative importance of any given type of items was determined. It was found that the best predictors of Otis I.Q. and Stanford Academic Achievement scores were co-ordination, balance and a combination of growth, motor fitness and kinesthetic items, in that order. These findings were achieved in the total group as well as boys and girls. Items geared to measure speed, power, strength, growth and kinesthesis have low predictive power for estimating intellectual achievement. These findings substantiate earlier work of psychologists and physical educators who found that growth and strength data added little to the prediction of intellectual achievement. However, these earlier investigators did not include measures of co-ordination, balance and kinesthesis in their research designs.

Kirkendall (1968) investigated the relationships between intellectual and non-intellectual performance. He concluded that motor co-ordination variables, especially those performed by the arms, were consistently and positively correlated with the intellectual variables.

Through the use of discriminant function techniques Kirkendall and Ismail (1969) examined the ability of motor performance variables in discriminating among 55 high, 95 medium and 55 low intellectually pre-adolescent children. It was found that the co-ordination items significantly discriminate beyond the 1 per cent level among the three intellectual groups. The items which had high discriminating power were: arms—eight counts followed by hop right and left, hop two right and two left, arms—four counts, in that order. In terms of importance, the general motor items followed the co-ordination domain. As to the balance items, they came third in the order of importance to discriminate among the intellectual groups. Finally it was concluded that the earlier results validated the findings obtained by Ismail and his co-workers.

Table 1 Results due to the application of the F-test pertaining to total group

	R^2		F	R^2		F	R^2		F
	Total Var.	Total Minus Co-ord.	d.f. (9,175)	Total Var.	Total Minus Bal.	d.f. (17,175)	Total Var.	Total Minus Bal. & Co-ord.	d.f. (26,175)
I.Q. (Otis)	0·655	0·481	9·64**	0·655	0·606	1·46	0·655	0·377	5·43**
Para. Mean. (Stanford Achiev.)	0·509	0·334	6·92**	0·509	0·425	1·76	0·509	0·175	4·58**
Word Mean. (Stanford Achiev.)	0·529	0·336	7·97**	0·529	0·458	1·55	0·529	0·195	4·77**
Arith. Reas. (Stanford Achiev.)	0·477	0·300	6·61**	0·477	0·427	1·03	0·477	0·199	3·59**
Arith. Comp. (Stanford Achiev.)	0·438	0·286	5·25**	0·438	0·363	1·37	0·438	0·160	3·33**
Total Stanford Achiev.	0·539	0·348	7·99**	0·539	0·467	1·58	0·539	0·203	4·88**

Table 2 Results due to the application of the F-test pertaining to boys

	R^2		F	R^2		F	R^2		F
	Total Var.	Total Minus Co-ord.	d.f. (9,86)	Total Var.	Total Minus Bal.	d.f. (17,86)	Total Var.	Total Minus Bal. & Co-ord.	d.f. (26,86)
I.Q. (Otis)	0·657	0·525	5·19**	0·657	0·589	1·42	0·657	0·385	2·62**
Para. Mean. (Stanford Achiev.)	0·537	0·365	3·55**	0·537	0·424	1·23	0·537	0·160	2·69**
Word Mean. (Stanford Achiev.)	0·513	0·361	2·98**	0·513	0·405	1·12	0·513	0·150	2·46**
Arith. Reas. (Stanford Achiev.)	0·465	0·320	2·59*	0·465	0·377	0·84	0·465	0·165	1·86*
Arith. Comp. (Stanford Achiev.)	0·428	0·321	1·70	0·428	0·348	0·71	0·428	0·190	1·38
Total Stanford Achiev.	0·533	0·382	3·09**	0·533	0·439	1·02	0·533	0·192	2·41**

Table 3 *Results due to the application of the F-test pertaining to girls*

	R^2		F	R^2		F	R^2		F
	Total Var.	Total Minus Co-ord.	d.f. (9,53)	Total Var.	Total Minus Bal.	d.f. (17,53)	Total Var.	Total Minus Bal. & Co-ord.	d.f. (26,53)
I.Q. (Otis)	0·840	0·720	4·42**	0·840	0·735	2·05*	0·840	0·459	4·86**
Para. Mean. (Stanford Achiev.)	0·700	0·584	2·28**	0·700	0·540	1·66	0·700	0·300	2·71**
Word Mean. (Stanford Achiev.)	0·774	0·638	3·55**	0·774	0·648	1·73	0·774	0·360	3·73**
Arith. Reas. (Stanford Achiev.)	0·732	0·605	2·79**	0·732	0·610	1·87*	0·732	0·351	2·90**
Arith. Comp. (Stanford Achiev.)	0·668	0·578	1·60	0·668	0·510	1·96*	0·668	0·280	2·36**
Total Stanford Achiev.	0·761	0·640	2·98**	0·761	0·625	1·77	0·761	0·351	3·51**

(*) Significant Reduction in Variance at 0·05 level due to the elimination of types of items.
(**) Significant Reduction in Variance at 0·01 level due to the elimination of types of items.

Using the univariate analysis Ismail and Kirkendall (1968) studied the power of discrimination of several motor domains among high, medium and low intellectual groups. They concluded that the co-ordination items in general discriminated significantly among the three discrete groups with the high intellectual group scoring higher than either the medium or low groups, in that order. The balance items as well as general motor ability items except for the 40-yard shuttle run failed to discriminate among the three intellectual groups.

Investigating the effect of statistical design on the results obtained when establishing the relationship between motor and intellectual performance, Dotson (1968) compared his canonical correlations solution with the multiple correlation results of Ismail and Gruber (1967) using the same data, concluding (1) co-ordination items were significantly related to academic performance in general; (2) low, insignificant relationships were found between academic performance and static balance, dynamic balance and general motor ability factors; (3) within academic performance in boys, girls, low-achievers and the total group the I.Q. and arithmetic reasoning variables tend to account for the underlying relationships with motor aptitude factors; (4) in high- and medium-achievers the Stanford Achievement Sub-tests tend to account for the underlying relationship between academic performance and motor aptitude factors; (5) the relationships between academic performance and the motor aptitude factors were higher in girls than boys. In summary, the multivariate and univariate solutions agree on the relationships between motor and intellectual performance.

The majority of the supportive findings pertaining to motor and intellectual developments are based on correlation techniques, and such findings should not be interpreted in terms of cause and effect relationship. Therefore, in an attempt to investigate the validity of the findings achieved by correlation, Ismail (1967) conducted an experiment at Fayetteville, Arkansas, during the year of 1964–5. The purpose of the study was to investigate the relative effectiveness of a one-year organized physical education program on I.Q. and intellectual achievement scores. Two matched groups consisting of 71 pre-adolescent children each were selected according to six criteria which included I.Q. and academic achievement scores, in addition to other criteria. A nested factorial design involving four factors was employed and the factors were sex, levels of achievement, paired subjects and groups (experimental and control). In this design, the paired subjects consisting of experimental and control groups were

21

nested under levels of achievement and sex. He concluded that an organized physical education program had no effect on I.Q. scores; however, it had a significantly favorable effect on intellectual achievement scores.

The statistically significant increase in intellectual achievement associated with the experimental group came as a slight surprise since the physical education program was conducted for a one-year duration which is relatively short. It is the writer's opinion that the effects of a quality physical education program on intellectual achievement should be much greater over a longer period of time. Speculating that the trend of improvement continues over a period of four years or more, greater difference would have been observed in favor of the experimental group. This may be due to the fact that the experimental group is exposed constantly to a better physical education program and thus develops better neurological bases for learning through two approaches, namely, the classroom as well as the gymnasium programs. Or, since the child can express himself through play activities, the psychological satisfaction of achievement through play may provide the child with additional motivation and feelings of adequacy which should assist in classroom work. At this moment the writer would like to propose that the experimental approach be adopted with children of all ages and grade levels. It is not clear what constitutes the optimum degree of exposure to an organized physical education program nor the mechanism involved which takes place due to such exposure on a child's intellectual development.

In summary, although some light has been shed on the relationship between certain motor variables and intellectual performance, this relationship has not yet been solidly confirmed relative to various motor domains except for motor co-ordination and intellectual performance. Adequate scientific evidence has been obtained as to the significant relationship between co-ordination items and intellectual performance.

Some of the difficulties which have been encountered by workers in this area are due to failure to (1) define motor items precisely; (2) define populations from which samples are drawn; (3) consider quality of measurements as well as quantity; (4) describe the testing set-up which affects performance; (5) consider previous experience of the child relative to items involved; (6) standardize directions for the administration of items involved; (7) select proper and relevant design; and (8) observe sources of biases which stem from the experimenter, the research assistants collecting data or early data returns.

Assuming that researchers correct for the above stated difficulties and others they might encounter, the relationship between motor and intellectual performance is likely to be less controversial.

Relationship between personality and intellectual measures

The investigation into the relationship between intellectual performance and personality is no different from the preceding areas discussed in that this area of endeavor has also been characterized by great diversity. Once again, the measures and experimental techniques vary from study to study and consequently reflect on the results.

Ames and Walker (1964) chose the Rorschach, given at the kindergarten level, in an attempt to predict fifth-grade reading ability as measured by the appropriate Stanford Achievement Sub-test. A correlation of 0·53 was obtained between the two measures while a correlation of 0·57 was obtained between the WISC I.Q. score given in kindergarten and the reading ability test. When both independent variables were used to compute a multiple correlation, the value of 0·73 was obtained.

Sontag, Baker and Nelson (1958) attempted to predict a future change in an intellectual variable (Stanford-Binet I.Q.) by use of a fourteen-factor personality scale which they developed. Seventy children were rated on these scales at age 6. Based upon these ratings and without knowledge of the child's present I.Q., the authors predicted whether a child was to ascend or descend in I.Q. during elementary school. The chi-square test was used to test the precision of the predictions and was found to be significantly different from chance. Aggressiveness, self-initiative and competitiveness were the best predictors for future I.Q. changes in elementary school years. In addition, the authors noted that if a child is highly dependent upon his parents, he is less apt to show an increase in I.Q.

Stagner (1933) in an attempt to predict the academic achievement and I.Q. of college students used the Allport, Laird, Moss, Neymann Kohlstedt, Thurstone and Bernreuter personality tests. In order to predict intellectual performance the Bernreuter test was used and 400 freshmen were selected as subjects. For intellectual predictions using the other personality tests, 195 upper-class college students were selected. In all cases, the intelligence test used was the American Council psychological examination and grade point average for achievement. No significant linear relationships between any of the personality tests and intelligence or achievement were found.

Lynn (1959) administered the Maudsley Personality Inventory to 115 male and 96 women university students and to 100 male apprentices and 67 female occupational therapy students. He found that the university students scored significantly higher on the neuroticism scale than the occupational group. Furthermore, the university group was less extroverted than the occupational group.

Studying 247 boys and 236 girls in the fifth grade, Semler (1960) found significant correlations ranging from 0·22 to 0·32 between scores on the Otis I.Q. and total Stanford Achievement and three measures of pupil adjustment. The measures of pupil adjustment were (1) peer acceptance as measured by the Ohio Social Acceptance Scale, (2) self descriptions as measured by the total score on the California Test of Personality (C.P.I.) and (3) teacher ratings.

Using the factors on the California Psychological Inventory, Gough (1964) developed regression equations for predicting the grade point averages of 571 high school boys, 813 high school girls and the total group. Seventeen of the eighteen correlations between the scales of the C.P.I. and academic achievement were found to be significant at the 0·01 level. In order to cross-validate the regression equations developed, they were tried out on an independent sample of 649 males and 722 female high school students. The respective predictive validities for the boys, girls and total group were 0·55, 0·55 and 0·56 in that order. Two scales of the C.P.I., namely, the Re and So, which indicate self-discipline, adherence to value and the management of impulse, were found to be consistently relevant in a positive manner in the prediction of achievement while the G_1 scale, indicating a trait of giving a good impression just for the sake of doing it, was consistently relevant in a negative fashion.

A number of researchers have investigated the personalities of over-achievers and under-achievers. Pierce (1961) studied 54 tenth- and 50 twelfth-grade boys with superior mental ability according to tests given to them in the fourth and seventh grades of school. The subjects were divided into high- and low-achievers on the basis of their academic grade performances during the preceding year. The C.P.I. was used to assess personality along with a personal interview, an interview with each boy's mother and a Parental Attitudes Research Instrument. The author concluded that high-achievers show more favorable personality characteristics, especially responsibility and tolerance. In addition, they have a somewhat higher level of motivation and are more active in achievement tasks as well as school-related activities than the low-achievers. Keimowitz and Ansbacher (1960) arrived at the same conclusion, using the same instrument, when comparing over-achieving and under-achieving eighth-grade boys. Similarly, Gill and Spilka (1962) found that 30 over-achieving high school junior and senior students were more intellectually efficient, resourceful, independent and socially mature as measured by the C.P.I. than 30 under-achieving high school juniors and seniors of comparable intellect. Using the C.P.I., Davids (1966) found the same results on high school over-achievers and under-achievers. In addition, he found the over-achievers to have more self-assurance and achievement potential.

Werner (1966) compared the scores obtained on Cattell's Children's Personality Questionnaire (C.P.Q.) by 20 boys and 23 girls who were achieving one year beyond their grade placement, and 27 boys and 17 girls 8 to 12 years of age with average performance. The over-achieving boys were more intelligent, emotionally mature, self-assured, venturesome, dominant, spontaneous and uninhibited but less conforming. The under-achievers generally showed a trend in the opposite direction. The over-achieving girls demonstrated more general intelligence, more dependency, conformity and conscientiousness, while the female under-achievers were more heedless, happy-go-lucky and acceptable than the norm group of girls. Furthermore, it was concluded that the C.P.Q. discriminated more in boys than in girls.

From the above information, it could be concluded that in general there are significant relationships between personality traits and intellectual performance. The magnitude of such coefficients are adequate for classifying individuals into different intellectual groupings. However, the amount of variance accounted for the existing relationships is not adequate for prediction purposes. In addition, Carter's (1959) conclusions of studies in this area present an adequate summary when he states:

1 For prediction of school achievement, the self-report inventories appear more promising than the projective measures which have been used.
2 There is great variation in the predictive value of the measures which have been used. Those which involved some subtlety of approach have been more effective than the inventories which have been quickly thrown together. The

correlations with measures of achievement vary from approximately zero to an upper limit which is usually not above 0·50.

3 It is clear that a variety of relatively independent predictors has been presented.

4 Measures of anxiety which have been used, so far have not been effective for prediction of school achievement. The authors of such scales have not necessarily intended them for this purpose, but other workers have tested the hypothesis that anxiety measures may predict achievement. The results tend to be negative.

5 Although the hypotheses have not been fully tested so far, there is inherent in the reports a clear suggestion that the devices which are useful for prediction of achievement will also be useful for prediction of continuation in school and completion of an appropriate program of studies, as indicated, for example, by college attendance.

Relationships among intellectual, motor and personality measures

The investigations reviewed in this section differ from those above in that variables from all three areas of interest, intellectual, motor and personality, have been measured on the same subjects. The Medford Study in Oregon has produced several studies of this nature. For example, using 95 13-year-old boys, Broekhoff (1966) administered physique type, maturity, body structure, strength and motor ability tests for the motor domain, the C.P.I. and an adjective check list for the personality domain and the Otis I.Q. and Stanford Achievement tests for the intellectual domain. When correlating intellectual and non-intellectual variables no significant coefficients were observed. However, there were significant correlations between the physical and personality variables, but in a consistently negative direction. Also, it was found that the taller boys who had high strength tended to be rebellious, defensive and uninhibited. It was suggested that the 13-year-old boy with advanced physiological development may have adjustment problems.

Another investigation growing out of the Medford Study was the one by R. M. Reynolds (1965). Personality traits as measured by the Davidson Adjective Check List were correlated with the physique, body size, strength, motor ability and mental characteristics of 215 13-year-old boys. For each adjective on the check list, the boys were divided into two groups, (1) the group which checked the adjective as describing them, or (2) the group which did not check the adjective. When comparing the two groups on the other variables in the study, boys who thought of themselves as being 'bossy' were more endomorphic and had less endurance, agility, power and speed. Those who thought of themselves as 'brats' were more endomorphic, had greater chest girth and less power. Those who checked the adjective 'bully' were more mature and less intelligent. Those who marked 'clumsy' were more mature, but weaker while those who thought they were 'cry-babies' were less mature, more endomorphic and had less strength and power. Boys who thought they were 'dependable' were superior in agility and power, while those who checked 'hard worker' were inferior in reaction time and mental ability, and those who thought of themselves as being a 'leader' were low in endomorphy, but superior in strength, agility, endurance, speed and explosive power. Finally, those who checked 'not eager to learn' or 'stupid' were in fact less intelligent.

Ruffer (1965) compared the personalities and academic achievements of 50 highly active junior and senior high school boys with the same measures of 50 other junior and senior physically inactive boys. The personality measures used were fifteen scales of the H.S.P.Q. by Cattell while the achievement measures used were the General Intelligence Scale of the H.S.P.Q. and academic grade averages. He found the highly active subjects were significantly more sociable, enthusiastic and extroverted, but also more tense than their inactive peers. In addition, the active group had significantly higher academic averages and scored higher on the General Intelligence Scale than the inactive boys.

Biddulph (1954) divided 461 high school boys into high and low athletic achievement groups on the basis of the California Classification Plan. Then the two groups were compared on the California Test of Personality, Henmon-Nelson I.Q., high school grade averages and teachers' ratings of social adjustment, scholastic achievement, attitude toward school, general appearance, grooming and positive or negative traits which best describe the student. It was reported that the superior athletic achievement group showed a higher mean score on the self-adjustment scale and the two social indices on the personality test, and were shown to have higher grade point averages than their peers. Furthermore, the upper group was rated higher on items of adjustment by teachers than was the lower group. However, it is interesting to note that no difference was shown in I.Q.

Slusher (1964) compared the personalities as measured by the

27

M.M.P.I. and I.Q.s as measured by the Lorge-Thorndike of various high school athletic groups with 100 non-athletes. The athletic groups were 100 baseball players, 100 basketball players, 50 swimmers, 50 wrestlers and 100 football players. All athletic groups scored significantly lower on the femininity scale of the M.M.P.I. than did the non-athletic group, and all athletic groups, except the swimmers, were shown to score significantly higher on the hypochondriasis scale than the non-athletes. Furthermore, the non-athletic subjects were reported to have significantly higher I.Q.s than all of the athletic groups. In addition, the author reported that the football and wrestling groups tended to have a strong neurotic profile on the M.M.P.I., while the basketball group were reportedly the most deviant of all groups studied as they displayed an overconcern with physical symptoms and a relative lack of repression.

In a correlational study, Weber (1953) obtained the relationships among scores on physical fitness, academic grade point averages, entrance examination and the nine scales of the M.M.P.I. obtained by 246 male college freshmen. The physical fitness score was a composite score made up of sit-ups for 2 minutes, 100-yard pick-a-back run and 300-yard shuttle run. The only significant correlation found was between the fitness scores and grade point averages.

Corder (1966) investigated the effect of an intensive twenty-day physical education program on intellectual, physical and social development of mentally retarded children between 12 and 16 years of age. The criterion measures were the WISC Full Scale mean scores for intellectual performance, the AAHPER Youth Fitness Test for the physical performance and the Cowell Personal Distance Scale for social behavior. The results showed significant gains on the intellectual, physical and social performance, especially between the training and control groups.

Smart and Smart (1963) used 28 nursery school children (aged 43 to 61 months) as subjects to investigate the relationship between the Kraus-Weber Adapted Test of Muscular Fitness, the Stanford-Binet, Form L-H and personality ratings by nursery school teachers. The personality variables correlated zero with age; positive, but insignificant with mental age, and significantly positive with the Kraus-Weber scores. Upon factor analyzing the correlation matrix, two factors were identified and named; those being an 'age' factor and an 'adjustment or lack of emotional disturbance' factor. The author noted that the Kraus-Weber scores had a high positive loading on the second factor.

Integrated development

Using the factor analysis technique, Kirkendall (1968) obtained a factor which was named 'intellectual performance'. He suggested that this factor might have easily been called 'integrated development'. The loadings on this factor indicated that intellectual proficiency is related to the motor co-ordination and personality traits of the child. In particular, it appeared that a child exhibiting superior intellectual ability may also exhibit a higher level of co-ordination, and his emotional traits may be described as more easy going, emotionally stable and natural than a child exhibiting a lesser degree of intellectual ability.

In a study by Klausmeier and Check (1959) four teacher personality ratings, in addition to the physical and intellectual variables, were included for the study of children 113 months of age. The investigators reported that in addition to the lack of any relationship between the intellectual and physical items, there were also no significant differences in the mean scores on any of the emotional items between intelligence levels or sex.

Brown (1964a, b) factor analyzed fifteen variables proposed to measure various aspects of intelligence, physical growth, physical performance and social-emotional traits. The measures were collected on the same 59 pupils when they were in the third, fourth and fifth grades. Factor analysis was performed at each grade. Four factors were extracted and named at grades three and four: (1) 'intellectual development' (high loadings on Otis I.Q. and the reading and arithmetic averages on the Stanford Achievement Test); (2) 'physical performance' (high loadings on standing broad jump, 50-yard dash, right- and left-hand grip); (3) 'physical growth' (high loadings on height and weight, moderate loadings on left- and right-hand grip); (4) 'emotional development' (moderate loadings on stability and social approachability scales of the SAS Personality Scale). At the fifth-grade level, the same four factors as above were extracted plus one additional factor named 'physical development' which had high loadings on weight and the Wetzel Developmental Channel. In addition, utilizing multiple regression in an attempt to predict reading and arithmetic achievement at the fifth-grade level, the author reported that physical growth and emotional development variables made the largest non-intellectual predictive contribution.

Barry (1961) using 65 university freshmen as subjects, factor analyzed twenty-nine variables measuring motivation, physical fitness and academic achievement. Twelve factors were identified and named. A factor named 'assertion by power' was extracted which had

29

high loadings on grade point average, assertion, self-sentiment, systolic blood pressure, mile run and standing broad jump.

Ismail, Kane and Kirkendall (1969) included the two scales of the Junior Maudsley Personality Inventory in addition to the motor and intellectual domains. They found that neuroticism and extroversion were loaded on four of the eight factors extracted, indicating some relationship with the motor and intellectual domains. However, the investigators were cautious about making further comment since the extent and direction of the association varied with the factor and the sex of the children.

Recently, Ismail and Kirkendall (1968) studied the discrimination power of personality traits and motor aptitude items to differentiate among various intellectual levels of pre-adolescent boys and girls. The 205 children involved were divided into three discrete groups according to several intellectual criteria. As a result, 55 children constituted the high intellectual group, 95 medium and 55 low intellectual group. The motor domain was assessed by twenty-one variables measuring athletic performance, leg and arm co-ordination and various kinds of balance items. As to the personality traits, they were measured by the Porter and Cattell C.P.Q. It was concluded that the co-ordination items in general discriminated significantly among high, medium and low intellectual groups than either balance or athletic performance variables. In addition, the three intellectual groups differed significantly on eight factors of the C.P.Q. The high-achievers were more outgoing, participating, emotionally stable, gay, venturesome, socially bold and less tender-minded than either the medium or low groups.

Little more can be added to the summary of this review of literature without becoming redundant. I conclude that the types of development—physical, intellectual, emotional and social—are not simply 'aggregates' or independent domains, but rather there are 'organic unities' among those domains. These organic unities are often characterized by the familiar dictum that they possess an organization which makes each of them 'more than the sum of its parts'. It is my opinion that researchers should devote their effort to studying the interactions—simple and complex—among the domains of development rather than the main effects, namely, the domains themselves.

Finally, it is pertinent to close with a quote from Cattell (1960) when he said:

In conclusion, I must apologize for having met your appetite for substantial findings by a rather meager serving of such actual results accompanied by a very large serving of methodological discussion. But, if I am right, research in this area has just reached the threshold of development at an entirely new level of conceptual precision, and it is most important that we cross the threshold with a more sophisticated vision of the methodological requirements and theoretical possibilities.

Bibliography

Altman, Joseph (1966), *Organic Foundations of Animal Behavior*, Holt, Rinehart & Winston, New York.
- (1968), 'The Postnatal Origin of Microneurons with Some Evidence of Their Selective Susceptibility to Harmful Environmental Influences', in Jervis, G. E. (ed.), *Expanding Concepts in Mental Retardation*, Thomas, Springfield, Illinois.
Das, G. C., and Anderson, W. J. (1968), 'Effects of Infantile Handling on the Morphological Development of the Rat Brain: an Exploratory Study', *Dev. Psychobiol.*, 1: 10–20.
Ames, Louise B., and Walker, Richard N. (1964), 'Prediction of Later Reading Ability from Kindergarten Rorschach and I.Q. Scores', *J. Educ. Psych.*, 55: 309–13.
Arnett, Chapelle (1968), 'Interrelationships between Selected Physical Variables and Academic Achievement of College Women', *Res. Q.*, 39: 227–30, May.
Barry, Alan J. (1961), 'A Factorial Study of Motivation, Physical Fitness, and Academic Achievement in College Freshmen', unpublished material, University of Illinois.
Bass, Ruth I. (1939), 'An Analysis of the Components of Tests of Semicircular Canal Function and Static and Dynamic Balance', *Res. Q.*, 10: 35–52, May.
Bayley, Nancy (1956), 'Individual Patterns of Development', *Child Dev.*, 27: 45–75.
Bender, Pauretta (1938), 'A Visual Motor Gestalt Test and its Clinical Use', *Amer. Orthopsychiat. Assoc. Res. Monogr.*, No. 3.
Bengston, Gwenn M. (1966), 'The Relationship between Perceptual-Motor Development and Motor Performance of Nine-Year-Old Boys', unpublished Master's thesis, University of Colorado.
Biddulph, L. G. (1954), 'Athletic Adjustment and the Personal Social Adjustment of High School Boys', *Res. Q.*, 25: 1–7, March.
Blatt, B. (1958), 'The Physical, Personality and Academic Status of Children who are Mentally Retarded Attending Special Classes as Compared with Children who are Mentally Retarded Attending Regular Classes', *Amer. J. Mental Deficiency*, 62: 810–18.
Bloomers, P. L., Knief, L. M., and Strand, J. B. (1955), 'The Organismic Age Concept', *J. Educ. Psych.*, 46: 142–50.

A. H. Ismail

Breckenridge, M. E., and Vincent, E. L. (1955), *Child Development*, W. B. Saunders, 4th edn, 20.

Broekhoff, Jan (1966), 'Relationships between Physical, Socio-Psychological, and Mental Characteristics of Thirteen Year Old Boys', Ph.D. dissertation, University of Oregon.

Brown, Roscoe C., Jr, (1964a), 'Prediction of School Achievement by a Developmental Index', paper presented at 79th Annual AAHPER Convention, 8–11 May.

(1964b), 'The Role of Physical and Motor Performance in Intellectual Development', *A Report-Symposium on Integrated Development*, Purdue University, June.

and Henderson, E. (1963), 'The Use of a Developmental Index to Predict Pupil Achievement', unpublished paper.

et al. (1962), 'Measuring Physical, Intellectual, and Social-Emotional Development', unpublished paper, presented at AERA, February.

Burley, L., and Anderson, R. L. (1955), 'Relation of Jump and Reach Measures of Power to Intelligence Scores and Arithmetic Performance', *Res. Q.*, 26: 28–35, March.

Carter, Harold D. (1959), 'Improving the Prediction of School Achievement by Use of the California Study Methods Survey', *Educ. Admin. Supervision*, 45: 255–60.

Cattell, Raymond B. (1960), 'Some Psychological Correlates of Physical Fitness and Physique', *Exercise and Fitness*, 138–51, Athletic Institute.

Corder, W. O. (1966), 'Effect of Physical Education on Intellectual, Physical and Social Development of Educable Mentally Retarded Boys', *Exceptional Children*, 32: 357–64, February.

Cratty, Bryant J, (1962a), 'A Comparison of the Learning of Fine Motor Skill to Learning a Similar Gross Motor Task, based upon Kinesthetic Cues', *Res. Q.*, 33: 212–21.

(1962b) 'The Influence of Small-Pattern Practice upon Large-Pattern Learning', *Res. Q.*, 33: 523–35.

(1964), *Movement Behavior and Motor Learning*, Lea & Febiger, Philadelphia.

(1966a), 'A Three Level Theory of Perceptual-Motor Behavior', *Quest*, 5: 3–10, May.

(1966b), 'The Perceptual Attributes of Mentally Retarded Children and, Youth', Department of Physical Education, University of California Los Angeles.

Crow, Lester D. and Crow, Alice (1968), *Child Development and Adjustment*, Macmillan, New York.

Cumbee, Frances Z., Meyer, M., and Peterson, G. (1957), 'Factorial Analysis of Motor Co-ordination Variables for Third and Fourth Grade Girls', *Res. Q.*, 28: 100–8, May.

Davids, Anthony (1966), 'Psychological Characteristics of High School Male and Female Potential Scientists in comparison with Academic Underachievers', *Psychology in the Schools*, 3(1): 79–87.

Day, James Albert (1965), 'Relationships Between Intelligence and Selected Physical, Motor and Strength Characteristics of Boys Nine, Thirteen and Seventeen Years of Age', Master's thesis, University of Oregon.

Delacato, Carl H. (1959), *The Treatment and Prevention of Reading Problems*, Thomas, Springfield, Illinois.

—— (1963), *The Diagnosis and Treatment of Speech and Reading Problems*, Thomas, Springfield, Illinois.

Denny, M. Ray (1966), 'A Theoretical Analysis and its Application to Training Mentally Retarded', in Normal R. Ellis (ed.), *International Review of Research in Mental Retardation*, Vol. 2, Academic Press, New York.

Doman, Glenn (1966), Lecture given at the Institute for the Achievement of Human Potential on 10 January.

Dotson, Charles O. (1968), 'An Investigation of Multivariate Test Criteria and their Application to Integrated Development Components', Ph.D. dissertation, Purdue University, August.

Duffy, Elizabeth (1962), *Activation and Behavior*, Wiley, New York.

Farmer, J. (1927), 'A Group Factor in Sensory Motor Tests', *Brit. J. of Psych.*, 17: 327–34.

Fleishman, E. A., and Hempel, W. E., Jr, (1954), 'Changes in Factor Structure of a Complex Psychomotor Test as a Function of Practice', *Psychometrika*, 19: 239–52.

Francis, R. J. and Rarick, G. L. (1959), 'Motor Characteristics of the Mentally Retarded', *Amer. J. Mental Deficiency*, 63: 792–811.

Frank, J. D. (1941), 'Recent Studies of the Level of Aspiration', *Psych. Bull.*, 38: 218–26.

Frostig, M., Levever, D. W., and Whittlesey, J. (1961), 'A Developmental Test of Visual Perception for Evaluating Normal and Neurologically Handicapped Children', *Perceptual & Motor Skills*, 12: 383–94.

Gates, A. I., Jersild, A. T., McConnell, T. R., and Challman, R. C. (1949), *Educ. Psych.*, Macmillan, 3rd edn.

Gill, Lois J., and Spilka, Bernard (1962), 'Some Nonintellectual Correlates of Academic Achievement among Mexican-American Secondary School Students', *J. Educ. Psych.*, 53: 144–9.

Gleason, G. T., and Klausmeier, H. J. (1958), 'The Relationship between Variability in Physical Growth and Academic Achievement among Third and Fifth-Grade Children', *J. Educ. Res.*, 51: 521–7.

Goetzinger, Cornelius P. (1961), 'A Re-Evaluation of the Heath Rail-Walking Test', *J. Educ. Res.*, 54: 187–91.

Gough, Harrison G. (1964), 'Academic Achievement in High School as predicted from the California Psychological Inventory', *J. Educ. Psych.*, 55: 174–80.

Guyette, Anna, Seymour, W., Henry, W., and John, D. (1964), 'Some Aspects of Space Perception in Mental Retardation', *Amer. J. Mental Deficiency*, 69: 90–100, July.

Hall, Calvin S., and Lindsey, Gardner (1957), *Theories of Personality*, Wiley, New York.

Heath, Roy S. (1942), 'Railwalking Performance as related to Mental Age and Etiological Type among the Mentally Retarded', *Amer. J. Psych.*, 51: 240–7, April.

Hebb, D. O. (1949), *The Organization of Behavior*, Wiley, New York.

33

A. H. Ismail

Henry, Franklin (1960), 'Increased Reponse Latency for Complicated Movements and a (Memory Drum) Theory of Neuromotor Reaction', *Res. Q.*, 31: 24–33.

Howe, C. (1959), 'A Comparison of Motor Skills of Mentally Retarded and Normal Children', *Exceptional Children*, 35: 352–4, April.

Ismail, A. H. (1967), 'The Effect of an Organized Physical Education Program on Intellectual Performance', *Res. in Phys. Educ.*, 1: 31–8, June.

— and Cowell, C. C. (1961), 'Factor Analysis of Motor Aptitude of Preadolescent Boys', *Res. Q.*, 32: 507–13, December.

— (1967), *Motor Aptitude and Intellectual Performance*, Merrill, Columbus, Ohio.

— and Gruber, J. J. (1965a), 'Predictive Power of Coordination and Balance Items in estimating Intellectual Achievement', *Proceedings of 1st International Congress on Psychology of Sport*, Rome, April.

— (1965b), 'Utilization of Motor Aptitude Tests in predicting Academic Achievement', *Proceedings of 1st International Congress on Psychology of Sport*, Rome, April.

Kane J., and Kirkendall, D. R. (1969), 'Relationships among Intellectual and Non-Intellectual Variables', *Res. Q.*, 40: 83–92, March.

Kephart, N., and Cowell, C. C. (1963), *Utilization of Motor Aptitude Test Batteries in Predicting Academic Achievement*, Technical Report No. 1, Purdue University, Research Foundation, August.

— and Kirkendall, D. R. (1968), 'Comparison Between the Discrimination Power of Personality Traits and Motor Aptitude Items to differentiate among Various Intellectual Levels of Preadolescent Boys and Girls', paper presented at the National Association for the Advancement of Science, Dallas, Texas, December.

Jacobson, J. M. (1931), 'Athletes and Scholarship in High School', *School Rev.*, 39: 280–7.

Jarmon, Boyd O. (1965), 'Interrelationships between Academic Achievement and Selected Maturity, Physique, Strength and Motor Measures of Fifteen Year Old Boys', Ed. D. dissertation, University of Oregon.

Jenny, John H. (1959), 'The M. Q. is as Important as I. Q.', *J. HPER*, 30: 3, April.

Johnson, G. B. (1942), 'A Study of the Relationship that exists between Physical Skill and Intelligence as measured by the General Intelligence of College Students', *Res. Q.*, 13: 57–9.

Kagerer, R. L. (1958), 'The Relationship between the Kraus–Weber Test for Minimum Muscular Fitness and School Achievement', unpublished Master's thesis, Purdue University.

Keeler, L. D. (1938), 'The Effect of Maturation on Physical Skill as measured by the Johnson Physical Skill Test', *Res. Q.*, 9: 54–8.

Keimowitz, R. I., and Ansbacher, H. L. (1960), 'Personality and Achievement in Mathematics', *J. Individ. Psych.*, 16: 84–7.

Keogh, B. K., and Keogh, J. F. (1970), 'Pattern Copying and Pattern Walking Performance of Normal and Educationally Subnormal Boys', *Amer. J. Mental Deficiency*.

34

Keogh, J. F. (1964), 'Motor Performance Measurement Problems when examining Relationship of Motor and Intellectual Functioning', *A Report-Symposium on Integrated Development*, Purdue University, June.

and Oliver, J. N. (1966), 'Physical Performance of Retarded Children, Diagnosis and Prescription', paper presented at the Joseph P. Kennedy, Jr Foundation—Scientific Symposium on Mental Retardation, Boston, Massachusetts, 11 April.

Kephart, Newell C. (1960), *The Slow Learner in the Classroom*, Merrill, Columbus, Ohio.

(1966), 'The Needs of Teachers for Specialized Information on Perception', in Cruickshank, William M. (ed.), *The Teacher of Brain-Injured Children*, Syracuse University Press, New York, 171–80.

Kirkendall, D. R. (1968), 'The Relationships among the Motor, Intellectual, and Personality Domains of Development in Pre-adolescent Children', Ph.D. dissertation, Purdue University, August.

and Gruber, J. J. (1969), 'Consistency of Arm and Leg Coordination Measures', unpublished material, University of Kentucky.

and Ismail, A. H. (in press), 'The Ability of Motor Performance Variables to Discriminate among Three Intellectual Groups of Boys and Girls', *Res. Q.*

Klausmeier, H. J. (1958), 'Physical, Behavioral, and Other Characteristics of High and Lower Achieving Children in Favored Environments', *J. Educ. Res.*, 51: 573–82.

Beeman, A., and Lehmann, I. J. (1958), 'Comparison of Organismic Age and Regression Equations in Predicting Achievement in Elementary School', *J. Educ. Psych.*, 49: 182–6.

and Check, J. (1959), 'Relationships among Physical, Mental Achievement, and Personality Measures in Low, Average, and High Intelligence at 113 Months of Age', *Amer. J. Mental Deficiency*, 63: 1059–68.

Feldhusen, J., and Check, J. (1959), 'An Analysis of Learning Efficiency in Arithmetic of Mentally Retarded Children in Comparison with Children of Average and High Intelligence', School of Education, University of Wisconsin, Madison, August.

Koppitz, Elizabeth M. (1964), *The Bender-Gestalt Test for Young Children*, Grune & Stratton, New York.

Kugel, R. B., and Mohr, J. (1963), 'Mentally Retarded and Physical Growth', *Amer. J. Mental Deficiency*, 68: 41–8, July.

Lynn, R. (1959), 'Two Personality Characteristics related to Academic Achievement', *Brit. J. Educ. Psych.*, 29: 213–16.

Magoun, H. W. (1958), *The Waking Brain*, Thomas, Springfield, Illinois.

Malpass, L. F. (1960), 'Motor Proficiency in Institutionalized Retarded and Normal Children', *Amer. J. Mental Deficiency*, 64: 1012–15.

McIntosh, P. C. (1966), 'Mental Ability and Success in School Sport', *Res. in Phys. Educ.*, 1: 20–7, October.

Miller, Jeffrey O. (1962), *A Study of the Relationships between Certain Fitness Variables and an Index of Scholastic Standing in a Selected*

A. H. Ismail

Sample of N.S.W. Public Secondary School Children, M.Ed. thesis, University of Sydney.

Namikas, G., and Archer, E. J. (1960), 'Motor Skill Transfer as a Function of Inter-Transfer Test Difficulty', *Exp. Psych.*, 59: 109–12.

Oliver, J. N. (1958), 'The Effect of Physical Conditioning Exercises and Activities on the Mental Characteristics of Educationally Sub-normal Boys', *Brit. J. Educ. Psych.*, 28: 155–65, June.

Olson, W. C. (1959), *Child Development*, D. C. Heath & Co., Boston, 2nd edn, ibid. pp. 220–1.

Pierce, J. V. (1961), 'Personality and Achievement Among Able High School Boys', *J. Individ. Psych.*, 17: 102–7.

Rabin, H. M. (1957), 'The Relationship of Age, Intelligence, and Sex to Motor Proficiency', *Amer. J. Mental Deficiency*, 62(3): 507–11, November.

Rarick, G. L., and McKee, R. (1949), 'A Study of Twenty Third-Grade Children Exhibiting Extreme Levels of Achievement on Tests of Motor Proficiency', *Res. Q.*, 20: 142–52.

Ray, Howard C. (1940), 'Interrelationships of Physical and Mental Abilities and Achievements of High School Boys', *Res. Q.*, 11: 129–41, March.

Reals, W. H., and Rees, R. G. (1959), 'High School Letter Men—Their Intelligence and Scholarship', *School Rev.*, 47: 534–7.

Reynolds, Robert Monti, (1965), 'Responses on the Davidson Adjective Check List as Related to Maturity, Physical and Mental Characteristics of Thirteen-Year-Old Boys', Ph.D. dissertation, University of Oregon.

Reynolds, W. F., and Chalmers, L. S. (1955), 'Comparison of Normals and Sub-normals in Mirror Drawing', *J. General Psych.*, 87: 301–8.

Ruffer, William A. (1965), 'A Study of Extreme Physical Activity Groups of Young Men', *Res. Q.*, 36: 183–96, May.

Ryan, Dean E. (1963), 'Relative Academic Achievement and Stabilometer Performance', *Res. Q.*, 34: 185–90.

Seashore, H. (1942), 'Some Relationship of Fine and Gross Motor Abilities', *Res . Q.*, 13: 259–74, October.

Semler, I. J. (1960), 'Relationship among Several Measures of Pupil Adjustment', *J. Educ. Psych.*, 51: 60–4.

Sengstock, W. L. (1966), 'Physical Fitness of Mentally Retarded Boys', *Res. Q.*, 37: 113–19, March.

Sheldon, William H. (1942), *The Varieties of Temperament*, Harper & Bros., New York.

Sherrington, Sir Charles (1940), *Man on His Nature*, Cambridge University Press, p. 213.

Sloan, W. (1951), 'Motor Proficiency and Intelligence', *Amer. J. Mental Deficiency*, 55: 394–406.

Slusher, Howard S. (1964), 'Personality and Intelligence Characteristics of Selected High School Athletes and Non-Athletes', *Res. Q.*, 35: 539–45.

Smart, R., and Smart, Mollie (1963), 'Kraus-Weber Scores and Personality Adjustment of Nursery School Children', *Res. Q.*, 34: 199–205.

Snoddy, L. M., and Shannon, J. R. (1939), 'Standardized Achievement Measurements of Athletes and Non-athletes', *School Rev.*, 48: 610–12.

Sontag, L. W., Baker, C. J., and Nelson, V. L. (1958), 'Mental Growth and Personality Development: A Longitudinal Study', *Monogrs. of the Soc. Res. Child Dev.*, 23: 1–143.

Stagner, Ross (1933), 'The Relationship of Personality to Academic Aptitude and Achievement', *J. of Educ. Res.*, 26: 648–60.

Steinhaus, Arthur (1964), 'The Role of Motor in Mental and Personality Development', *A Report-Symposium on Integrated Development*, Purdue University, June.

Strong, C. H. (1963), 'Motivation related to Performance of Physical Fitness Test', *Res. Q.*, 34: 497–507.

Teuber, Has-Lakas (1965), 'Exploring Brain Functions', National Institute of Mental Health Research Project Summaries, No. 2, *Public Health Service Publications*, No. 1208–2, pp. 39–44.

Thurstone, Thelma Gwinn (1959), 'An Evaluation of educating Mentally Handicapped Children in Special Classes and in Regular Classes', Cooperative Research Project Contract #OE-SAE,6452, U.S. Office of Education, School of Education, University of North Carolina.

Travis, R. C. (1945), 'An Experimental Analysis of Dynamic and Static Equilibrium', *J. Exp. Psych.*, 35: 216–34.

Turnquist, D. A., and Marzolf, S. S. (1954), 'Motor Abilities of Mentally Retarded Youth', *Journal of AAHPER*, 25: 43–4, March.

Van Dalen, D. B., Mitchell, E., and Bennett, B. (1953), *A World History of Physical Education*, Prentice-Hall, New Jersey.

Verduzco, Roger (1969), 'The Relationship Between Motor and Intellectual Performance among Educationally Subnormal Children', unpublished material, Purdue University, August.

Weber, Robert J. (1953), 'Relationship of Physical Fitness to Success in College and to Personality', *Res. Q.*, 24: 471–4, December.

Werner, Emmy E. (1966), 'CPQ Personality Factors of Talented and Underachieving Boys and Girls in Elementary School', *J. Clin. Psych.*, 22: 461–4.

Woodworth, Robert S., and Sheehan, Mary R. (1964), *Contemporary Schools of Psychology*, Roland Press, New York.

2

Perception and movement behavior

Bryant J Cratty

Researchers in psychology, education and physical education have, within recent years, begun to take a closer look at relationships between perception and movement. The frequent appearance of such terms as perceptual-motor and sensory-motor is indicative of the fact that the various stimulus conditions supportive of motor output are more and more being scrutinized by various scholars. Some of the findings arising from studies in which the perceptual bases of motor activities have been explored offer obvious guide-lines for the improvement of instruction in motor skills, while other information emanating from these investigations contributes to more basic understandings of how humans perceive and move.

Perception and movement behavior is considered in several contexts within this chapter. For example I have attempted to delineate just how these two facets of the human personality function independently; and conversely, the ways in which various perceptual attributes interact directly with observable actions might be reviewed.

The subject has also been approached developmentally. Various ways in which perceptual processes and motor processes mature and interact in the changing infant and child have also been explored in the following pages (Cratty, in press).

Another way in which movement behavior and perceptual processes may be studied is to determine the interaction of attributes denoting efficient management of input, during the learning of a gross or fine motor skill. Investigations of this type have produced information important to those attempting to improve movement efficiencies of children and adults. The data from research of this nature are also summarized in the following discussion (Fleishman and Hempel, 1954).

Critical to a coherent discussion of this nature is the formulation of reasonably acceptable definitions of perception and motion. In general, perception may be defined as the process of organizing and interpreting sensory information. Movement as used in this discussion refers to observable activity of the skeletal muscles. In general, the material which follows will be primarily concerned with two types of sensory stimulation that are received via the visual apparatus and information arising from the sensory end organs in the muscles, tendons and joints. The perceptions of a more global nature, i.e. the total self-concept, or the performing 'self', which might also be covered in an essay of this type, have been excluded from this chapter. Similarly, space will not be devoted to summarizing research dealing with olfactory and auditory sensations as their interactions with voluntary movement are rather oblique.

Developmental aspects of perception and motion

Some writers have speculated that perception and motion in the developing infant are inseparable. It has been written that adequate perceptual development is directly dependent upon the acquisition of adequate motor competencies and that if the infant lacks movement capacities and/or is denied movement experiences, he will likely evidence concomitant perceptual inadequacies. Piaget and others have argued for the imperative nature of the sensory-motor period which undergirds the ability to interpret and to think (Kephart, 1960; Piaget, 1954).

It is believed that this type of 'lamination theory' is not adequate to explain the complexities of human maturation. Nor is it adequate to explain intellectual competencies seen in children and adults whose movement capacities are either lacking or have been seriously impaired. In a text by the author a more elaborate theoretical framework through which to explain the development and interactions of perceptual and motor attributes was attempted (Bower, 1966). To summarize, it was proposed that the attributes of the infant and child can be conceived of as developing along several parallel channels. The child matures verbally, motorically, perceptually and cognitively. These channels undergo a diffusion or branching as the child grows older, as new attributes appear. At the same time, as maturation continues, numerous bonds are formed between attributes contained within various of these four attribute channels.

It was also proposed that some of these bonds may tend, as the child ages, to become obliterated in order to facilitate more efficient functioning.

It is believed that reviewing some of the experimental evidence which supports this 'lattice-work' theory may reveal the manner in which various perceptual attributes are related to indices of motor development in the maturing infant. Furthermore, it is believed that the available evidence makes it clear that at times certain visual perceptual abilities emerge, proliferate and evolve relatively independent of any type of movement behaviour or motor skills.

One example of the manner in which movement and visual perception first develop independently and then later become welded together in various ways is illustrated in the emerging drawing behavior of infants and children (Cratty and Duffy, 1967).

During the first days of birth it has been demonstrated that infants can visually discriminate between various geometric figures placed over their crib. Later, at about the age of 8 months, the child begins to 'exploit objects' in various ways as he hits blocks together, stacks them and in general finds different things to do with them. These manipulative attributes proliferate, and when his 18th month is reached he will usually begin to find that when manipulating one classification of objects (crayons and pencils), interesting marks may be made on available tables, walls and sometimes even on paper.

Not until the age of 3 to 4 years, however, will sufficiently numerous and strong bonds be formed between the infant's previously developed ability to discriminate perceptually between the characteristics of geometric figures and his ability to draw them in an accurate manner with his pencil or pen. Indeed, one of the first geometric figures *perceptually* recognized by the infant seems to be the triangle, while this same three-sided figure is one of the last which can be accurately inscribed on paper via *motor* output. Not until about the age of 6 or 7 can children draw accurate triangles, while they may be 8 or older before symmetrical diamonds are drawn (Cratty and Martin, 1969).

This same phenomenon of early independent development of perceptual and motor attributes, followed by their later welding together, is illustrated by data from studies in which infants have been asked to discriminate between solid three-dimensional figures including cylinders, cubes and spheres. By the age of 20 *days*, it has been found that infants are able to discriminate between the shapes of these figures, as well as between objects having three dimensions and two-dimensional figures, discs, squares and the like (Bower,

1966). And yet, not until about the age of 10 *years* can children be expected to draw these same figures accurately (Judd, 1908).

Further evidence of the complex interactions between intelligence, attitude, as well as perception and motion are revealed to us when we administer a drawing test to children with perceptual-motor problems in our program at the University of California (Los Angeles) (Cratty and Martin, 1969). Essentially the child must copy, in correct order, a number of figures superimposed on each other so that the final drawing looks like this (Cratty and Martin, 1969).

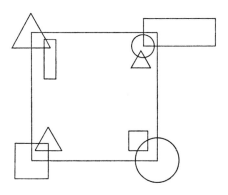

The task starts as the tester draws the larger square, and then the child must follow. Second, a triangle is added to one corner by the tester, and again the child must attempt to replicate it exactly. The results of just these initial two sub-tasks are often revealing of the complexities of neuromotor functioning. For example, if the child produces a drawing like this:

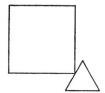

it may be due to the fact that he cannot guide his hand effectively and/or to the fact that he cannot perceive the similarities between the two figures. So that in the former case one child realizing that he could not control his hand effectively, said that he had 'drawn a rock'. This same child when asked if the two figures looked the same said they were not. Thus he was deficient in only one perceptual attribute, i.e. the ability to guide his hand visually, while in his ability to compare visually the differences and similarities inherent in the two forms he evidences no difficulty.

Another child might produce a drawing like this when asked to copy the original figure

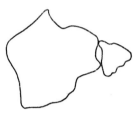

thus evidencing either of two other difficulties. He may not be able to perceptually organize the up-down, left-right of his space field with accuracy, or upon questioning him, it might be discovered that he doesn't feel that it really makes any difference! Thus in the first case the child is exhibiting a perceptual deficit, while in the second simply his *attitude* about the exactitude with which he should copy the two figures, and their relationship to each other has altered his rendition. A spoon is a spoon to a 4-year-old child, whether it is hanging on the wall, lying on a table or resting on the floor. Many children of this age see no reason why numbers and letters must be structured within exact spatial limits (i.e. an E facing to the right, etc.), even though they are able to perceive differences between an E and an X.

Another possibility in this copying task of course, is a drawing in which the child evidences both an inability to copy the figures correctly, as well as perceptual deficits relative to gross left-right, up-down orientation, resulting in a figure like this:

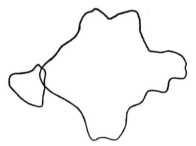

Even more dramatic is the manner in which perceptual and motor attributes become bonded as children learn to intercept small balls which are projected at them from some distance. Again the perceptual components of the task seem to emerge prior to the motor competencies required. Also, similar to the examples outlined above, the final bonds between the appropriate perceptions and motions are formed several years from the dates at which the necessary motor and perceptual components appear separately in the child (Williams, 1967).

The infant is attracted briefly by moving objects at birth. By the age of 6 months he can usually track, using both eyes together, the movements of objects over his crib in both vertical and horizontal directions through arcs of about 90°. Later, at about the age of 1 year, he learns how to walk, and by 2 years will evidence rudimentary running (Peiper, 1963). During his second year, if the opportunity arises, he may trap a large ball lofted to his outstretched arms by his interested parents. But by the age of 5 and 6 he still has little idea of where small balls projected from a distance will finally terminate. Not until the age of 9 or 10 years, according to the research by Williams[1] can children move accurately and quickly to the location of small balls projected in their direction at some distance; objects which they may have been capable of visually tracking perfectly by the age of about 6 months (Williams, 1967).

Other examples also confirm this kind of uneven maturation of perceptual and motor attributes in infants and children, with the visual perceptual development usually preceding the maturation of motor competencies.

As children mature there are numerous instances which might be cited in which bonds previously formed between perceptual and motor traits are 'erased'. For example, the infant at 1 year must carefully visually monitor his moving feet as he makes his first tentative efforts to walk. However by the age of 2 or 3 years this type of visual-motor bond has disappeared in the normal child, and he no longer has to watch his alternate foot movements during his efforts at locomotion. Many other simple and complex tasks when first mastered by the infant require that strong bonds by formed between visual-perceptual

[1] In this investigation children from 6 to 12 years of age were tested in their ability to predict the terminus of a ball projected so that they could only view the initial part of the arc. The children were placed, one at a time, under a large roof; they viewed a ball-throwing machine at the end of the roof, and after the ball was projected, they attempted to run to the spot under the roof where they felt the ball would land (if the overhead roof did not stop it). The subjects stood on switches connected to the ball-throwing machine, and to a stop-clock, so that reaction time as well as the accuracy of their responses could be determined.

processes and movement; while their later performance is not apparently dependent upon an inordinate amount of guidance from his eyes.

In addition to the formation and dissolution of bonds between various perceptual-motor attributes it also seems apparent that a marked dependence upon one channel of attributes (i.e. vision) may tend to blunt the development of the other channel (i.e. movement). At the same time, if the maturing child engages in too much movement (is hyperactive) it may impair the development of attributes within the other channels.

The findings from the research by Burton White and Richard Held offer evidence of the possible interference of visual activity with motor development (White and Held, 1958). Babies exposed to experimental conditions which included an inordinate amount of handling and visual displays of various types (i.e. watching stabiles placed over the crib), evidenced an average *delay* of the onset of hand regard of over 3 weeks as compared to infants who had not been exposed to this type of visual environment.[2]

In nearly every study in which the activity level of children with learning and/or reading difficulties has been compared to measures of activity evidenced by normal children, it has been found that hyper activity is more prevalent in the former (Cratty and Martin, 1969). Nancy Bayley found that the relatively inactive male baby during the middle of his second year tends to be more intelligent in childhood and adolescence (Bayley, 1968).

Evidence from a variety of studies has purported to substantiate the fact that motor experience is imperative to perceptual development in children and infants. The advocates of this type of perceptual-motor theory usually state that *direct interaction* with the environment in qualitative and quantitative ways is necessary for the complete perceptual maturation of the young.

The classic studies of Held and his colleagues at MIT have been referred to frequently to substantiate the preceding hypothesis. In a number of interesting investigations they have explored what has been termed the influence of 'self-induced movement' upon the emergence of various perceptual attributes in both animal and human subjects (Held, 1965). When animals (i.e. cats) have been

---

[2] It was found, however, that once the visually-enriched group began to engage in manipulative behavior the measures obtained were larger quantitatively than those for children whose visual surroundings had been more bland.

employed they have been placed in situations in which they are either walking and looking, or could simply look at their surroundings.[3]

In general it has been found that simple visual-motor responses, including eye blink to approaching objects, are elicited only in the animals who had been given the opportunity to both walk and look while traveling within the confines of a large cylinder. When adult subjects are employed the influence of 'self-induced' (i.e. initiated and controlled by the subject himself) movement is assessed as the subject attempts to resolve various visual distortions created by looking through distorting lenses. As in the animal studies, subjects who were permitted to walk through the experimental environment wearing the lenses were better able to resolve various visual-motor distortions caused by the lenses than were subjects who were wheeled through these environments. In similar studies humans who were permitted to move their hands under prisms were better able to locate the intersection of grid lines while observing them through the same prisms than were subjects who had their hands moved for them while they watched through the same lenses.

Although Held and his colleagues at first suggested that basic visual-motor integrations occur in the lower levels of the mid-brain, it has been suggested, as the result of more recent experiments, that these integrations occur at higher levels in the neurocortex (Held and Mikaelian, 1964; White and Held, 1958). When Judd and others in similar experiments afforded their subjects information to *think* about the amount of distortion that was occurring, they found that resolution of these distortions could also be resolved (Judd, 1908). Kilpatrick, as a result of experiments in which distorted rooms were used, suggested that perceptual organization occurs in two primary ways. Some percepts may be the result of direct motor interactions with the environment, while others may be made vicariously by inspecting and thinking about the forces, movements and other phenomena in space caused by the efforts of others (Kilpatrick, 1946).

French, upon polling subjects concerning how they made judgments about space, suggested that there are two ways to achieve high scores on various perceptual tests, (1) to analyze cognitively the situation with which an individual is confronted, and/or (2) to interpret sensory information without conscious effort (French, 1965). It is probable that children as they mature engage in both processes, depending upon the type of perceptual judgment which

[3] The animals are reared in the dark prior to being placed in the experiment.

they are required to make and unique experiences and capacities which they possess.

Olin Smith, after finding that perceptual judgments in children are divisible into several distinct and independent factors,[4] suggested that perceptions concerning near space and depth (the relative distances of objects in relation to the perceiver) may be aided by locomotor and manipulative activity, while judgments of distance (the relative distances between objects in space) are the result of separate perceptual processes (Smith, 1966).

In summary, the available data concerning the perceptual-motor relationships in the maturing infants suggests that visual-perceptual attributes mature before the motor abilities to which some of the former may later be paired. The successful early development of skills dependent upon visual-motor co-ordinations are heightened by the formation of helpful bonds between perceptual and motor attributes, previously independent of one another. As the skill becomes engrained into the memory of the child, however, its performance may be marked by the apparent dissolution of a formerly helpful perceptual-motor bond. He no longer must watch every movement of his hand as his handwriting gains fluidity nor must he fixate more than once per word as he gains proficiency in reading; just as he needs no longer to observe his running feet as he passes into middle childhood (Cratty, in press).

It appears that while the development of some perceptual attributes may be dependent upon movement experiences, the efficient human animal may also structure his space field without direct physical contact with his environment. While this latter 'tactic' is more likely to be employed by the child whose motor capacities may be blunted in some way, the normal child may also quickly and accurately perceive objects in three-dimensional space without the need for direct contact even before he acquires capacities for efficient manipulation and/or locomotion (Bower, 1966).

Physical educators, when attempting to develop sports skills with normal youngsters or to improve the movement attributes of atypical children, must at times aid in the formation of helpful bonds between perceptual and motor attributes, as they teach them, for example, to track and to intercept the soaring ball. At other times they must help the child to become more efficient by 'erasing' bonds between vision and movement which may elicit less efficient functioning, i.e.

---

[4] Visual acuity, visual tracking, distance perception, depth perception, fractionalizing space, etc.

watching the hand while writing or inspecting the feet while walking and running.

Educators attempting to improve the perceptual-motor functioning of children should also be well acquainted with the manner in which various movement attributes mature, and proliferate due to ageing. At the same time they should become familiar with the literature dealing with ocular maturation and the maturation of perceptual functions. Movement may aid in the development of certain perceptual attributes, but to be scholarly one should delineate precisely what specific perceptual attributes may be modified by just what types of movement experiences.

Motor learning and perceptual functioning

A number of studies have supplied information important to educators concerning the interactions between motor learning and perception. In general it has been the intent of the investigators to delineate the relative importance of a number of perceptual and motor factors during various stages in the learning of complex skills. Fleishman, for example, has analyzed the manner in which various factors elicited from a variety of tests contribute to the early, intermediate and final stages of the learning of various co-ordination tasks requiring the integration of visual information with hand and foot movements (Fleishman and Hempel, 1954; Fleishman, 1957; Fleishman and Parker, 1962; Fleishman and Rich, 1963; Freedle, 1968).

The usual finding is that, early in learning, various perceptual factors make more significant contributions to the performance scores elicited than do motor factors. During the final stages of learning the motor factors assume paramount importance. For example, it appears that scores evaluating such qualities as the performer's ability to organize mechanical principles, to make various judgments concerning the spatial dimensions of the task are more important during the time the individual begins to learn about the motor task. It is during the first part of the learning process that he is deciding upon the strategies he will employ when attempting to master it and the precepts he formulates are more dependent upon his intelligence and the perceptual attributes he brings with him to the task than on his capacities for movement (see Figure 1).

As the task is mastered, errors eliminated and speed and accuracy are achieved, movement capacities exert more influence upon performance levels reached. Scores in tasks evaluating kinesthetic judgments, movement speed and reaction time are more likely to correlate to the performance measures obtained from the complex co-ordination tasks employed in these investigations than are the scores from measures of perceptual accuracy as was true during the initial stages of learning.

In perhaps the most important investigation in motor learning Fleishman attempted to determine whether an application of these findings would result in significantly better terminal learning. It was assumed that if different factors were important to various stages of learning, that instructional cues comparable to the factors which were important at various stages would result in significantly higher performance being reached at the final trials (Fleishman and Parker, 1962).

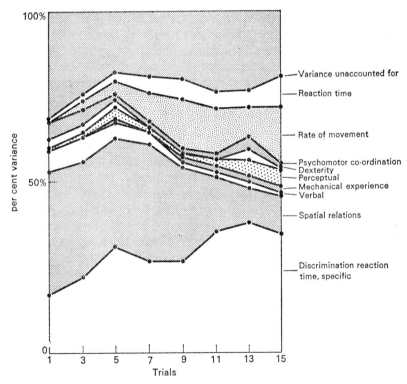

Figure 1 Percentage of variance represented by each factor at different stages of practice on the Discrimination Reaction Time Task.
(Percentage of variance is represented by the *area* shaded in for each factor.) After Fleishman and Hempel (1955).

48

It was thus attempted to insert instruction during the initial stages which emphasized the spatial dimensions of the task, its mechanical principles and other qualities which had been researched as important initially. During the middle and final trials instruction designed to anticipate the emergence of important factors was afforded the experimental group. The findings supported the hypotheses. Instructional cues varied in this manner exerted a significant influence upon final performance.

Only a relatively few experimental tasks have been analyzed in this exact manner, and thus are amenable to this kind of flexible instruction. However, in further investigations a variety of sports skills might be investigated in a similar manner, and following this kind of analysis, guide-lines for more effective instruction should be forthcoming.

In more recent studies within this same experimental program, individual differences in learning have been explored (Fleishman and Rich, 1963). The learning curves of subjects scoring well on perceptual tests have been compared to similar measures obtained from subjects who scored high on tests evaluating motor competency. As might be expected, the progress of the two learning curves in the two comparisons were different. The subjects who were adroit perceptually evidenced initial quick improvement but levelled off during the later stages of learning; while the reverse trend was noted in subjects whose motor competency outweighed their perceptual efficiency. In this latter group their initial progress was relatively slow, but as the demands of the task began to coincide with the attributes they possessed in abundance, their performance curves rose markedly (Figure 2).

Other authors have become interested in the ways in which individual differences influence the learning of motor and intellectual skills. An important difference in people apparently seems to be the perceptual attributes they bring with them to a task. Further investigations should further illuminate just what visual perceptual attributes are important in the initial stages of a greater variety of perceptual-motor tasks (Gagne, 1967).

Data of this nature presents several important lessons for physical educators and for others interested in the improvement of movement attributes in education, industry and in the maturing infant. For example, it is apparent that teaching strategies should be varied not only from task to task, but also as various stages of learning within an individual task are reached. Over-teaching is a traditional detriment

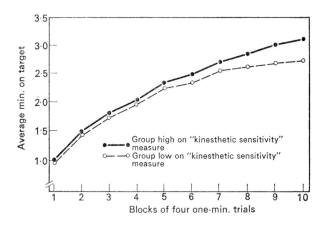

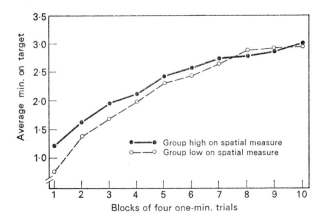

Figure 2 Comparison of two-hand co-ordination acquisition curves for groups high and low on spatial ability and kinesthetic sensitivity. Data from Fleishman and Rich (1963).

to acquiring proficiency in motor skills; it is probable that fewer but more appropriate instructional cues will do more to hasten improvement in athletes and school children than will rigid adherence to preconceived methods of teaching in which little variation is shown. Furthermore, this kind of information also suggests that teachers should take into account individual differences when teaching skills. They should not be discouraged, for example, when little initial improvement is recorded by some of their students, for in fact these individuals may later 'blossom' as their capacities for movement coincide with the demands of the task, after early stages of learning are passed.

Kinesthetic and visual feedback

Visual control in skill

A reasonably strong case can be made for the fact that all voluntary movement is undergirded by perceptual processes. This kind of statement receives substantial support if the definition of perception includes the duration, intensity and/or velocity of movement. For all complex voluntary movements are dependent upon the manner in which the individual 'blends' the initial portions of the movement into the task components which follow.

In a similar manner when complex tasks are performed slowly and/or they are learned initially, they are usually visually monitored. A number of interesting research programs have explored the interaction of vision and movement during the execution of complex motor tasks. K. U. Smith and his students at Wisconsin, for example, have evolved a theory largely from data emanating from studies in which various types of visual distortions have been visited upon individuals attempting to learn and to perform a variety of complex motor skills (Smith, K. U. and Smith, W. M., 1962; Smith, K. U. and Smith, M. F., 1966). And while the neurogeometric theory of human motion they propose has been subjected to critical reviews by several scholars,[5] the findings have pointed to the exact ways in which visual inspection contributes to the performance of motor tasks.

[5] Howard and Templeton and others have criticized the experimental protocols used by Smith as failing to discriminate between several possibly influential variables, i.e. displaced vision and the location of the arm completing the task, etc. The space receptors referred to by Smith in the formulation of his theory are also somewhat difficult to locate within the human nervous system (1966).

Elaborate apparatus has been employed in these studies including television equipment which is used to delay, invert and/or reverse the image transmitted to the subject as he views his hand moving through the task. By placing the observing camera in various locations relative to the subject and to the task it has been possible apparently to remove the subject's eyes from their heads! For example, it is usually found that if the visual feedback emanating from the task is in the least distorted as the subject is permitted to inspect his efforts, there is likelihood that disruptions of the motor components of the task will also occur. These investigations have pointed out that not only are the spatial qualities of the task important as the individual monitors his own movements but have also illustrated that of even greater importance are the temporal aspects of the performance situation. Severe disruption in motor performances have been achieved when, through the use of a video-tape playback arrangement, the visual feedback upon which the individual depended when performing the various tasks was delayed by a short period of time (Smith, K. U. and Smith, W. M., 1962).

Although the theoretical findings arising from these experiments by Smith and his students are controversial, their data makes it apparent that motor performance is highly specific, and that co-ordinated actions are influenced in rather exact ways by the nature of the temporal and spatial interactions between vision and movement.

Kinesthesis

Studies of kinesthesis have appeared for years in the experimental literature. Indeed, the initial studies of psychophysics by Wundt in the last century were of just noticeable differences in hand-held weights, a measure of kinesthetic perception (Wundt, 1894).

As experimenters gained knowledge and obtained more sophisticated measuring equipment additional information was gained concerning the so-called 'muscle sense'. Guthrie and others based entire learning theories upon assumptions gained from studies of kinesthesis. They suggested that knowledge was stored in the form of kinesthetic impressions derived from thoughts translated into lip and tongue movements used when forming words (Guthrie, 1952).

By the turn of the century basic information was collected by Goldscheider and others which remained relatively unaltered when similar qualities were explored by scholars in the 1920s and 1930s (Goldscheider, 1898). Measures of the 'position sense' were obtained when the subject positioned or moved his own limbs (active movement), and when the subject's movements were under the control of the experimenter (passive movement). Perceptions formed about the extent, speed, angular and linear velocities, accuracy of limb positioning, the replication of tension and similar qualities of limb and body movements were researched. Analysis of the data revealed that indeed kinesthetic perception was not a unitary but a multi-dimensional human attribute (Scott, 1955). It was not often that significant correlations were obtained between the measures obtained in studies in which several tests of kinesthesis were employed. For example, it was not possible to predict the accuracy with which a subject could position a small circular dial with his hand and when this same subject positioned a similar but larger mark which required arm movement.

It is also probable that the neurological mechanisms controlling the various movement sensations are dependent upon the complexity of the pattern the individual is attempting to reproduce, as well as the speed with which the action is to be replicated. Recent findings relative to the gamma efferent system suggest that muscular tensions contributing to fine adjustments of rapid complex movements are not consciously 'called up' from the individual's memory bank of learned skills, but function at the reflexive level (Howard and Templeton, 1966).

Thus if complex movement is practised slowly during the initial stages of learning, the manner in which kinesthetic impressions unite to contribute to the total gestalten may be controlled by different neuro-anatomical structures than those controlling the more rapid execution of the movement.

Further recent studies suggest that kinesthetic impressions may be transitory and easily distorted by just previous movement experiences (Cratty and Hutton, 1964; Cratty and Duffy, 1967). Jackson, for example, found that holding an arm position for as short a time as 5 seconds significantly alters the accuracy with which an individual can reposition the same arm (Jackson 1954). Studies in our laboratory have produced similar findings. It is usually found that rather marked distortions of the sense of position can be produced if the individual is required to hold a prior position for a time (usually about 20 seconds produces maximal distortion). The reader may attempt one of these experiments in kinesthetic after-effects by first holding his arms out horizontally to the front, elbows straight and even with each other. Following this initial brief positioning, he may then place one arm

45° above the horizontal and the other 45° below the horizontal and hold this position for from 15 to 25 seconds (eyes may be closed or open at this point). After this second position has been held, he should then try, with his eyes closed, to reposition his arms to the horizontal again, attempting to make them parallel with each other. Inspection of the results of the final attempt should convince anyone that unless both the duration of time between positionings in standard tests of kinesthesis, and the positions which the limbs assume between measured attempts to relocate a position are controlled and specified, the data emanating from studies of kinesthesis are questionable, to say the least. Nevertheless studies in which these variables have not been controlled still appear in the literature (see Figure 3).

A number of studies have been carried out in which an attempt has been made to 'heighten kinesthetic sensitivity' to various sports skills through blindfolded practice. In general, the findings from these studies have not proved supportive of blindfolded practice as a teaching technique.

The investigations of the various parameters of kinesthesis suggest that it is a complex and relatively inaccurate type of perception, and thus attempting to somehow heighten movement sensations by instituting practice methods in which vision is eliminated are less than promising. With further study important teaching guide-lines may emerge, particularly when the role of the various sensory receptors within the muscle spindles, joints and tendons are more fully explored.

The term 'movement sense', however, seems to be incorrect. One should rather refer to a total classification of specific impressions involving various dimensions of movement sensitivity. Until the interactions of these movement sensations with themselves and with other facets of sensory input are more fully understood, valid principles applicable to the teaching of sports skills and physical education are at best difficult to formulate, and at worst could produce confusions and impediments to learning.

The complexity of the movement sense is revealed in the extensive list of kinesthetic judgments contained in the text by Howard and Templeton (1966), including threshold of movement; position judgment, and repositioning judgments; threshold of direction of passively moved limbs; accuracy of direction of passively moved body parts; judgment of amplitude of passive movements; judgment of speed of movements controlled by experimenter; steadiness of movement; accuracy of the reproduction of muscular tension;

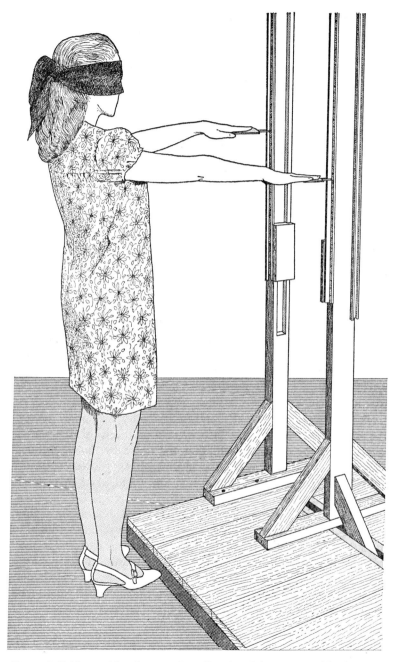

Figure 3 Subject evidencing an after-effect involving arm positioning.

accuracy of direction of movements initiated by the subject; and accuracy of speed of movement controlled by the subject.

The accuracy of the kinesthetic judgments obtained from experiments of this nature are also influenced by the peripheral muscular fatigue which may be present, the amount of ancillary muscular tension evidenced by the subjects, just where within the space field (relative to the subject) the measurement is obtained, as well as the speed with which the judgment must be made. The direction of the movement (relative to the subject's body) is also a relative variable, as are the personality traits of the subjects and their previous experiences in movement.

In general it is found that more accurate judgments of the position sense are made within the space field adjacent to the visual apparatus, immediately in front of the body. Athletes seem able to reproduce muscular tension better than non-athletes. If judgments in reproducing repetitive movements of various lengths are made rhythmically, a speed of more than 40 beats per minute will likely result in a decrease in accuracy.

Perceptions of both complex and simple movements arise from a number of peripheral and central neural mechanisms. The so-called 'somesthetic' area of the brain contains areas which mediate movement, while stimulation of the body-image area of the motor cortex usually results in a rather global report of movement sensations on the part of the subject. Complex movement responses are the result of total neuromotor 'program' contributed to by the motor cortex, the somesthetic areas, the associational portions of the cortex activated by the reticular formation and timed by the cerebellum. This involvement of virtually the entire brain suggests complicated ways in which movements are sensed and acquired as perceptual-motor activities.

It is possible, for example, as gymnasts and dancers have long believed, that conscious concentration on limb positions and bodily attitudes will heighten performance. These same performers may heighten position sensations by wearing tight-fitting clothing during performances which seem to make them more aware of their bodies by combining tactual (the touch of cloth on skin) with kinesthetic sensations arising from the joint receptors. However, verification of these assumptions awaits further research.

Summary

The research reveals many subtle and obvious interactions between perceptual attributes and movement behaviors of various kinds. Developmentally it seems that the infant evidences behaviors in which movement and several components of visual-perceptual perception interact in helpful ways, and at the same time evidences a proliferation of visual-perceptual attributes which operate independently of emerging capacities for movement. The extent to which various components of visual perception and movement may pair is thus dependent upon the age of the child, the nature of the task and the practice the child has received in the task.

In general, perceptual attributes seem more important in motor learning during the initial stages of task acquisition. At the same time experimental evidence demonstrates that exact knowledge of the relative importance of various perceptual and motor factors can contribute to more effective teaching and to higher levels of final performance in perceptual-motor skills.

Kinesthetic perception is, upon consulting the available research, a rather imprecise term. At the same time, specific measures of kinesthesis are transitory and easily influenced by a number of variables, including just prior movements and positions held. Blindfold practice does not seem to hold as much promise for skill acquisition as does effectively pairing visual information gained from self-observations of limb and body positions with the 'feel' of the movements themselves derived from the various kinesthetic receptors.

Bibliography

Bayley, Nancy (1968), 'Behavioral Correlates of Mental Growth, Birth to Thirty-Six Years', *Amer. Psych.*, Vol. 28, No. 1, 1–17, January.
Bower, T. G. (1966), 'The Visual World of Infants', *Scientific American*, 215: 80–97.
Cratty, Bryant J. (in press), *Perceptual and Motor Development in Infants and Children*, Macmillan, New York.
and Duffy, Kirt (1967), 'Relationships Between Figural After-Effects elicited by Selected Bodily Movements, Part I', monograph, University of California, Los Angeles.
and Hutton, Robert S. (1964), 'Figural After-Effects resulting from Gross Action Patterns', *Res. Q.*, 35: 116–25.
and Martin, Margaret Mary (1969), *Perceptual-Motor Efficiency in Children*, Lea & Febiger, Philadelphia.

Bryant J. Cratty

Fleishman, Edwin A. (1957), 'A Comparative Study of Aptitude Patterns in Unskilled and Skilled Psychomotor Performances', *J. Appl. Psych.*, 41: 54–63.

(1967), 'Individual Differences and Motor Learning', in Gagne, R. M. (ed.), *Learning and Individual Differences*, Merrill, Columbus, Ohio.

and Hempel, Walter E., Jr (1954), 'Changes in Factor Structure of a Complex Psychomotor Test as a Function of Practice', *Psychometrika*, 19: 239–52.

and Parker, J. F., Jr. (1962), 'Factors in the Retention and Relearning of Perceptual-Motor Skills', *J. of Exp. Psych.*, 64: 215–26.

and Rich, Simon (1963), 'Role of Kinesthetic and Spatial-Visual Abilities in Perceptual-Motor Learning', *J. of Exp. Psych.*, 66: 6–11.

Freedle, Roy Omer, Azvala, Albert, and Fleishman, Edwin A. (1968), 'Studies of Component-Total Task Relations: Order of Component-Total Task Practice and Total Task Predictability', *Human Factors*, 19: 3, 283–296.

French, J. W. (1965), 'The Relationship of Problem-Solving Styles to Factor Composition of Tests', *Educ. Psych. Measurement*, 25: 9–28.

Gagne, Robert M. (1967), *Learning and Individual Differences.*, Merrill, Columbus, Ohio.

Goldscheider, A. (1898), 'Physiologie des Muskelsinnes: Gesammelte', *Abhandlungen*, 2.

Guthrie, E. R. (1952), *The Psychology of Learning*. Harper & Row, New York.

Held, Richard (1965), 'Plasticity in Sensory-Motor Systems', *Scientific American*, 213: 5, 1–9.

and Mikaelian, H. (1964), 'Motor-Sensory Feedback Versus Need in Adaptation to Rearrangement', *Perceptual & Motor Skills*, 18: 685–8.

Howard, I. P., and Templeton, B. (1966), *Human Spatial Orientation*. Wiley, New York.

Ilg, Frances L., and Ames, Louise Bates (1965), *School Readiness*, Harper & Row, New York.

Jackson, C. V. (1954), 'The Influence of Previous Movement and Posture on Subsequent Posture', *Q. J. Exp. Psych.*, 6: 72–8.

Judd, C. H. (1908), 'The Relationship of Special Training to General Intelligence', *Educ. Rev.*, 26: 28–42.

Kephart, Newell C. (1960), *The Slow Learner in the Classroom*, Merrill, Columbus, Ohio.

Kilpatrick, F. P. (1946), 'Two Processes in Perceptual Learning', *J. Exp. Psych.*, 36: 187–211.

Peiper, Albrecht (1963), *Cerebral Function in Infancy and Childhood*, Consultants Bureau, New York.

Piaget, Jean (1954), *The Construction of Reality in the Child*. Basic Books, New York.

Scott, M. Gladys (1955), 'Measurement of Kinesthesis', *Res. Q.*, 26: 324–41.

Smith, Karl U., and Smith, William M. (1962), *Perception and Motion*, W. B. Saunders, Philadelphia.

and Smith, Margaret Foltz (1966), *Cybernetic Principles of Learning and Educational Design*. Holt, Rinehart & Winston, New York.
Smith, Olin W. (1966), 'Development Studies of Spatial Judgments by Children and Adults', *Perceptual & Motor Skills*, 22: 3–73. Monograph Supplement I-V22.
Weinstein, S., Sersen, E. A., Fisher, L., and Weisinger, M. (1964), 'Is Re-Afference Necessary for Visual Adaptation?' *Perceptual & Motor Skills*, 19: 641–8.
White, Burton L., and Held, Richard (1958), 'Plasticity of Sensorimotor Development in the Human Infants', in Harlow, H., and Woolsey, C. (eds), *Biological and Biochemical Bases of Behavior*, University of Wisconsin Press, Madison.
Williams, Harriet G. (1967), 'The Perception of Moving Objects by Children', unpublished study, Perceptual-Motor Learning Laboratory, University of California, Los Angeles.
Wundt, W. (1894), *Lectures on Human and Animal Psychology*. Sonnenschein, London.

3

Learning motor skills

H T A Whiting

The proliferation of research findings in the motor skill area in recent years and in particular, the comprehensive overviews presented in standard textbooks (Knapp, 1964; Holding, 1965; Bilodeau, 1966; Fitts and Posner, 1967; Welford, 1968; Whiting, 1969) makes the task of presenting a comprehensive survey within the scope of a single chapter an impossible one. Instead, a decision has been made to select some general areas of interest and to draw on relevant literature which in the main has not been collated in any one place. In so doing, it is hoped that the reader will have another viewpoint of the field of study to add to those which he will obtain by reference to the standard works quoted.

The decision to limit this chapter to the learning of motor skills is primarily dicated by the need to focus attention on one particular category of human performance. It should not necessarily imply that the learning of motor skills is essentially different from the learning of verbal skills, social skills or perceptual skills. In many ways—and particularly from an explanatory point of view—the designation motor skills is a misnomer since it would be difficult to think of any skilled behaviour in which only efferent activity was involved.

Fitts and Posner (1967) distinguish between perceptual-motor skills and language skills but at the same time recognize that both categories involve perceptual and motor abilities in their performance. Welford (1968) suggests that a distinction is commonly drawn between sensory-motor and mental skills but that such differentiation is difficult to maintain completely. The subject is further complicated by Elkind and Weiss's (1967) contention that patterns of visual exploration (which would normally be classed as perceptual learning)

60

are in effect, motor skills. Thus, decisions to delimit particular areas of human performance would appear to be dictated by the need to adopt a classifactory system which brings some meaning and order into what is virtually the totality of overt behaviour. In talking about motor skills in this chapter, attention is being focussed primarily on those tasks in which the motor aspects of the skill are dominant. At the same time, it is implicitly accepted that such skills involve afferent as well as efferent activity.

The important relationship which exists between the perceptual and motor aspects of skilled performance is emphasized by Argyle and Kendon (1967) in defining skill as 'an organised, co-ordinated activity in relation to an object or a situation which involves a whole chain of sensory, central and motor mechanisms'. A definition as general as this can be applied to all categories of skills. It is however interesting to note that Argyle and Kendon are primarily concerned with the acquisition of social skills.

Fitts (1964) has discussed a number of models which have usefully been established as an aid to the understanding of the process of skill learning and human performance. One of the most useful and heuristic models is that developed by such workers as Crossman (1964) and Welford (1968). This model reflects a systems-analytic approach emphasizing the links between perceptual, translatory and effector systems and their related feedback loops. A similar model has been adopted by Whiting (1969) in relation to the acquisition of ball skill.

In discussing the learning of motor skills, the concern is with bringing about changes in skilled behaviour. Learning can in fact be considered to be the process underlying the change in behaviour itself (Gagne, 1963) or in the potential for such change. The latter statement emphasizing that learning does not always manifest itself as a change in behaviour at the time when learning is deemed to have taken place. Performance—as will be demonstrated below—is manifested behaviour. It does not necessarily accurately reflect the learning which may have occurred. Inferences about such learning from observed behaviour should be made with caution although such behaviour will generally reflect the learning that has taken place.

Learning and performance

The distinction made in the literature between learning and performance is largely the outcome of modern learning theory (Eysenck,

1965). It is not difficult to understand the need for such differentiation—particularly outside the artificial laboratory situation—when the number of variables which contribute to overt behaviour are called to mind.

Perhaps the easiest way to clarify the issue is to give an example of the way in which groups of subjects performing a primarily motor task under different conditions of practice produce radically different performance curves (Figure 1). The two matched groups of subjects performed under either massed or distributed practice on the Minnesota Rate of Manipulation Test for a total period of 10 minutes. This task requires that 1-inch diameter pegs be removed from a hole turned over and replaced. A specially constructed board contains rows of such pegs and the subject is required to proceed from hole to hole in some prescribed sequence. The conditions of massed practice were 30 seconds work and 10 seconds rest and of distributed practice, 10 seconds work and 30 seconds rest. Although the performance of the massed practice group is markedly inferior to that of the distributed practice group, it would be wrong to infer that the one group had learned more than the other. This is demonstrated when after a rest period following on the 10-minute work session, the massed practice group are made to perform under distributed conditions and the distributed group under massed conditions (Figure 1). It is worth drawing attention to the relatively short periods of work and rest in both the massed and distributed practice sessions. These are typical of the times reported in studies dealing with the phenomenon. It would be difficult to use similar explanations to those found in the literature for longer periods of work and rest typical of physical education situations and perhaps more appropriately referred to as 'block practice' (see Holding, 1965).

Reminiscence

A phenomenon related to massed practice which manifests itself in tasks of a repetitive nature such as that described, is reminiscence, defined differentially as 'increments in *learning* which occur during a rest period' (Hovland, 1951) and 'a temporary improvement in *performance* without practice' (Osgood, 1958) (my italics). (An example of reminiscence is apparent in Figure 1 when the massed practice group after a rest period begin work on the task once again.) Eysenck (1965) has attempted to resolve the distinction being made by postulating that memory-trace consolidation (a learning pheno-

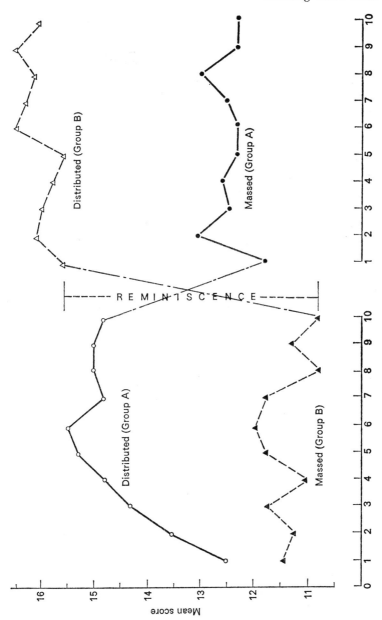

Figure 1 Effects of massed and distributed practice on performance of the Minnesota Rate of Manipulation Test (Barrett, Davies, Hart and Woods, 1966).

63

menon) and reactive and conditioned inhibition (performance phenomena) contribute differentially to the process of reminiscence— the relative contributions of such processes being task specific. It is further proposed that differences in drive conditions, personality, fatigue, drug administration and other variables have important bearings on reminiscence. Stelmach (1968) has attempted to verify experimentally Eysenck's (1965) three-factor theory of reminiscence using a large muscle motor task in the form of a ladder climb. The experiment attempted to interfere with the consolidation process by giving subjects additional tasks to perform in the rest intervals. The findings of this experiment did not support Eysenck's interpretation but it is possible that the task used was not suitable for testing the hypothesis.

The effects of massed and distributed practice in the terms described in the experimental psychology literature do not appear to have been exploited in the area of skill acquisition in a physical education context. Where links have been attempted, it would appear that experimentalists are considering largely different phenomena. It is possible that there is no direct carry over of the effects of massed and distributed practice and reminiscence as described in the laboratory situation to the kind of skill in which physical educationalists are primarily interested. In considering this effect on performance, physical educationalists should bear in mind that such effects are in the main confined to taks of a repetitive nature using work and rest periods of very limited duration. Interpretation of the effects of such practice are largely in terms of a central (brain) effect rather than a peripheral one based on actual energy expenditure. It may well be that the laboratory interpretation would apply to the kind of repetitive training situation involved in athletics and swimming which is commonly referred to as 'interval training' but this is a hypothesis which has yet to be substantiated (Whiting, 1963).

Performance curves

Although examples of learning curves are still reported in the literature it will be appreciated that a more correct terminology would be that of performance curves. The rate at which motor skills are acquired and the subsequent level of performance achieved is limited by the previous experience of the individual, the characteristics of the task set (e.g. relative degree of difficulty) and personal variables (musculature, nervous system, personality, etc.). Thus, it would be expected that individual performance curves would differ in terms of initial starting point, rate of learning and final level of performance. Such differences are reflected in the individual results of a ball-catching task (Figure 2) with limited opportunities for viewing the ball in flight (Whiting, Gill and Stephenson, 1969). It is important in this context to differentiate between backwardness reflecting a failure to produce performance of which the individual should be capable and that of the inherently slow-learner. The latter person may show a rate of learning well below that of his contemporaries but in as far as this reflects the rate of which he is capable, he cannot be considered to be backward (Tanner, 1961).

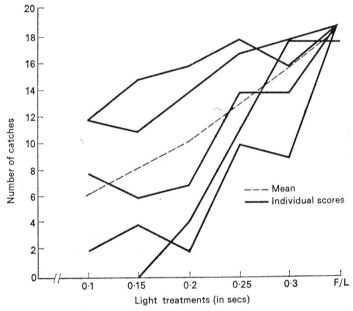

Figure 2 Individual differences in performance on a ball-catching task under restricted viewing conditions (Whiting, Gill and Stephenson, 1969).

Plateaux in performance

In the past, many workers in the field of skill acquisition have reported plateaux—periods of no apparent improvement—in the performance of their subjects. Some of the earliest reports of this nature were the results of the classic experiments by Bryan and Harter (1897) on the sending and receiving of morse code and Book

H. T. A. Whiting

(1925) on the acquisition of skill in the use of the typewriter. While (as Fitts and Posner (1967) point out) later investigators support the findings from these experiments of a progression from perception of letters to the perception of words, they found little evidence that improvement in performance ceases as the shift is being made. Such plateaux may therefore be artefacts of the way in which the experiment was carried out or more particularly the way in which the results were monitored. There is, however, another consideration which needs to be pointed out. Performance curves usually reflect the results of individuals or groups on particular criterion measures *in which the experimenter is interested*. Where plateaux do occur in such performance curves, it may well be that there is a period of no apparent improvement *on that particular criterion* but it does not follow that the subject is not improving his ability to perform on some other unrecorded variable which contributes to total task improvement. This point is illustrated by the individual curves of performance (Figure 3) obtained on a continuous ball-throwing and catching task (Whiting, 1967) where plateaux are apparent on the criterion variable

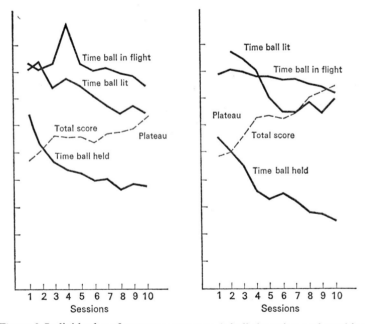

Figure 3 Individual performance curves on a ball throwing and catching task (Whiting, 1967).

(total score) but other aspects of performance (time ball was held, time ball in flight, etc.) continued to show improvement. Thus plateaux might equally well be artefacts of the particular response variables on which the experimenter chooses to focus.

Learning and teaching

In spite of close on a century of the most elaborate laboratory experimentation and attention to the learning process, the contribution of such findings to the educational field has been very limited. Part of this difficulty must lie with the failure of experimental psychologists to consider teaching in relation to learning. This particular failing has been highlighted by Meredith (1967) as follows:

> Now it is sometimes scientific to attend to one thing at a time and to ignore other things so long as the things ignored exert only a negligible influence on the thing studied. But to treat learning as if it were unaffected by teaching suggests a large and quite astonishing blind spot in the conceptual framework of the learning theorists.

The role of the teacher in the learning of motor skills is not always easy to define. At one extreme, if the opportunity to learn a particular skill is not presented then the skill obviously cannot be acquired, while at the other extreme, the presentation of the opportunity to learn a particular skill can often result in the attainment of proficiency at the skill even in the absence of a teacher. While many skills are acquired fortuitously in this way in everyday life, teaching of a more formal kind normally makes a fundamental contribution to the learning process and imposes limitations both on what skills are learned and the level to which they are developed.

To talk of skills being acquired fortuitously, hides a wealth of implication. What is meant here, is that the role of an identifiable teacher of such skills is minimal. In order for any skill to be acquired, the individual must inherently have the potential for acquiring such behaviour and the environment must provide the opportunity for that particular skill to be developed. The question whether the role of the teacher is primarily that of structuring an environment in which learning might take place (such as Montessori, 1912, 1949, in particular advocated) leaving the individual relatively free to choose his activity and teach himself or to dominate the learning situation cannot be answered categorically. It will depend amongst other things on the stage of learning reached, the particular skills in which interest lies, the methods and the objectives which the educator has in mind. It may also depend on the end product in which the teacher is interested and to what extent he considers the way in which the skill is acquired to be more or less important than the end gained.

In some instances, combinations of opportunity together with minimal teaching may be all that is necessary for the learning to take place. This type of procedure is utilized by Wassef ('Pendennis', 1969) working in the primitive village of Harrania in Egypt. He has demonstrated impressive examples of Egyptian tapestries produced on looms by children recruited without selection and apparently never having seen any work of art. He teaches the children only the basic rudiments of weaving and lets them get on with it. Such a procedure is reminiscent of 'social facilitation' (Thorpe, 1963) and its usage is probably more universal than might be expected. It is manifested for example in many of the children's programmes on television where demonstrations are given of the construction of simple models and toys. Seldom do children sit down to follow exactly the stages in the procedure or to make notes on the instructions. Instead, they get a general idea of what is intended and at some later stage proceed to acquire the necessary skill in their own construction of the model.

Perhaps nowhere is the dichotomy between a formalized system of training and an experimental creative approach more apparent than in the division which exists between the teaching of gymnastics by the so-called education gymnastics approach (Pallett, 1965) and that of the traditional approach (although a parallel probably exists in the teaching of foreign language skills in which there has been a major revolution in the past few years). The difficulty has not been resolved and in terms of skill level achieved probably will never be. Good performances in gymnastic skills are produced by both methods. The fundamental question once again, is the criterion on which success is being measured. If this goes beyond the aim of producing top-level gymnasts and concerns itself more with allowing individuals to proceed at their own level and by their own methods, the choice is a more obvious one.

The other major bone of contention is that of giving children a wide general movement experience as against teaching them specific skills or, more accurately, specific activities such as those used in gymnastics, athletics, games, outdoor activities and dance. There is perhaps less argument about the usefulness of the former procedure than on the age at which it should take place. Much of the difficulty over this question arises from a failure in the main factorial studies to show up a general factor of human performance (Fleishman, 1964). It must however be recalled that most of such studies have been carried out with adolescent children and adults. It would be dangerous to extrapolate from such findings to younger age groups. Learning is a hierarchical process. During the early months of a child's development its whole education is based upon movement experience. While it is not possible to demonstrate unequivocally the value of wide movement experience or what this would imply in specific terms, some indication can be had from examining the deleterious effects which ensue when an organism is deprived of movement experience (Newton and Levine, 1968). It is possible that limitations imposed by restricted environments—such as most children experience—leads to the development of particular abilities such as Fleishman (1967) describes. This should not however lead educationalists to suppose that different opportunities and the removal of limitations imposed by particular space-time frameworks might not lead to greater all-round development.

Too little research at the present time has gone into the teaching of skills and to the teaching of particular skills at particular age levels. Concepts of age of readiness and 'critical periods' are bandied about with little firm evidence in the field of human behaviour. As Connolly (1968) suggests, failure or great difficulty on the part of a child to learn a given response has frequently been accounted for in terms of the child's not being ready, or not being able, to learn the response at the time whereas more concern should be centred around the efficiency of the teaching techniques adopted.

Limitations imposed by lack of opportunities for learning particular skills have been emphasized by Biesheuvel (1963) in relation to African populations. He suggests that failure to provide the right psychomotor experience at particular maturational stages will prevent the full realization of potential ability. While the maturational concept might be questioned, he does raise the interesting proposition as to whether limited opportunities for learning certain basic movement habits in the tribal or urban African environment may be responsible for the difficulties which Africans experience in acquiring the manual dexterities needed for certain skilled trades. The discrepancy which exists between the performance of tribesmen and educated white or African groups is illustrated in Figure 4 for a two-hand co-ordination task. Biesheuvel suggests that a prima facie case exists for providing African children with more opportunity to manipulate, to diversify their motor responses and habits and to exercise these basic skills more continuously. A point already made in connection with giving children wider opportunity for acquiring skill. This area needs investigation.

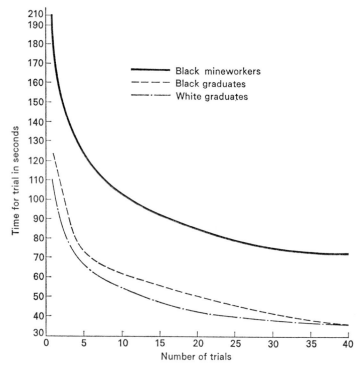

Figure 4 Psychomotor learning on two-hand co-ordination test by white and black adults at different educational and cultural levels (Biesheuvel, 1963).

Learning and maturation

Fitts and Posner (1967) describe what they term universal skills which although reflexive in nature are not necessarily unaffected by learning. Nevertheless, their basic patterns are considered to be inherent in the genetic structure of man. Breathing, digesting, coughing and sneezing would come into such a category. The idea of maturational skills in which learning plays a limited part and is only appropriate when a particular level of maturation has been reached, is also an accepted category of skilled behaviour. Of particular interest in this respect are the locomotive skills on which so much later gross body skill learning depends. It is not possible on the basis of current information to assess the limitations of retardation in the development of such skills on later skill learning, or on development in general, or whether such limitations are transitory in nature.

The classical study illustrating the limitation of practice on children learning to walk, is Dennis's (1940) description of the Hopi Indians who bind their children on to cradle-boards for most of the day. These children develop the ability to sit, creep and walk just as rapidly as children who are never bound. What is often missed in such explanations is the opportunity for other learning and development which is possible under such restrictions. It would appear for example that one of the reasons for binding children on to cradle-boards is that they can be carried on the mother's back. It is to be assumed therefore that such children do not suffer the perceptual (at least visual, auditory and haptic) deprivation which is the lot of children in more restricted environments. The point being made here, is that the concept of maturation applies to the organism as a whole and is not specific to some part of it.

Schaffer and Emerson (1968) make the further suggestion that

the sheer weight of evidence has been such as to give strong support to the view that early development is not just a maturational unfolding of inherent capacities at predetermined rates, but is based on processes occurring in the context of environmental conditions that may foster or impede the individual's progress to varying degrees.

Beceause it is the norm for children to walk at particular ages in a given culture, it should not be assumed that particularly favourable opportunities to learn in the general sense might not accelerate the potential age at which walking is possible or particularly unfavourable conditions put back the age. The same reasoning could be applied to other 'maturational' skills. This point is well made by comparing the Geber (1958) studies on native-reared Baganda children who show precocious motor behaviour (including walking) in the first eighteen months of life and some of Spitz's findings on institutionalized children (1958, quoted in *Review of research in deprivation of maternal care*, W.H.O. Public Health Papers, No. 14, p. 83). According to Geber, the Baganda children walk on average at 10 months of age. Spitz on the other hand followed up 21 children who remained in a foundling home up to 4 years of age. Of these, the youngest was 2 and the oldest 4 years and 1 month. Only 5 of the 21 could walk unassisted, 8 could walk with assistance, 3 could sit up but not walk and 5 were incapable of locomotion. These children had suffered severe sensory and perceptual deprivation which presumably had delayed the maturational process.

Variations in the onset of a maturational phase conducive to walking which would be difficult to interpret in terms of genetic endowment can be found if an attempt is made to quote European norms for the onset of walking behaviour which can be contrasted with those of the native-record Baganda. Significant discrepancies were found by Hindley et al. (1966) in a longitudinal study of age of first walking in five European samples. Figure 5 shows the age of first

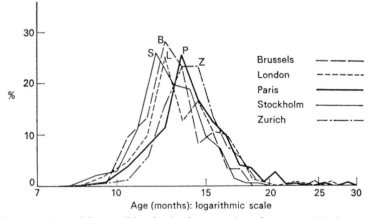

Figure 5 Age of first walking in the five samples—frequency distributions (Hindley et al., 1966).

walking plotted on a logarithmic scale (resulting in approximately normal distributions). If the cumulative distributions of logarithm of age of walking are plotted on probit paper (which results in straight-line plots when the underlying distributions are normal—Finney, 1952) all curves are very close approximates to straight lines between the 5th and 95th percentiles (Figure 6). Table 1 gives the mean and median ages in months for the five samples. Differences between the means were highly significant ($P < 0.001$) with Stockholm and Brussels differing significantly from the other three means and London differing significantly from Paris. There were no significant sex or social class differences within any of the samples. Presumably, therefore the

observed differences represent underlying population variations
which might be genetic, environmental or combinations of the two.

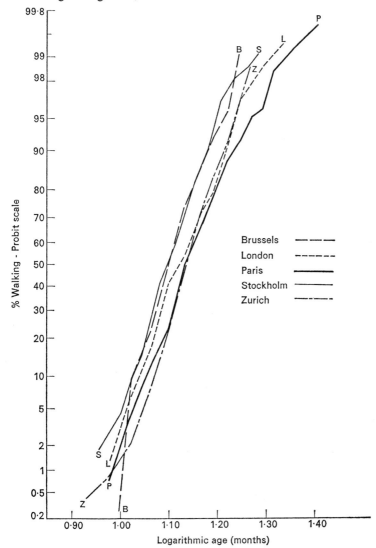

Figure 6 Age of first walking—cumulative frequency distribution
(Hindley et al., 1966).

Spitz (1945) has further suggested that the mother provides security
for the child in the field of locomotion. He suggests that it is the

73

'emotional bait' offered by the mother calling her child that 'teaches' him to walk. This he claims, is a partial explanation of the above eatastrophic findings.

Table 1 *Mean and median age of walking in each sample (Hindley et al., 1966)*

	N	Total Sample Mean (Months)	Median (Months)
Brussels	211	12·65	12·48
London	152	13·31	13·23
Paris	272	13·81	13·58
Stockholm	209	12·51	12·44
Zurich	233	13·59	13·63

The idea that the helpful presence of an adult who teaches the child or at least encourages his efforts in the development of even maturational skills is an interesting one and supposedly firmly entrenched in the child-rearing practices of most civilized communities. This is so much the case, that paediatricians in reporting stages in development often include such descriptions as 'sits with help', 'stands with help', 'walks with help'. The question which naturally arises in this respect is whether such adult interference helps the development of such skills or whether it is merely the perpetuation of habits which give primary satisfaction to the parent as the child is put through socially desirable movements. A recent study by Pikler (1968) provides useful evidence in this respect and the conditions she reports in the National Methodological Institute for infant care and education in Budapest must be almost unique. For here, as far as can be ascertained the institute withholds teaching in any form. By teaching is meant the systematic practice of certain motor skills by holding or keeping the child in a certain position, whether by adults or by equipment, or in any way causing him to make movements that in everyday life he is not yet able to execute by himself. Further, workers avoid encouraging children to move in some particular way since performances required by adults according to certain norms are considered potentially harmful and disturbing to normal development. Table 2 gives a comparison of the motor development stages and the ages achieved from the Pikler study and other textbooks of paediatrics. The discrepancies in regard to the ages at which such stages are reached are apparent. There is also further disagreement on the principal stages of gross motor development and their sequences. It is interesting to note that Pikler reports stages a, b, c, h and i to follow one another regularly in the given order while sequence d, e, f, g is not constant but each of these stages always occurs after c and precedes the stage i. Stages d, e and f occur at approximately the same time; stage g precedes stage h in 90 per cent of the cases.

Pikler (1968) concludes from ten years' observation in such a setting, that direct teaching by adults is not a necessary condition for infants achieving gross motor skills if they are of normal mental level and are kept under appropriate conditions for self-movement; and children kept under appropriate conditions for independent learning achieve stages of gross motor skills without appreciable delay in comparison with instructed children reported in the literature.

Table 2 *Comparisons of motor development (mean ages in weeks) (after Pikler, 1968)*

Development	A	B	C	D	E	F	G
a Turns from back to side	18		28	20			18
b Turns from supine to prone	25	32		24	28	21	18
c Turns from prone to supine	30			24	24	21	26
d Creeps on level ground	46		39	40	44	28	30
e Sits up from prone	47		47	44	40	32	33
f Kneels by self	48						
g Stands up by self	51	41	47	40	36	39	41
h Starts walking	70	62	69	65	56	58	49
i Walks well (uses walking for locomotion)	75			78			58

A = Pikler (1968) E = Illingworth (1960)
B = Brunet and Lezine (1951) F = Schmidt-Kolmer (1956)
C = Buhler and Hetzer (1953) G = Schelovanov and Aksarine
D = Gessell (1941)   (1960)

Differences between earlier and later learning

A concept of this nature can be viewed in terms of (1) contribution to skill learning with the inference that the quality of the early experiences in childhood determine to a large extent the child's potential for skill learning of all kinds at some later stage of development; and (2) nature of and relationship between the early and the later stages of acquiring a particular skill.

(1) The former interpretation has already been raised in reference to the effects of favourable opportunities for varied and useful experience in the general sense on the onset of particular maturational stages. It was also implicit in the discussion on the giving of general movement experience as against the teaching of specific skills. Hebb (1949) in particular has propounded a theory which predicts that animals that have had a large amount of perceptual experience early in life will prove better learners than others deprived of such experience. The magnitude of such a facilitative effect is within rough limits inversely related to the age at which the perceptual experience is gained (Beach and Jaynes, 1954).

Although evidence from the field of human behaviour is less conclusive than that from the animal world it has only recently been discovered how important for mental development are the effects of early experience. Hebb (1966) proposes that sensory stimulation from the early environment is necessary for the maintenance of some neural structures which would otherwise degenerate and also for the occurrence of learning which is essential for normal adult behaviour. Early experience is said to build up the 'mediating processes' (neural activity of the brain which can hold the excitation delivered by a sensory event after this event has ceased) which once established make possible the very rapid learning of the mature adult. Hebb (1949) suggests the formation of cell-assemblies—hypothetical reverberating systems within the brain—as the basis of such mediating processes.

(2) Fleishman (1967) in particular has drawn attention to the finding that abilities which contribute significantly to performance early in the learning of a skill may not be the same abilities which contribute to later stages of learning. In the learning of complex skills early learning will usually necessitate visual monitoring of the display. As the skilled behaviour of the subject develops with practice as a result of learning some of the constancies in the task situation, there will be a transfer of some of the monitoring functions of vision to proprioception as Fitts (1964) and Fleishman and Rich (1963) have demonstrated. The subject 'knows' where his hand or other member is without looking. He can place it in position either on the basis of feedback information from the muscular system (kinaesthesis) or by a pre-programmed action. One of the problems associated with an

interpretation of this nature has been highlighted by Connolly (1968). How is an equivalence between the visual and kinaesthetic analysers of the C.N.S. to be developed? He proposes that this might be done by operant conditioning techniques in which control over a response would be established by giving visual feedback and then using this feedback to teach the child to identify an equivalent kinaesthetic signal and discriminate this from noise.

Fleishman and Hempel (1955) have drawn a further distinction between earlier and later learning in suggesting that performance in perceptual-motor tasks becomes increasingly a function of habits and skills acquired *in the task itself*. This is a reinforcement to the specificity principle of skill learning and the need to practice a skill in context for maximum proficiency.

In the learning of skills involving a moving object (such as a ball) which has to be tracked in space, it is necessary to obtain information about a number of its characteristics. Position and direction have an obvious importance but for the development of *anticipation* it is necessary for proficient performance, not only to know where the object is now, but where it will be at some future time. That is to say, information is necessary about the trajectory, the velocity and possibly the acceleration characteristics of the flight. It would seem likely that in the early learning of tasks of this nature or of particular tasks involving unfamiliar flight paths, that the learner unable to deal with all the information in the display, focuses his attention on positional information and behaves in consequence with many errors. With more familiarity with the situation, the learner comes to detect the constancies in the situation—to assess not only the positional/directional aspects of the flight path but also the velocity/acceleration characteristics. In consequence, being able to anticipate, his behaviour becomes more adaptive. Garvey and Mitnick (1957) have in fact proposed that with training the behaviour of the human control systems progressively becomes a more complicated servomechanism such that later in training velocity characteristics of the input data and acceleration characteristics are the major influences in control. Fitts, Bahrick, Noble and Briggs (1961) refer to such a procedure as the 'progression hypothesis'. Fuchs (1962) has further postulated a 'progression-regression hypothesis' to account for the finding that, under unfavourable conditions such as stress, the learner reverts to an earlier level of control and his performance suffers accordingly.

Verbalization in the learning of motor skills

The observation that people (and children in particular) talk or mutter to themselves while performing a motor task is not a new one. What is less clear is the efficacy of such a procedure in task completion. Flavell, Klein and Higgins (1963) quoted by Jarvis (1968) report the results of a survey in which they found that over 90 per cent of parents of young children affirmed that their children used some kind of speech-for-self behaviour. Following on the work of Vygotsky (1962) the Russian psychologist, Luria (1961) has hypothesized that there is a stage in development during which instructing a child to verbalize (in the sense of giving himself instructions) while he is performing a sensory-motor task will improve his performance if he tells himself what to do, but hinder his performance if he tells himself what not to do. While Luria's experiments gave some support for this hypothesis, they have been criticized from a methodological and design point of view by Jarvis (1968). This worker invokes the Rosenthal (1963) effect as a possible explanation of Luria's results. (Experimenter expectations regarding the outcome of an experiment can have an effect on that outcome.) In a similar experimental set-up but with safeguards imposed to prevent such an effect from operating, Jarvis found no support for Luria's hypothesis. Verbalization did not appear to have a significant effect on performance of a button-pushing/not pushing task in response to a blue or yellow light.

In an attempt to develop right-left directionality in a group of mentally retarded children, Hill et al. (1967) required half of the experimental group to use a directional verbal label for the body part used. While the group as a whole showed significant improvement after four months of training (20 minutes per day) on activities requiring oral and motor responses to visual stimuli as well as physical exercises and games, there were no significant differences between those who verbalized and those who did not. Hill et al. interpret this finding as showing that the lag in development of a concept of right-left awareness with these retarded children is not due to a deficit in verbalization per se.

Training perceptual-motor skills

The placing of emphasis on the 'means whereby' a skill is acquired or on 'structuring an environment' in which learning might take place, reflects less concern with the end product achieved than with other less tangible gains by the learner. These will often involve social, emotional and philosophical determinants—fundamental considerations of educationalists. In contrast, training although being a part of the educational process has more clearly defined objectives which may be stated quite explicitly and which give rise to measurable results (Holding, 1965).

There is no one fixed type of training particularly suited to *all* tasks on *all* occasions, but rather a diversity of such procedures adopted by different trainers under different circumstances. Gaines (1967) has suggested a useful four-fold classification of training procedures which while not exhaustive would account for a large percentage of reported methods: (1) fixed training—in which the terminal performance is designated at the outset and the trainee is expected to learn it outright; (2) open-loop training—a suitably graded and fixed sequence of tasks given to the trainee who is found to be able to follow or 'remain stable' (e.g. the procedure utilized in 'linear' programmed learning); (3) feedback training—the trainer determines the next task according to the current ability of the trainee (e.g. the procedure utilized in 'branching' programmed learning—see Lumsdaine and Glaser, 1960, for discussion of both types of programming); and (4) adaptive training—the trainer's branching strategy is modified trainee by trainee so as to become best suited to the population of trainees (thus, the trainer may also be considered to learn!).

In view of the interest and considerable amount of work and research which has gone into programmed learning for the cognitive skills and the diversity of teaching machines for presenting such programmes in which feedback may be automatically presented, it is surprising that there has been little attempt to relate such procedures to the training of primarily motor skills. Some of the reasons for this can be traced to the difficulty of *operationally defining* such skills (discussed below) in a way which would enable a machine to be built which would simulate the defined operations. Other difficulties are presented by individual physical differences which would necessitate many adjustments to such 'standard' machines. This would add to the technological difficulties and the expense of fabricating such designs.

At a simple level, Cook et al. (1963) have demonstrated a machine for teaching the correct path through a punchboard maze. In addition to reinforcement (in terms of a light going on over the correct button) being provided immediately upon the subject making a correct response, a second experimental usage informed the subject of the correctness of the response *before* he made it! (The latter procedure incidentally was shown to be a superior training technique to the former.) A similar procedure was adopted in the teaching of keyboard operations such as typewriting or punched card preparation in the manual task trainers developed by Pask (1958). Gaines (1967) has described a teaching machine for tracking skills in which the task is to maintain a marker within a given region of the display (meter or oscilloscope) by manipulating a control (joystick or push-buttons). This was largely in the nature of an experimental piece of apparatus which promised to give rise to further machines designed for specific training procedures.

It is interesting to note that Cook (1963) in the experiment already described used a 'guidance' technique in the form of what they termed *prompting*. The use of *heavy prompting* in maze learning was a characteristic feature of Carr (1921) and his co-workers in the early twenties. The same kind of technique is of course a feature of the teaching machine method of verbal learning. Holding (1966) has coined the term 'artificial learning' to describe the procedure involved when a required response is arrived at by an artifice of the trainer, rather than through the efforts of the learner. The more usual term is that of 'guidance' and Holding and Macrae (1964, 1965, 1966) have made a major contribution to experimental work in this area involving perceptual-motor rather than verbal skills. These workers distinguish between 'forced-reponse' methods in which the learner is physically put through the movement and 'restriction' techniques in which the subject is free to make his own response but is prevented from making an incorrect response by the use of stops or mechanical guides. In addition, Macrae and Holding (1966) have shown that 'hinting' (partial response forcing) produces satisfactory gains in performance. Implicit in all these procedures, is that the trainer 'knows' the correct movement which he is guiding. While this may be relatively straightforward in simple tasks or in primarily perceptual skills (as Holding and Macrae (1964) demonstrated for the task of drawing 4-inch lines), the operational analyses (on the motor side) for complex skills present greater problems. It is in this area that on-going biomechanical analyses of human movement are likely to make a contribution. Further help in this respect will come with the development of kinetographic descriptions of skilled behaviour (Preston-Dunlop, 1963; Causley, 1967) currently undergoing elaboration and experimental analysis.

Simulators

A training procedure currently attracting a great deal of interest in the industrial and commercial field (but by no means a new idea) is the use of simulators. While such procedures may incorporate aspects of guidance training, they cannot truly be called teaching machines until feedback can be incorporated into the system (Gaines, 1967). Hammerton (1967) has discussed simulators in the following way: 'Stripped to its essentials, the use of simulators in training involves an operator learning some skill S with a device d (the simulator) in the hope or expectation that he will then perform some skills with a device D (the real equipment).'

The use of simulators as a development of general systems research, is beginning to gain momentum. They have been constructed for application to problems as diverse as 'handling vehicles under emergency conditions' (McHenry, 1969) to simulating a community comprising criminals, non-criminal populations and police detectives teams as an aid to the training of police officers (Malik, 1969).

The use of simulators is often dictated purely from an economical point of view. Thus, the increasing capital and running costs involved in highly technical industrial equipment precludes its usage as a training medium. Furthermore, such equipment may be easily damaged by a mistake on the part of an incompetent operator and because of the complexity of the operating skills required, more training time is demanded which would necessitate the withdrawal of such apparatus from active production. One of the earliest devices of this kind was the link-trainer of the early thirties which was used up to the second world war as a pilot training device.

If a simulator is to be effective, it must enable the operator who trains on it to transfer his learned techniques to the actual equipment (Hammerton, 1967). This kind of transfer of training situation is dissimilar to that normally encountered in the literature in which transfer is usually looked for between related but not necessarily similar tasks. The simulator designer however attempts to imitate as closely as possible the *relevant* features of the equipment simulated. Hammerton and Tickner (1967) go further in suggesting that ideal simulation must go beyond the equipment per se and take account of both adequate background texture and accurate depth scaling. Absence of the former can produce stimulus confounding and of the latter mis-estimations. Once again, one of the primary difficulties becomes that of a suitable operational analysis by which to isolate such features.

Two main criteria have generally been utilized for assessing the transfer of training effectiveness of simulators: (1) how much time (or how many trials) on the real equipment is saved by using the simulator (savings measure); (2) how will a trainee cope with the real equipment the first time he uses it, after a simulator training (first-shot measure). Hammerton (1966, 1967) suggests that savings measures are always better than first-shot measures and are good even when the latter are poor. Simulators are particularly valuable where the saving of time is what matters most. By considerable elaboration good first-shot transfer can be obtained but this has to be weighed against cost and accident risk.

Simulators are not altogether a novel idea for the physical educationalist. In 1927 Mesple patented a mechanical figure for teaching golf. It is not clear from the patent what operational analyses were carried out on the stroke simulated or by what criterion it was accepted, neither has any information been found on the efficacy of the machine in practice. Patents of a similar nature were taken out for teaching children to walk (1900), teaching swimming (1898) and the teaching of walking and dancing (1928) (U.S. Patent Office). The use of simulators in the form of magnetic tables for demonstration of tactical situations within particular field games is of course a normal procedure. The effectiveness on transfer to the game situation does not appear to have been assessed.

Another important feature of the simulator, is that it not only reproduces the essential features of the learning situation in a more convenient form, but that it can modify certain aspects of the field situation to suit the individual. Thus, freedom to manipulate the situation provides the trainee with the opportunity to concentrate upon his weaknesses if necessary and so make him better equipped to deal with the natural situation when he is confronted with it. Particularly useful simulators of this nature in the field of physical education are the cricket, tennis and table-tennis ball propulsion machines which can be infinitely varied for pace, direction and in some cases, spin.

Laterality and the learning of motor skills

The predominance of a right-handed majority in the performance of many perceptual-motor skills has led to the assumption that right-handedness is normal and proper (Clark, 1957). Speculation as to the causes of handedness has ranged through hereditary predisposition to environmental and temperamental circumstances or combinations of such factors. Similar problems arise regarding eyedness and preferential use of the foot, although these are less self-evident to the casual observer.

Primitive tribes would seem to have a greater degree of left-handedness or at least of ambidextrality. The fact that early neolithic tools found in England are far more frequently shaped for left-handed use than the present incidence of left-handedness would have indicated leads to speculation as to whether there has been a decline in the incidence of left-handedness or rather a suppression of it under the changing demands of society (Clark, 1957). Certainly, we now live in a right-handed world and the production lines of factories are designed to turn out equipment for the right-handed majority. Seldom do right-handers consider the difficulties encountered in everyday life by the left-handed minority. Not only is nearly everything used specifically made for the right-hander, but there is still an historical prejudice which militates against the person who has a preference for performing acts with the left side (Barsley, 1966).

The idea that heredity plays a fundamental part in determining laterality has led to the suggestion that the dominant limb or eye is on the opposite side to the dominant hemisphere of the brain, which is generally taken to be congenitally determined. However, it is fairly clear—particularly in the case of left-handedness—that many supposedly congenitally determined left-handed people become trained right-handers so that the position is somewhat confused. This has led to the term 'preference' being substituted for dominance (Clark, 1957), and to handedness being defined not as the predominant use of a specific hand in a particular activity, but as a constant tendency or preference to undertake new skills with one hand rather than another (Schrecker, 1968). The concept of cerebral dominance is, as Semmes (1968) suggests, little more than a label, a restatement of the finding that lesions of one hemisphere produce deficits that lesions of the other hemisphere do not.

Lund (1932) discussing the case of eye–hand adjustments calling for close co-ordination suggests an advantage in having 'the directing and controlling eye' on the same side as the 'controlling member'. In a target aiming test, he was able to show superior performance when subjects used their dominant eye than with the non-dominant eye. The best scores of all were obtained with both eyes open

83

suggesting that ocular dominance is not a simply explained pheno-menon. Lund's findings were substantiated by Fink (1938) who found the use of the dominant hand and dominant eye resulted in the highest degree of co-ordination.

In more gross co-ordination tasks (such as ball game skills) opinion would appear to be different. Adams (1965) in discussing the effect of eye dominance on baseball batting suggests that speculation amongst American coaches had led to the belief that the batter of the crossed-lateral type (i.e. left-eyed—right-handed or right-eyed—left-handed) has a distinct advantage over the unilateral batter because of the position of the batter's dominant eye in relation to the pitch of the ball. Adams compared the batting performance of players from college baseball teams divided into two groups of crossed laterals and unilaterals. The unilaterals scored better than the crossed laterals in most batting categories. He also showed that the batting stances of the unilateral players significantly affected their perfor-mance in certain batting categories. This led him to suggest that eye dominance may have some effect on certain aspects of baseball batting.

The question of dominance can be seen to be a confused one and it seems that many workers in this field have not fully appreciated the complexity of the problem. Berner and Berner (1938) for example differentiate between what they term the 'controlling eye' and the 'sighting eye'. The former is considered to be the one which guides binocular pattern. Apparently, the controlling eye is not always the same as the eye that sights in monocular tasks. Using a large group of subjects, these workers were able to show that the controlling eye was the same as the sighting eye in only two-thirds of the subjects.

Whiting and Eastwood (1969) compared the performances of left- and right-hand preferent children at different ages in a target throwing situation. Amongst other findings, it was noted that dominance related to accuracy of throwing is not as well established at 6 years of age as it is at 9 years and 13 years.

The results of this experiment and the ideas proposed by Semmes suggest that if Shrecker's (1968) plea for the development of 'approx-imate ambidextrality' is to be put into practice, it should be encouraged before the discrepancy between the right and left hand due to normal cultural training becomes too well established. 'Approximate ambidextrality' is defined as the ability to carry out the gross activities in which mainly large muscles of the arm are involved, with the inferior hand and arm as efficiently or almost as efficiently as with the dominant upper extremity. Schrecker quotes an interesting study by Grundlingh Malan on the attainment of approximate ambidextrality in a throwing task. Two groups of 25 children around 8 years of age were matched for handedness. Prior to the beginning of the experiment, Group 1 were accustomed to carry their books in the inferior hand and to do other simple routine activities with it. Throwing practice was then carried out for a period of 6 months but whereas children in Group 1 were taught to use left and right hand equally in all the activities, Group 2 were allowed to give preference to their better hand. Children were tested initially and after the training period for throwing distance, accuracy and other measures not of immediate concern. The results of these findings showed superior improvement by Group 1 in throwing distance with the left hand as might be expected. The gain in skill shown by the target aiming scores was in favour of the group trained in approximate ambidextrality.

Environmental effects on the establishment of limb preference have also been reported by Provins. In a review of the literature on handedness and perceptual-motor skill performance Provins (1967) suggests that there is little or no difference in the relative performance of the right and left sides on tasks involving simple movements but that differences do occur when the serial organization of muscle activity is an important factor. These results are interpreted in terms of a *differential training hypothesis.*

Provins and Glencross (1968) tested this hypothesis in groups of trained touch typists and non-typists working on typewriting exercises. A comparison of the performance of the two sides showed, for the typists, no difference between the sides or a difference in favour of the left hand and for the non-typists a difference between hands in favour of the right side in two of the three comparisons. A similar finding occurred on a handwriting performance task. Provins and Glencross postulate that different individuals have different capacity to acquire motor skill so that if training is held constant for a given group of subjects (i.e. they all 'overlearned' the task with both hands or one hand only as in the typewriting and handwriting experiments respectively), those subjects who did well with one hand would be expected to do well with the other. They further note that there appears to be a reasonable basis for suggesting that a minimum level of general intelligence and motor capacity is necessary for the acquisition of motor skill and that without these, handedness is also unable to develop. Given an adequate capacity for the acquisition of motor skill in these terms, the level of performance achieved by an individual in a motor task appears to depend on the extent of his training on this or similar tasks and that in so far as the training of the two sides has been dissimilar, then the level of performance achieved on the two sides are dissimilar.

In a paper already referred to in this section, Semmes (1968) reports one of a series of studies carried out on brain-injured war veterans. She proposes that elementary functions are *focally* represented in the left hemisphere favouring integration of *similar* units and consequently specialization for behaviours which demand fine sensor motor control such as manual skills and speech. Conversely, *diffuse* representation of elementary functions in the right hemisphere may lead to integration of *dissimilar* units and hence specialization for behaviour requiring multimodal co-ordination such as the various spatial abilities. Such a proposal of concentration of function on the left and diffuseness on the right argues for hemispheric specialization in different aspects of behaviour. On such a basis, small lesions in the focally organized hemisphere and the diffusely organized hemisphere of a similar magnitude would result in more deficit being produced by the former and leading to what Semmes denotes pseudo-dominance.

Semmes further suggests that spatial function might depend on convergence of unlike elements—visual, kinaesthetic, vestibular—combining in such a way as to create through experience a single supramodal space.

Bibliography

Adams, G. L. (1965), 'Effect of Eye Dominance on Baseball Batting', *Res. Q.*, 36: 3–9.

Argyle, M., and Kendon, A. (1967), 'The Experimental Analysis of Social Performance', in Berkowitz, L. (ed.), *Advances in Experimental Social Psychology*, Vol. 3, Academic Press, New York.

Barrett, J., Davies, W., Hart, J., and Woods, J. (1966), unpublished Diploma in Physical Education dissertation, Leeds University.

Barsley, M. (1966), *The Left Handed Book*, University of London Press, London.

Beach, F. A., and Jaynes, J. (1954), 'Effects of Early Experience upon the Behaviour of Animals', *Psych. Bull.*, 51:3 239–63.

Berner, G. E., and Berner, D. E. (1938), 'Reading Difficulties in Children', *Arch. Ophthalm.*, 20: 829–38.

Biesheuvel, S. (1963), 'The Growth of Abilities and Character', *S. Afr. J. Sci.*, 59: 375–85.

Bilodeau, E. A. (ed.) (1966), *Acquisition of Skill*, Academic Press, New York.

Book, W. F. (1925), *The Psychology of Skill*, Gregg, New York.

Bryan, W. L., and Harter, N. (1897), 'Studies in the Physiology and Psychology of the Telegraphic Language', *Psych. Rev.*, 4: 27–53.

Brunet, C., and Lezine, I. (1951), *Le Développement Psychologique de la Première Enfance*, Presses Universitaires, Paris.

Buhler, C., and Hetzer, H. (1953), *Kleinkindertests*, Barth, J. A. Munich.

Carr, H. A. (1921), 'The Influence of Visual Guidance in Maze Learning', *J. Exp. Psych.*, 4: 399–417.

Causley, M. (1967), *Benesh Movement Notation*, Max Parrish, London.

Clark, M. M. (1957), *Left Handedness*, University of London Press, London.

Connolly, K. (1968), 'The Applications of Operant Conditioning to the Measurement and Development of Motor Skill in Children', *Dev. Med. & Child Neur.*, 10: 6, 697–705.

Cook, J. O. et al. (1963), '"Superstition" in the Skinnerian', *Amer. Psychologist*, 18: 8, 516–18.

Crossman, G. R. F. W. (1964), 'Information Processes in Human Skill', *Brit. Med. Bull.*, 20: 1, 32–7.

Dennis, W. (1940), 'The Effects of Cradling Practices upon the Onset of Walking in Hopi Children', *J. Genetic Psych.*, 56: 77–86.

Elkind, D., and Weiss, J. (1967), 'Studies in Perceptual Development, 3: Perceptual Exploration', *Child Dev.*, 38: 2, 553–61.

Eysenck, H. J. (1965), 'A Three-Factor Theory of Reminiscence', *Brit. J. Psych.*, 56: 2 and 3, 163–81.

Fink, W. H. (1938), 'The Dominant Eye: its Clinical Significance', *Arch. Ophthalm.*, 19: 555–82.

Finney, D. (1952), *Probit Analysis*, University Press, Cambridge.

Fitts, P. M. (1964), 'Perceptual-Motor Skill Learning', in Melton, A. W. (ed.), *Categories of Human Learning*, Academic Press, New York.

Bahrick, H. P., Noble, M. E., and Briggs, A. E. (1961), *Skilled Performance*, Wiley, New York.

and Posner, M. I. (1967), *Human Performance*, Brooks/Cole, Belmont.

Fleishman, E. A. (1964), *The Structure and Measurement of Physical Fitness*, Prentice-Hall, New Jersey.

(1967), 'Individual Differences and Motor Learning', in Gagne, R. M. (ed.), *Learning and Individual Differences*, Merrill, Columbus, Ohio.

and Hempel, W. E. (1955), 'Changes in Factor Structure of a Complex Psychomotor Test as a Function of Practice', *Psychometrika*, 18: 239–52.

and Rich, S. (1963), 'Role of Kinaesthetic and Spatial Visual Abilities in Perceptual Motor Learning', *J. Exp. Psych.*, 66: 6–11.

Fuchs, A. H. (1962), 'The Progression-Regression Hypothesis in Perceptual Motor Skill Learning', *J. Exp. Psych.*, 633: 177–82.

Gagne, R. M. (1963), 'A Psychologist's Counsel on Curriculum Design', *J. Res. in Sci. Teaching*, 1: 27–32.

Gaines, B. R. (1967), 'Teaching Machines for Perceptual-Motor Skills', in Unwin, D., and Leedham, J. (eds), *Aspects of Educational Technology*, Methuen, London.

Garvey, W. D., and Mitnick, L. L. (1957), 'An Analysis of Tracking Behaviour in Terms of Lead-lag Errors', *J. Exp. Psych.*, 53: 373–8.

Geber, M. (1958), The Psychomotor Development of African Children in the First Year and the Influence of Maternal Behaviour', *J. Soc. Psych.*, 47: 185–95.

Gessell, A. (1941), *Developmental Schedules*, Psychological Corporation, New York.

Hammerton, M. (1966), 'Factors Affecting the Use of Simulators for Training', *Proc. J.E.E.*, Vol. 113, No. 11, 1881–4.

(1967), 'Measures for the Efficiency of Simulators as Training Devices', *Ergonomics*, 10: 1, 63–5.

and Tickner, A. H. (1967), 'Visual Factors Affecting Transfer of Training from a Simulated to a Real Control Situation', *J. Appl. Psych.*, 51: 1, 46–9.

Hebb, D. O. (1949), *Organisation of Behaviour*, Wiley, New York.

(1966), *A Textbook of Psychology*, Saunders, London.

Hill, S. D., McCullum, A. H., and Sceau, A. G. (1967), 'Relation of Training in Motor Activity to Development of Right-Left Directionality in Mentally Retarded Children: Exploratory Study', *Perceptual & Motor Skills*, 24: 363–6.

Hindley, C. B., Filliozat, A. M., Klackenberg, G., Nicolet-Meisten, D., and Sand, E. A. (1966), 'Differences in Age of Walking in Five European Longitudinal Samples', *Human Biol.*, 38: 4.

Holding, D. H. (1965), *Principles of Training*, Pergamon, London.

(1966), 'Artificial Learning', unpublished paper, Experimental Psychology Society Annual General Meeting.

and Macrae, A. W. (1964), 'Guidance, Restriction and Knowledge of Results', *Ergonomics*, 7: 289–95.

(1966), 'Rate and Force of Guidance in Perceptual Motor Tasks with Reversed or Random Spatial Correspondence', *Ergonomics*, 9: 4, 289–96.

Hovland, C. I. (1951), 'Human Learning and Retention', in Stevens, S. S. (ed.), *Handbook of Experimental Psychology*, Chapman & Hall, London.

Illingworth, R. S. (1960), *The Development of the Infant and Young Child, Normal and Abnormal*, Livingstone, London.

Jarvis, P. E. (1968), 'Verbal Control of Sensory-Motor Performance—a Test of Luria's Hypothesis', *Human Dev.*, 11: 172–93.

Knapp, B. (1964), *Skill in Sport*, Routledge & Kegan Paul, London.

Lumsdaine, A. A., and Glaser, R. (eds) (1960), *Teaching Machines and Programmed Learning*, Nat. Educ. Assoc. Dept. Audio-Vis. Instruct., Washington.

Lund, F. H. (1932), 'The Dependence of Eye-Hand Coordination upon Eye Dominance', *Amer. J. Psych.*, 44, 756–62.

Luria, A. R. (1961), *The Role of Speech in the Regulation of Normal and Abnormal Behaviour*, Josiah Macy Foundation, New York.

Macrae, A. W., and Holding, D. H. (1965), 'Method and Task in Motor Guidance', *Ergonomics*, 8: 315–20.

McHenry, R. R. (1969), 'Handling Vehicles under Emergency Conditions', unpublished paper, Cornell Aeronautical Laboratories Inc., Buffalo, New York.

Malik, R. (1969), 'The 72 Hour Day', *New Scientist*, 41: 632, 125–6.

Meredith, G. P. (1967), 'Teaching: a Hard Look', *Guardian*, Manchester.

Mesple, J. L. (1927), 'Mechanised Figure for Teaching Golf', U.S. Patent Office, patent no. 1, 703, 403.

Montessori, M. (1912), *The Montessori Method*, Heinemann, London.

(1949), *The Absorbent Mind*, Theosophical Publishing House, Madras.

Newton, G., and Levine, S. (eds) (1968), *Early Experience and Behaviour*, Thomas, Springfield, Illinois.

Osgood, C. E. (1958), *Method and Theory in Experimental Psychology*, Oxford University Press, New York.

Pallett, G. D. (1965), *Modern Educational Gymnastics*, Pergamon, London.

Pask, G. (1958), 'Electronic Keyboard Teaching Machines', in A. A. Lumsdaine and R. Glaser (eds), *Teaching Machines and Programmed Learning*, Nat. Educ. Assoc. Dept. Audio-Vis. Instruct., Washington.

'Pendennis' (1969), 'We are all Artists', *Observer*, London, 2 March.

Pikler, E. (1968), 'Some Contributions to the Study of the Gross Motor Development of Children', *J. Genetic Psych.*, 11: 27–39.

Preston-Dunlop, V. (1963), *Introduction to Kinetography*, Macdonald-Evans, London.

Provins, K. A. (1967), 'Motor Skills, Handedness and Behaviour', *Aust. J. Psych.*, 19: 137–50.

and Glencross, D. J. (1968), 'Handwriting, Typewriting and Handedness', *Q.J. Exp. Psych.*, XX: 3, 282–9.

Rosenthal, R. (1963), 'On the Social Psychology of the Psychological Experiment', *Amer. Sci.*, 51: 268–83.

Schaffer, H. R., and Emerson, P. E. (1968), 'The Effects of Experimentally Administered Stimulation on Developmental Quotients of Infants', *Brit. J. Soc. Clin. Psych.*, 7: 61–7.

Schelovanov, I. M., and Aksarine, I. M. (1960), *Voszpitanyie Gyetyej Rannevo Vozrasta v Gyetskih Ucsrezsdenijah*, Medgiz, Moscow.

Schmidt-Kolmer, E. (1956), *Die Pflege und Erziehung unserer Kinder in Krippen und Heimen*, Volk und Gesundheit, Berlin.

Schrecker, K. A. (1968), 'Approximate Ambidexterity—Why and How', *J. Sports Med. & Phys. Fit.*, 8: 1, 44–8.

Semmes, J. (1968), 'Hemispheric Specialisation: a Possible Clue to Mechanism', *Neuropsychologica*, 6: 11–26.

Spitz, R. A. (1945), 'Hospitalism: an Enquiry into the Genesis of Psychiatric Conditions in Early Childhood', *Psychoanal. Stud. Child.*, 1: 53–74.

and Wolf, K. M. (1946), 'Anaclitic Depression: an Enquiry into the Genesis of Psychiatric Conditions in Early Childhood, II', *Psychoanal. Stud. Child.*, 2: 313–42.

Stelmach, G. E. (1968), 'Reminiscence and Consolidation in a Gross Motor Task', *Perceptual & Motor Skills*, 27: 1075–8.

Tanner, J. M. (1961), *Education and Physical Growth*, University Press, London.

Thorpe, W. H. (1963), *Learning and Instinct in Animals*, Methuen, London.

Vygotsky, L. S. (1962), *Thought and Language*, Wiley, New York.

Welford, A. T. (1968), *Fundamentals of Skill*, Methuen, London.

Whiting, H. T. A. (1963), 'Personality and the Athlete', *A.A.A. Coaching Newsletter*, 25: 2.

(1967), 'Visual Motor Coordination', Ph.D. thesis, Psychology Department, Leeds University.

(1969), *Acquiring Ball Skill—a Psychological Interpretation*, Bell, London.

and Eastwood, P. (1969), 'Handedness and Accuracy of Throwing with Age', *Res. in Phys. Educ.*

Gill, E. B., and Stephenson, J. (1969), 'Critical Time Intervals for Taking in Information in a Ball Catching Task', *Ergonomics*, 12.

4

Personality, body concept and performance

J E Kane

Organismic theory emphasizes the interaction and interdependence of mind and body functioning. Physical educationists are closely concerned with the body and the development of physical abilities but they are also aware of associated personality outcomes. The way an individual characteristically perceives his body has long been held as an important factor in forming his image of himself and his general integration. Recently, increasing importance has been directed to the way in which the neurophysiological functioning accounts for the integration and modulation of diverse body processes and may explain personality and performance differences. From another point of view, the extent to which personality factors may account for differences in gross physical abilities has begun to attract the interests of researchers.

The purpose of this chapter is to consider some ways in which physical factors (in particular the body, physiological functioning and physical abilities) may be linked with personality and behaviour. For convenience, it is divided into three parts; the first dealing with body concepts and personality, the second outlining physiological explanations of personality and performance and the third part presenting current evidence of the relationship between personality and physical (athletic) abilities.

Part I The body and personality

The term 'body image' (and relatively synonymous terms, such as 'body percept' and 'body schema') is used in psychology to indicate the attitudinal framework defining the individual's concept of his body and his characteristic way of perceiving it. An increasing number of psychological researches are exploring the body-image dimension with a view to predicting other behavioural variables. In perceiving his own body, an individual is uniquely ego-involved and it is proposed that he may introduce systematic biases which may tell a great deal about him. The concept of body image is a dynamic one, to be considered not merely as the sum of a number of visual, tactile and kinaesthetic sensations but as a responsive and changing organization of the physical elements by which our perceptual schema of our body is constantly affected by new experiences and activities. Concerning the way in which body image is considered to be connected with personality, Fisher (1965) writes:

> With increasing study of the body image, we have learned that the normal individual's attitude towards his body may mirror important aspects of his identity. An individual's feeling that his body is big or small, attractive or unattractive, strong or weak may tell us a good deal about his self concept or his typical manner of relating to other people. There is evidence that the individual has a unique way of perceiving his own body as contrasted to non-self objects. As such, this body image or body concept frequently serves as a screen or target upon which he projects significant personal feelings, anxieties and values.

The child's conception of his body develops and becomes differentiated as he grows through an interplay of the forces that shape his personality. Witkin (1965) has suggested that achievement of a differentiated body concept is a manifestation of the child's general progress towards greater psychological complexity. It is proposed that, at an early age, the child experiences himself and his body as a 'continuous body field matrix'. As he grows and develops the differences between his body and the non-self world are formed and later he becomes aware of the differentiation between parts of the body and their interrelatedness, so that his body concept and perception become less global and more articulated in terms of the body parts and body boundaries.

During this process, body attitudes are formed which may have long-term effects on behaviour. Kagan and Moss (1962) have demonstrated that fearfulness about their bodies among adults is linked with the level of fearfulness developed in early childhood. They also found that body anxieties in children may encourage long-term attitudes and modes of behaviour towards certain bodily experiences. Boys, for example, with a high body anxiety were found to avoid athletic activities and to give an increasing amount of time to intellectual tasks.

Increasing efforts have been made by researchers to identify the major dimensions of the body image and concept—that is to say, the organized impression an individual forms of his body, both cognitive and affective. Researchers have reported on a range of body-image variables, such as body anxiety, body awareness and narcissism (Secord, 1953), body orientation in space (Witkin et al., 1962), concept of body size (Nash, 1958), plasticity of body schema (Schneiderman, 1956), preferred body proportions (Jourard and Secord, 1955), body attention patterns (Fisher, 1966), body type (Sugerman and Haronian, 1964). These and other studies continue to clarify the nature of body perception and the way in which it is linked with the personality processes. One series of experiments (Fisher, 1963; Fisher and Cleveland, 1958) have demonstrated, for instance, that an individual's perception of his body boundaries is associated with personality traits of self-assertion, self-expression and mastery. Fisher (1964) has also found aggression linked with body-size perception. It is of interest also to note that the dynamic nature of the body image is supported by research findings indicating, for instance, that body attitudes seemed to change during psychotherapy (Cleveland, 1960), and that success or failure differentially affects body evaluation (Popper, 1957). An interesting and recent exposition of the success-failure effect on body and self-image has been made by Read (1969). He found that constant winners in competitive physical education activities had significantly higher mean body image and self-concept scores than constant losers. He also concluded, on the basis of pre- and post-experimental measures of body image and self-concept, that competitive physical education activities may have a detrimental effect on those who consistently lose.

At this point, it would appear to be useful to identify a number of notions concerning body perception appearing in the experimental literature.

Orientation in space

Witkin and his collaborators reported, in their book, *Personality through Perception* (1954), a detailed summary of their long-term researches concerning the way in which an individual's way of perceiving was related to his personality. This early work demonstrated through the use of a number of ingenious tests of spacial orientation that a developed differentiated body concept (body image) is a manifestation of personality development. Later, Witkin (1962) in reviewing his findings wrote: 'It became clear, at a certain point in the investigations, that the way in which a person orients himself in space is an expression of a more general preferred mode of perceiving which is linked, in turn, to a broad varied array of psychological functioning.'

Throughout his work, the assumption was made that the body concept (image) guides perception. The main outcome of Witkin's earlier studies was to identify those who, in their perceptual functioning, were more or less dependent on the prevailing visual 'field'. Individuals were therefore rated on a continuum which extended from 'field-dependent' (i.e. those who depend for their orientation on their surroundings), to 'field-independent' (those capable of orientation with relative independence of the surroundings). To put it in another way, the individual's body-concept development was reflected in the orientation tests by the extent to which the body was experienced as clearly segregated from the 'field'. The orientation characteristics of the 'field-dependent' person were mainly demonstrated by two of Witkin's tests—the rod and frame test, and the body-adjustment test.

In the rod and frame test, the subject sits in complete darkness facing a luminous rod surrounded by a luminous frame, both pivoted at the same centre and seen by the subject in a tilted position. His task is to adjust the rod to an upright position (through instructions to the experimenter) while the frame stays in the tilted position. There are some subjects, at one extreme, who can only perceive the rod to be upright when it is aligned with the tilted frame, which is interpreted as indicating that their perception is dictated entirely by the surrounding 'field'. At the opposite extreme are those who are able to adjust the rod to an upright position irrespective of the angle at which the frame is tilted and this ability is indicative of their field independence. In the body-adjustment test, the subject is seated in a tilted chair in a tilted room and required to adjust his chair to the upright position while the room remains tilted. As in the rod and frame test, there are those who are guided by the axes of the surrounding visual field rather than by sensations from within their bodies and these perceive their bodies as upright even though they are being tilted as much as 35°.

From these and other performance tests of orientation a difference can be identified between those who experience the body as distinct from the field and those who experience a fusion of body with field. Those with a heightened and articulated body concept are those whose body awareness is more differentiated and who experience the body as a discrete entity, quite separate from field. The Witkin proposition is that the extent to which the body concept is more or less articulated is associated with a tendency to experience the self and the surrounding world in a similar way and is reflected in a 'style of life'. This personality characterization of 'field-dependent' and 'field-independent' subjects constitutes the other half of the Witkin thesis which is also supported by a large volume of research. Field-dependent people do not readily locate a familiar figure hidden in a complex design; they have difficulty in picture completion, object assembly and parts of intelligence tests; they produce poorly detailed and unrealistic proportioning in the drawing of a person and they are changeable and stimulated to feelings of aggression. These and other behavioural characteristics, found by Witkin to be linked with field dependence-independence, reflect the nature of the individual's experience of his surroundings, the sensitivity of his body awareness, his interpersonal relationships and the structure of his personal defences. Witkin (1962) summarizes the importance of the association between an individual's generalized way of experiencing body, self and the outside field in those terms:

> The dynamic linkage that exists between sense of body and sense of self suggested that the ready fusion of body and field in experience may, in turn, signify a self which is limited both as to segregation and inner structure. Evidence from subsequent studies, in fact, showed, as we see later, that people with a relatively field-dependent way of perceiving have a less developed sense of their identity and of their separateness from others than do field-independent perceivers. A self which is only limitedly segregated from the field—or which, in experience, easily 'loses' its field—is characteristic of people who tend to experience the body or any object as 'fused' with its surroundings. If we think of the self as corresponding to a segment of experience, we may consider that greater or more limited articulation represents a common quality running through much of a person's experience.

Body boundary

It was Fisher and Cleveland (1958) who first proposed that a fundamental aspect of the body image is the individual's perception of his body boundaries. Apparently, individuals vary in the extent which they experience their bodies as being clearly and sharply bounded and distinct from what is 'out there'. The degree of boundary definitiveness may be assessed as a 'barrier score' based on the number of responses, elicited by ink-blot stimuli, which emphasize protective, containing, decorative or covering functions. A number of studies by Fisher and Cleveland (1965) have demonstrated the relationship between the barrier score and various behavioural (and physiological) variables. In particular, subjects with high barrier scores were found to be more autonomous, to have higher achievement motivation, to communicate more with others and to be helpful and active in providing integration in small groups. Further studies firmly established an association between an individual's barrier score and the prominence of his sensation and perception of interior body regions (e.g. stomach and heart) as against exterior regions (e.g. skin and muscle); the higher the barrier score the greater the sensations from the exterior boundary regions.

Another proposed measure of body boundary was formulated which emphasized (in ink-blot percepts) the penetrability of the body in terms of its weakness, lack of defence and insecure boundaries. This measure (Fisher and Cleveland, 1958) is referred to as the 'penetration score' and typical ink-blot responses illustrative of the penetration concept were found to be 'bullet piercing flesh,' 'X-ray of inside the body,' 'soft material,' 'person bleeding' and 'house burning.'

While the barrier index appears to have a relatively stable relationship to persisting attitudes and personality dimensions, the penetration index seems to be particularly sensitive to situational changes (Fisher and Cleveland, 1965) in significant life experiences such as pregnancy and recovery from psychotic disorganization.

Body cathexis

Secord and Jourard (1953) focused attention on the aspect of body perception concerned with the individual's relative satisfaction (or cathexis) towards different parts of his body and the way in which attitudes towards the body are 'of crucial importance to any comprehensive thesis of personality'. These investigators were able to demonstrate a connection between attitudes towards parts (and functions) of the body and anxiety, insecurity and feelings towards self. In addition, they made implications for mental health, having found, for example, that college students who had positive satisfaction towards the body also felt more secure, self-confident and freer from inferiority feelings than those who had negative body feelings. They conceive of the body as a foundation point for the more generalized and inclusive concepts of self and have offered support for their contentions by showing a significant relationship between objective measures of body cathexis and self-cathexis. Body cathexis, described as 'the degree of satisfaction or dissatisfaction with the various parts of the body' was initially measured by a test which consisted of forty-six words describing body parts and functions against which subjects recorded their reactions on a 5-point scale of intensity. The self-concept was assessed by a self-cathexis inventory which listed fifty-five items believed to represent a sample of factors related to satisfaction of self, and these were also assessed for intensity and direction on a 5-point scale. These investigators presented correlations between body cathexis and self-cathexis of 0·58 for males and 0·66 for females and subsequent researches have shown this degree of relationship to be well founded (e.g. Johnson, 1956; Rosen and Ross, 1968).

Johnson (1956) found that the degree of body dissatisfaction was associated with somatic symptoms especially amongst women and that women tended to have a lower body-cathexis score than men. Of the measurable factors that may be related to liking or disliking parts of the body, it appears that size is of particular importance. Large size, but not weight, seems to be a desired quality among males according to Jourard and Secord's (1954) report, in which body cathexis and actual body measurements were significantly related. In a recent study investigating the possible threat to self-esteem of small body size among young and healthy naval men, size, as measured by height, seemed to have a pervasive effect on self-evaluation in general. Short underweight and short overweight groups had the most unfavourable self-images, but no general relationship was established between these perceived inadequacies and military performance but it was noted that individuals who were both very short and overweight frequently expressed dissatisfaction with themselves and also scored low on performance tests.

In a study of the ideal female figure and body cathexis, Jourard and Secord (1955) had as subjects, students enrolled at Emory University who were graduates, nurses and art college undergraduates with an average age of nearly 23 years. The subjects were given the body cathexis test, had twelve body parts measured and for each of these parts were asked to estimate the size and indicate what they considered to be an ideal size for it. The two major findings were that (1) body cathexis was positively related to the size of the selected body parts, (2) 'ideal' size for weight, hips and waist was smaller than the measured size, while 'ideal' bust size was larger. The investigators concluded that there was a shared ideal among college women for certain dimensions of the female figure and that the restrictive nature of these ideal dimensions may be, in some cases, a source of anxiety and insecurity.

Body type

The proposed relationship between body type (physique) and personality has a long history in psychology. In the field of constitutional psychology certain basic human types have been proposed in an effort to simplify the large observable variations among individuals. Such constitutional types are presented as a characterization of the individual as a whole in terms of his physical intellectual and emotional traits. Of the more scientific studies, Sheldon's (1940) stands out as proposing the strongest association between physique and temperament. Sheldon elaborated on Kretschmer's (1925) propositions and introduced more sophisticated procedures for quantifying the related dimensions with greater accuracy before launching on long-term investigations to clarify the way in which he considered personality to be an extention of an individual's biological structure as represented by his somatotype. Sheldon's primary evidence was derived from a study of 200 university men aged between 17 and 31, ways in which the three somatotype dimensions, endomorphy (fat), mesomorphy (muscle) and ectomorphy (linearity) were significantly related to the three corresponding Sheldonian temperamental scales, visceratonia (relaxed), somatotonia (energetic) and cerebretonia (detached) as follows: endomorphy and visceratonia 0·79; mesomorphy and somatotonia 0·82; ectomorphy and cerebretonia 0·83.

These correlations are higher than any found by other investigators and where independent measures of body type and personality have been used few, if any, significant results have been established (Fiske,

1944; Smith, 1949; Kane, 1969). Sugerman and Haronian (1964) are critical of subsequent attempts to replicate Sheldon's work mainly because inappropriate or unsophisticated procedures have been used to 'elucidate the highly intuitive insights of Kretschmer and Sheldon'. In their recent investigation of physique and temperament, Cortes and Gatti (1966) claim to have utilized more objective methods with greater scientific rigour than those employed by Sheldon. In particular, they avoided the two major errors attributed to Sheldon—that of the experimenter rating both somatotype and temperament himself and of using what, in the last analysis, is a subjective body-typing procedure. Cortes and Gatti used Parnell's (1958) objective techniques for body typing and a self-description (adjectival) questionnaire which was specially structured to give scores equivalent to the three Sheldonian scales, viceratonia, somatotonia and cerebretonia. The subjects in this investigation were 97 young men, 120 young women and a small (N=20) group of criminals.

When the young men were grouped according to their body dominance (either endomorphic, mesomorphic or ectomorphic) and their temperamental component scores considered it was found that (1) endomorphs rated themselves significantly more often as viceratonic (i.e. 'relaxed, warm'); (2) mesomorphs described themselves significantly more often in terms of somatotonia (i.e. 'confident, energetic'); and (3) ectomorphs considered themselves significantly more often as cerebretonic (i.e. 'detached, tense').

The intercorrelations between the corresponding components were moderately high for both the men and women ranging from 0·31 and 0·74. The criminals as a group, were highly mesomorphic and the correlation between this component and somatotonia was again highly significant. The authors felt confident that a clear and substantial association between physique and temperament had been demonstrated. Unlike the Sheldon experimental design they felt that they had loaded their design against a significant relationship occurring in that their sample was so heterogeneous. However, their self-descriptive questionnaire is both short (six terms) and subject to self-flattery error and its validity is not reported. Moreover, the conclusions in this study rest heavily on the significance of correlations between the separate body-type components and the temperamental traits.

The importance in this area of finding appropriate statistical and experimental procedures to take account of the 'three-dimensional' nature of the body type is not merely academic. Parnell (1958) has pointed to the conceptual and experimental weakness of considering body type as three separate unit components arguing that a particular score in any one component is relatively meaningless, its significance only becoming evident in association with the scores on the other two components. A recent investigation in this area (Kane, 1969) attempted to allow for the three-dimensional nature of body type by using two kinds of analyses: (1) discriminant function analyses between discrete body-type groups of subjects plotted on a somato-chart according to their component scores considered as a whole; (2) canonical correlation analyses in which the three components were optimally weighted in a body-type vector. In this study, the Parnell method of body typing and the well standardized Cattell (1965) 16 P.F. questionnaire procedures were employed with 400 men and women college students. Neither for the sample as a whole nor for the men and women subjects taken separately were any significant associations found between body type and personality. This would seem to be an interesting finding in view of the fact that the statistical procedures used maximized the possibility for a significant association to be demonstrated. The nature of the body type/personality relationship would seem to require a great deal of further clarification. It may be that the relationship is more general than specific and may be observed experimentally only when reliable but rather global measures of psychological functioning are used. Such measures were used in a study by Sugerman and Haronian (1964) in which they explored the relationship between body type and sophistication-of-body concept among men students. Body type was assessed by both the Sheldon and Parnell methods and Witkin's (1962) simple 5-point scale was used to ascertain the degree of primitivity or sophistication of the body concept as it is reflected in human figure drawings. The authors found a moderate positive link between sophistication-of-body concept and mesomorphy (muscularity) and a moderate negative association between the body sophistication scores and endomorphy (fat). They accounted for these significant correlations in terms of Sheldon's new somatotyping component, the Trunk Index (ratio of thorax to abdomen) which tends to differentiate between mesomorphs and endomorphs.

It has been argued earlier that body concept is a crucial aspect of the self-concept which underpins behaviour and general psychological adjustment. It is surprising therefore, that few studies have investigated the way in which the actual body type is related to body concept. The study just reported is one of the few indications that such an association does exist and in particular, it shows that body-type sophistication goes with a broad-shouldered, narrow-hipped mesomorphic physique. If, as seems likely, body-concept sophistication is a manifestation of body cathexis (i.e. satisfaction with the body and its parts) it may be that the development of a positive body concept will depend to some extent on the differential, social and personal approval given to varying physiques. On this point, McCandless (1960) writes: 'For us in the United States, the beautiful body serves purposes related to fantasy, displacement, projection and wish fulfillment; heroes of popular novels and in the movies and on the television screen are broad-shouldered, narrow-hipped, possess flat abdomens and are muscular.' Some research support is now available for the existence of stereotyped behavioural description relating physique to social image. Brodsky (1954) for instance, found that among medical and dental students, the mesomorphic figures (in various body-type silhouettes) were given the most favourable ratings as being most popular, confident and likely to make the best athlete, the best soldier and the most successful military leader. The extreme ectomorph was rated less favourably and indicated as the most likely to have a nervous breakdown before the age of 30, to be a chain-smoker, to suffer over critical decisions and to have fewest friends. The endomorph was given the most negative ratings, a poor athlete and soldier, a heavy drinker, unaggressive and least preferred as a friend.

More recently, it was found (Kiker and Miller, 1967) that college students ranked, with significant agreement, eleven somatotype photographs on six personality/behaviour concepts and Miller and Stewart (1968) demonstrated the concordance of stereotyped female physique using fourteen boys as judges. On concepts such as 'lazy', 'physically fit', 'religious', 'attractive physique', 'well-adjusted' and 'best-liked', a group of middle-aged men ranked twelve somatotype photographs in an investigation by Sleet (1969). Mesomorphs were rated highest in all the concepts with the exception of 'religious' and the endomorphs lowest. The findings from these complementary researches appear to substantiate the hypothesis that stereotyped social images of individuals based on their physique exist among men. Such stereotypes will undoubtedly affect the way in which an individual perceives his physique and himself.

Another possible explanation of the apparent importance of mesomorphy to body concept is that mesomorphic males are more likely to take part in strenuous physical activities and competitive sports.

Through participation in these activities they will tend to develop a highly developed image of the body and its boundaries. Athletes presumably in the process of achieving necessary control and sensitivity of body orientation and body movement also acquire well-defined and articulated body concepts. The degree of athletic participation might, therefore, be a behavioural factor mediating the relationship between physique and body concept. One study at least has thrown some light on the relationships. In an extension of the study by Sugerman and Haronian (1964) quoted earlier, athletic participation rating was correlated with the body-type assessments and the sophistication-of-body concept scores. The results are shown in Table 1.

Table 1 *Correlation of athletic participation with body type assessments and body-concept scores*

Variable		r	P
Body Concept		0·27	0·01
Trunk Index		0·28	0·01
Endomorphy	(Sheldon)	0·16	NS
Mesomorphy	(Sheldon)	0·46	0·001
Ectomorphy	(Sheldon)	−0·25	0·01
Fat	(Parnell)	0·17	NS
Muscularity	(Parnell)	0·31	0·01
Linearity	(Parnell)	−0·38	0·001

As expected, mesomorphy (muscularity) and body concept are significantly and positively related to high athletic participation while ectomorphy (linearity) is associated with low athletic involvement. A further analysis demonstrated that the negative correlation between ectomorphy and athletic participation score is due to the ectomorphs lacking mesomorphy so that it is mesomorphy alone of the somatotype components which is independently related to athletic participation. It would seem then that athletic participation is positively linked with sophistication-of-body concept but apparently the correlation depends essentially on the mesomorphic component of physique.

Mesomorphy also appears to be of particular importance in recent interesting attempts to indicate a continuity between physical and psychological energy. Mesomorphs were found by Cortes and Gatti (1965) to rate themselves more often as being confident, energetic, adventurous and enterprising. In a later investigation (1966) the same authors hypothesized that mesomorphy would correlate positively with the type of psychological motivation expressed in need for achievement (n Ach). McClelland (1961) has described a person with high scores in n Ach as one who is concerned with accomplishing and doing well and who is energetic, competitive, enterprising and adventurous—in summary, a person who typifies physical and psychological energy. The results of the investigation supported the hypothesis. For two groups of 100 young men significant correlations were found ranging from 0·20 to 0·54 between measures of n Ach and mesomorphy. It is reasonable to speculate on the basis of these results that if n Ach represents high psychological energy which is linked in behaviour with entrepreneurship, innovation and competitive striving, those individuals who are by nature particularly well endowed with superior physical resources will be particularly suited to this type of motivation.

Some implications

It is often claimed by physical educationists that in some unspecified ways, physical activity, physical education and sports experiences are of psychological benefit to the individual. As yet this assumption does not rest on any well-established scientific findings but rather on a generalized philosophical notion of the body-mind relationship.

The body and its reactions are the fundamental concerns in physical education. The vocabulary in physical education is full of terms which reflect the central concern with the body—body development, body sensitivity, body awareness, body control, body expression. It would seem, therefore, that an appreciation of the body image and its implications for self-image may be of importance to the physical education teacher who anticipates psychological outcomes from his work. There is a substantial amount of support—of which some has been outlined above—for the physical educationist who considers that body experience and awareness are vital aspects of total personality development. Freud (cf. Trent, 1961) emphasized this point in commenting, 'the ego is first and foremost a bodily ego.' The special relationship of the way to the self is due no doubt to the unique closeness of the individual's body to himself as a perceiver. His body is the only object in his perceptual field which at once is perceived by him and is also part of himself. Its special closeness increases the possibility of reflecting his personal concerns and feelings. One way in which this works has been demonstrated by Wapner and Krus (1959) who found that failure experiences resulted in subjects perceiving themselves as shorter in stature than they really were. Success and failure as the inevitable outcome of competition is widely used as a motivation procedure in physical education. A study by Read (1969) indicated that constant winning and constant losing influence the concepts of body and self. What is not clear from the study is the position of the critical point beyond which losing begins to have a deleterious psychological effect. The subjects falling within the middle range, i.e. not winning or losing all the time, were found not to have changed either self- or body-concepts in any significant way. The question for the physical educationist is clearly one of controlling competitive situations in such a way that while benefiting the physically capable, they are not a source of threat to others.

The body-image correlates of motor ability and motor performance have been investigated in a number of recent studies at the University of Maryland aimed at increasing understanding in the way physical education experiences are related to psychological dynamics. In one of these investigations among adolescent girls, Schulz (1961), administered balance, co-ordination and power tests of motor performance together with two tests, a Semantic Differential Test and the Draw-a-Person Test which were designed to reveal the individual's body image. Highly significant correlations were found between the combined physical performance measures and both the body-image assessments. In another Maryland University study, Sloan (1963) used a body cathexis test and a body scale to ascertain the body image of young men whose motor performance was scored on the Barrow Motor Ability Test. Again a significant relationship between body image and motor performance was demonstrated. Taken together, these two studies are indicative of a link between the motor experiences which form part of the physical education programme and integrated personality.

Physical educationists would additionally like the possibility of considering notions of body and self-concepts in terms of an awareness of the body in motion. It would seem likely that the development of perceptions relative to body boundary, body cathexis, body sophistication and body orientation are increased by movement experiences in, for example, dance and sports. Some possibilities seem to have been opened recently in this area by Zion (1965). In her study of the relationship between body and self-concept of college women, she used body-concept measures which included scales of physical qualities in body movement, expressiveness and masculinity-femininity. Her conclusions based on significant correlations between self concept and these (and other) body-concept scales were that the security one has in one's body and its functional abilities (especially those reflected in attitude to movement and expression) is related to the security with which one faces one's self and the world.

In the area of movement therapy there seems to be some reason for considering the possibility of body-concept changes being involved. Max Cogan (1963) questions whether the mental and physical improvement among educationally subnormal boys, reported by Oliver (1958), as a result of a systematic course in physical activities was not in some way linked with positive change in body concept. Cogan also refers to the early work of Elsa Gindler in Germany and Marian Chace in the United States as examples of ways in which a development of body awareness through various forms of movement education helps in psychological readjustment. Wooten (1959) also reports that movement diagnosis and therapy have been developed in England based on principles of Rudolf Laban.

Of particular interest and challenge to the physical educationist will be Witkin's suggestion of perceptual styles linked with field dependence-independence. Of all the body concepts this discriminatory index appears to be the most stable over time and would seem likely to repay careful consideration of those interested not only in the body-mind relationships, but also in factors affecting motor learning and performance. It is conceivable that a field-independent individual will have less difficulty in acquiring skills that depend on body orientation, especially in those skills (i.e. diving and gymnastics) where accurate body awareness is crucial. It is also a possibility that field dependency may be more of an advantage than a disadvantage in the performance of 'open' skills which require the performer to relate the skill or technique to the environment as in many team sports. Indeed, Poulton's (1957) interesting suggestion of a classification of skills into 'open skills' (in which the reading of the environmental display is vital) and 'closed skills' (in which there is relative independence of environmental factors) might seem to be particularly meaningful when considered together with the body orientation concept of field dependence-independence which emphasizes the distinction between figure and ground. The study (Kreiger, 1962) undertaken in this area, indicated that figure-ground perception is positively and significantly related to spatial adjustment in tennis. One would like to see findings from similar attempts to relate modes of perceiving to other skills abilities and to movement concepts such as space, time and force which appear to be founded on figure-ground orientation.

Some concern has been expressed by Vincent and Dorsey (1968) as to whether we may or may not infer, from the various measures of body concept, that there are a number of interrelated and integrated aspects of the individual's perception of his physical self. What evidence there is tends to indicate that there are a number of dimensions which together go to form the fully structured body image and concept. The authors have hypothesized the existence of three dimensions, a sensory-spatial dimension, an existential dimension and a valuative dimension. The sensory-spatial dimension is meant to represent those perceptions related to body conformation, spatial position, etc. The existential aspect of body concept is suggested to represent the perceptions pertaining to substantiveness, realness and vulnerability. The perceptions constituting the proposed valuative dimension are those concerned with the value of the body's appearance and functions.

This conceptual model of the body-concept dimensions offers both a possible integrative explanation of the various approaches to the assessment of the physical self and a testable hypothesis for a much needed research. In the meantime, the model is a useful basis for the physical educationist who is so closely concerned with the instrumental body. The term 'body awareness' is used freely in physical education to generalize about planned or incidental outcomes of various types of physical activity. It might be useful for physical educationists and others to consider the strong possibility of there being at least three ways in which 'body awareness' has meaning, in terms of sensory-spatial awareness, existential or phenomenal awareness and valuative awareness.

In his fascinating book, *Joy-Expanding Human Awareness* (1967), Schutz considers the search for joy through the realization of one's potential must begin with a consideration of the body as the origin of emotional and mental states. Concerning the many social and personal factors which coalesce to make it difficult for an individual to be acquainted with his real feelings and desires and to function effectively and joyously Schutz writes:

Our bodies, too, can inhibit the development of joy. Poor physical condition, physical trauma and emotional problems (converted into physical ailments, weakness and malformations) limit a person's capacity for full realization. A pained, tired, deadened or unfeeling body cannot experience itself fully and cannot hold the feeling required for optimal fulfillment of the individual.

Part II Personality and performance

The postulated association between personality and performance would seem to be best supported by attempts to explain a common neuropsychological base for both. An increasingly strong line of reasoning attempts to explain personality in terms of neural arousal and there is interesting evidence to suggest that differences in arousal may affect performance in psychomotor tasks.

No psychologist has been more systematic than Eysenck in offering physiological and neurological explanations of his descriptive dimensions of personality. Eysenck (1965) has developed two broad personality scales, E (extraversion-introversion) and N (neuroticism) which give a description of the phenotype but do not in themselves represent any theory of causation. He has continued to emphasize, however, that underlying causal substrates of personality may be at the genotypic level and has continued to develop and refine a theory linking the overt personality characteristics with their causal biological source. His notion of behavioural causation emphasizes the neural level: neuroticism is explained as the lability or excitability of the autonomic nervous system and extraversion-introversion is seen as reflecting the strength of the excitatory and inhibitory functions of the central (cortical) nervous system. More particularly, Eysenck (1967) has recently proposed two separate but interrelated neural circuits to explain his two main personality dimensions. The first with which extraversion-introversion is identified involves a recticular cortical loop and the second, associated with neuroticism, is identified with the hypothalmus. Claridge (1967) has therefore suggested two sources of personality arousal, sensory-recticular arousal and autonomic (hypothalmic) arousal.

In the elaboration of the causal genotypic links with the descriptive phenotype, Eysenck (1965) suggests four strata or levels. The first level is considered to be constitutionally determined and controls the balance of excitation or inhibition. (Teplov (1964) has indicated that workers in Pavlov laboratories first conceived the idea that variations in the excitatory and inhibitory functions of the nervous system could account for personality differences.) Strong excitatory and weak inhibitory potentials would typify the introvert and the opposite emphasis would typify the extravert. The second level reflects the individual differences in experimental behaviour: extraverts should condition more poorly, show greater reminiscence, dislike repetitive tasks, etc. At the third level environmental factors begin to influence behaviour and therefore the more complex observable phenomena of personality are to be seen visualizing the traits of introversion-extraversion, including sociability, impulsiveness and ascendance. The fourth level represents social attitudes and habits of thought, especially tough-mindedness versus tender-mindedness.

Certain criticisms have been made of this theoretical schema mainly because of the relative emphasis on the extraversion dimension and the relative neglect of the neuroticism dimension and also because of the explanation and interpretation of excitation and inhibition.

Concerning the causal basis and neural structure supporting emotionality or neuroticism, Eysenck is less elaborate than in attempting an explanation of the nature of the other main personality factor, extraversion-introversion. Emotionality or neuroticism is simply explained in terms of instability of the autonomic nervous system. It is held that autonomic reaction is basically dependent on the individual's constitutional structure which mediates the strength of sympathetic reaction to incoming stimuli. Although there seem to be characteristic ways in which individuals react to the stimulation of the sympathetic and to the way in which control is indicated by the parasympathetic system, the autonomic nervous system is nevertheless considered to be the most likely basis for individual differences in emotionality.

Eysenck's interpretations of the introversion-extraversion dimension are based on the balance between cortical excitation and inhibition. Excitation in neural and behavioural terms refers to the facilitation of perceptual, congitive and motor responses in the central nervous system and inhibition refers to just the opposite effect, that is, to the depression of those responses. The use of this kind of causative physiological model of behaviour derives from the earlier premises of Pavlov and their revision by subsequent Soviet psychologists, especially Teplov (1964). Pavlov offered a three-fold description of neural processes fundamental to behaviour as 'strength', 'balance of arousal and inhibition' and 'mobility'. In recent studies emphasis has been given to the ways in which these three processes interact so that neural 'strength' is currently being described in terms of the ability of the nervous system to endure prolonged arousal without unusual inhibitory action and the conception of neural mobility as being expressed in terms of 'the ease of formation of inhibitory and facilitative associations' (Klein, Barr and Wolitzky, 1967).

In his generalized explanation of the processes of neural excitation and inhibition, Eysenck (1965) introduces, for the purposes of illustration a demon who is to be regarded

> as a kind of homunculus, sitting near the point where the long pathways of the central nervous system enter into the lower parts of the brain. He has his hands on two levers, one marked 'excitation' and the other marked 'inhibition'. Whenever sensory stimuli are coming in through these pathways, he presses sometimes one lever, sometimes the other and sometimes both. Stimuli produced by the levers are then sent on into the brain, where they either facilitate the passage and the interplay of the incoming neural stimuli or suppress and inhibit them.

The illustration is taken further in behavioural terms to propose that there are two kinds of demons, the ones particularly given to pulling the excitation lever who inhabit the central nervous systems of introverted people and the others inclined more to pulling the inhibition lever who inhabit the central nervous systems of extraverted people. Extraverts are, therefore, more liable to inhibitory potentials and introverts more subject to excitation. In support of these explanations of the biological basis of introversion-extraversion a great deal of assiduous empiric research has been undertaken by Eysenck and his collaborators mostly in studies of perceptual and psychomotor performance. The inhibition to which the extravert is subject and which is accountable for the differences in experimental performances quoted above causes a kind of 'stimulus hunger'. This need and desire of the extravert for strong sensory stimulus to sustain his required level of arousal against the depressing affects of inhibition would seem to explain the behavioural pattern of the typical extravert. There is a good deal of evidence (Eysenck, 1965) to support this notion in that extraverts are found to be fond of noise, loud music and bright colours; and to be more disposed than introverts to alcohol, drugs, cigarette smoking and other forms of stimulation. It may be also that the characteristic sociability of the extravert derives from his stimulus hunger so that he seeks the company and reaction of other people. The extravert's inhibition of incoming stimuli may, of course, be of some advantage in pain tolerance. For a given amount of pain, the extravert will tend to experience less and the introvert more because of the differential effects of inhibition and excitation on the sensory input.

A number of attempts have been made to interpret Eysenck's excitation-inhibition hypothesis of personality in terms of arousal. Claridge (1967) in particular has reinterpreted Eysenck's postulates from the point of view of physiological arousal or activation. Arousal theorists such as Elizabeth Duffy (1962), Malmo (1958) and Hebb (1955) have taken the theoretical position that variations in arousal occur along a continuum from sleep, at the lower end, to emotional excitement at the upper end. It is suggested that changes along this continuum are reflected centrally (by EEG) and peripherally by somatic reactions such as muscle tension, heart rate, blood pressure, respiration rate and skin resistance. Duffy (1962) has reviewed a considerable amount of research evidence to support the arousal hypothesis and to demonstrate associated personality functioning.

Claridge (1967) has made the point in support of his interpretation that although Eysenck has seldom explained differences in performance measures in terms of excitation, it could often be used as appropriately as inhibition to account for the demonstrated differences. Moreover, Claridge concluded from a factor analysis of perceptual and perceptual-motor performance of normal and psychiatric subjects that the so-called excitation-inhibition balance was the net result of an interaction between *both* Eysenck's personality dimensions (E and N). He identified two major factors in his analysis: the first was a factor 'extraversion' which had high loadings in the appropriate objective tests and on the Eysenck E scale; the second was identified as 'drive' because it showed moderate to high saturation of excitation-inhibition measures (vigilance decrement, pursuit motor performance level and spiral after-effect), and of the Eysenck N scale. These findings allowed Claridge to translate and elaborate Eysenck's theory into an equivalent arousal model which gave more emphasis to the excitatory rather than the inhibitory processes. In doing so, he demonstrated the possibility of considering *both* Eysenck's personality dimensions, extraversion and neuroticism, as contributing to arousal. Neuroticism, it was argued, contributed substantially to the identified 'drive' factor in the analysis referred to above and also was known to correlate with anxiety (Eysenck, 1959) while both drive and anxiety have been linked with recticular arousal (Malmo, 1957).

It may be useful at this point, to comment briefly on the neuro-physiological explanation of arousal. This may serve to give a more detailed account of the proposed link between arousal and person-ality as suggested by Claridge and may also serve as an important background against which to consider the relationship (to be discussed later) between arousal and performance.

The 'ascending recticular arousal system' which is situated in the brain stem is known to exert a generalized tonic arousal influence on the cortex and the subcortex and thereby controls the activation level and regulation of the various body organs and systems. The recticular formation is considered to be an accessory of the classical afferent sensory pathways at the point when they pass through the lower brain stem. Impulses passing to the cortex along the afferent path-ways are also carried through the recticular formation by collateral fibres giving rise to recticular discharges. The effects of this lateral recticular stimulation are transmitted upward in the brain producing widespread cortical activation associated with behavioural arousal (Duffy, 1962). In addition to the part of the recticular formation lying in the brain stem there is a discreetly organized portion which has been identified as 'the diffuse thalmic projection system' which appears to have a shorter-lasting effect on limited areas of the cortex. This thalmic portion of the recticular formation is regarded as a scanning or screening mechanism which controls the distribution and integration of impulses to the cortex. In this connection, it also provides a kind of inhibitory influence. The integrated recticular formation may be considered therefore to account for general control of cortical arousal affecting the level of activation which provides the energizing aspects of motivation, drive and general behaviour. The excitatory and inhibitory regulation of the arousal system apparently depends on the delicate interplay of cortical and subcortical circuits which interact to maintain a dynamic equilibrium by processing and filtering sensory impulses and which protect the brain from excessive stimulation. Claridge suggests that there may be, in fact, two functionally related arousal mechanisms; the first is identified as a 'tonic arousal system' which is concerned with main-taining an individual's gross level of arousal and the second is suggested as 'the arousal modulating system' which controls the level at which the tonic arousal system functions and also integrates the stimulus input by appropriate facilitation or suppression.

The particular importance and function of the recticular formation in arousal and personality is emphasized by studies of the effect of drugs on the central nervous system. Depending on the nature of the drug and the dosage used, some drugs may apparently exert differential effects on different areas of the nervous system and cause not only changes in activation and arousal but also in behaviour. In particular, the so-called stimulant and depressant drugs have a strong effect on the various parts of the recticular formation. Amphetamine and caffeine, even in small concentration, have been shown to raise both the arousal reaction and the level of overt activity while the depressant barbiturates, well-known inducers of relaxation and sleep, seem to reduce activation through their particular effect on the mesencephalic recticular formation which in turn seems to lengthen the recuperation time of neurones on the sensory cortex (Duffy, 1962). Eysenck (1965) has postulated that depressant drugs have an extraverting effect by increasing inhibitory potential and that stimulant drugs have an introverting effect by decreasing inhibition and increasing excitation. In support of this notion, he quotes the results of a study of delinquent boys. On the assumption that the subjects were extraverts, a stimulant (d-amphetamine) was given to one experimental group in the hope of providing an introverting effect which might also reduce their delinquent behaviour. It was found that those who were given the stimulant drug showed a very significant decline in delinquent symptoms while control and placebo groups demonstrated a slight increase in symptoms during the period of the study. When drug administration was stopped, the experimental group gradually returned to its original level of delinquency. It seems that human behaviour and performance can effectively be controlled by drug administration and that this control is mediated through the recticular arousal system.

Arousal and performance

The proposed causal explanations of personality in terms of arousal outlined above have implications for motor performance. There are good reasons to suppose that differences in arousal may affect not only sensory responses but also various aspects in the performance of tasks. On this point, Welford (1968) has suggested that, in considering the relationship between performance and Eysenckian personality dimensions, it may be useful to 'assume that introverts are more chronically aroused than extraverts and that 'unstable' (i.e. neurotic) people become aroused more easily than 'stable people'. This generalization would necessarily lead to the expectation of poorer task performance among extraverts compared with introverts and more particularly of poorer performance among stable extraverts. Performances according to these expectations were, in fact, demonstrated in a study of the examination results obtained by engineering students (Furneaux, 1962). Other studies have shown that extraverts perform less well than introverts when it would appear that arousal is low, as for instance after loss of sleep (Corcoran, 1965) and when tests are given late in the day (Colquhoun and Corcoran, 1964). Noise, which may be regarded as increasing arousal and attention, prevented the decline in vigilance tests among extraverts studied by Davies and Hockey (1966) and the superiority of the extravert over the introvert in performance tasks undertaken in the evening, when presumably the extravert has had time to be aroused, are reported by Welford (1968).

It would seem reasonable to consider chronic anxiety as being associated with arousal level which reflects autonomic and cortical activity. Some support that such an association does exist is provided by evidence of, for example, higher palmar sweating, higher cardiac response, higher blink rate and longer spiral after-effects among anxious subjects. Breen (1959) found that 16 P.F. anxiety and three primary traits factors contributing to it, factor O (insecurity), factor Q_4 (ergic tension) and factor C (instability) were consistently related to high pulse rate, high systolic and diastolic amplitude and to diastolic surge among college students. He interpreted his results as indicating that general anxiety was linked with poor physical fitness as reflected in resting measures of cardiovascular reaction. Wells (1958) also found that physical fitness performances were poor in students of high anxiety. He reported that the IPAT Anxiety Scale was significantly and negatively correlated with the Cureton Motor Fitness Test (-0.27), with the Larson I.C.D. test (-0.31), with chins (-0.29) and with dips (-0.36). It would seem that while the higher levels of arousal and alertness associated with chronic anxiety may lead to higher initial cerebral task performance it makes for poorer physical endurance which depends on a relatively low cardiovascular response to work load.

Stable extraverts may be considered as being low in both arousal and arousability which may put them at a disadvantage in mental tasks but may enable them to be superior performers in physical endurance tasks which capitalize on their low physiological activation. However, the way in which arousal affects performance of any kind is not entirely clear and there appear to be a number of factors affecting the relationship, for example, the difficulty of the task, the individual's ability and previous training and the situational (stress) anxiety associated with the task.

Optimal performance

Long before the discovery of the arousal function of the lower brain centres such as the ascending recticular formation (Moruzzi and Magoun, 1949) such terms as 'degree of excitation' and 'energy mobilization' were used by Elizabeth Duffy (1934, 1941) to explain behavioural phenomena from the viewpoint of generalized organismic arousal. More recently (Duffy, 1962) has elaborated her notions of behavioural causation in terms of 'activation' which may be taken to be roughly equivalent to general arousal. It is proposed that the level of activation is the product of action and reaction taking place within the organisms as a whole.

There appears to be an optimal level of activation for various kinds of performances. That activation or arousal may be too high or too low for producing the best quality of performance has a good deal of empiric support. If activation is too low, as in drowsiness, it might be expected that the individual might lack alertness and attention so that his response would be inadequate. On the other hand, if activation is too high, the cortex may become 'bombarded' by a stream of impulses with which it is unable to cope. The optimal level of performance in a given task will clearly depend on a number of factors such as the nature of the task, previous training and habituation and the individual's tonic arousal level. However, the relationship between activation and performance seems to be best expressed by an inverted U-shaped curve in which performance improves with arousal or activation from a low level up to an optimum after which performance deteriorates with further increases in activation (Figure 1).

Supporting research in this field is reviewed by Duffy (1962) who describes a number of studies which appear to give only indirect evidence of the inverted-U function relating activation with performance. Ideally, one would like to see evidence of a systematic variation of activation level from low to high related over the whole range to corresponding changes in performance. However, the weight of experimental evidence, both direct and indirect, tends to confirm, in general, the inverted-U hypothesis. In an early study by Yerkes and

Dodson (1908) fewer errors in learning were recorded when an electric shock of medium intensity was applied to mice than when shocks of low or high intensity were applied. When the tasks in two studies were made more difficult the optimum shock for most efficient learning was found to be progressively weaker. This classical study with mice has stimulated a number of studies with human subjects where different tasks and incentives were used and similar results have been found. Some of the methods used to manipulate activities in these studies, giving indirect confirmation of the inverted-U association, were to deprive subjects of sleep (e.g. Malmo, 1958), to reduce different levels of muscular tension (Eason and White, 1961) and to put the subjects into frustrating situations (i.e. Burgess and Hokansson, 1964). In each instance, moderate levels of activation were associated with optimum performance.

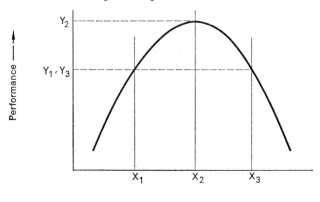

Arousal ———▶

Figure 1 The inverted-U relationship between arousal and performance. Arousal levels up to X_2 are positively linked with performance but thereafter negatively. $X_2 - Y_2$ represents the optimal relationship. However, arousal levels X_1 and X give rise to the same performance level Y_1, Y_3.

While the linking of rise of activation to improved performance can be readily accepted, the fall in performance at high levels of activation is more difficult to explain. In general, the research evidence indicates motor performance such as ball tossing, speed of tapping, manual pursuit and mirror drawing deteriorate when activation level is high. High levels of anxiety and stress (e.g. dangers, annoyances and incentives) have been shown to have some kind of disorganizing effect on performance. In this connection, Welford (1968) quotes the observations of Mira (1944) of fear reaction during the Spanish Civil War. Mild degrees of fear led apparently to prudent actions and caution which led to improved achievement. Severe states of fear led, however, to alarm and the breakdown of high-grade skill and later to panic and uncontrolled activity. Fear of failure (F.F.) has been clearly identified as a cause of poor performance arising from anxiety. Apparently, arousal levels may run high when F.F. subjects feel threatened as in unfamiliar, complex, speeded, competitive and non-game achievement settings (Birney, Burdick and Teevan, 1969). In some way, F.F. subjects became confused and disorganized in these situations and fail to perform according to their ability.

One recent study (Sjoberg, 1968) which systematically examined the hypothetical inverted-U function relating efficiency to arousal used bicycle ergometer work to manipulate arousal level over a wide range. It was assumed that graded variations in work load would be associated with consistent changes in heart rate which has been regarded as one of the most reliable measures of arousal. A visual choice reaction task (pressing appropriately left- or right-hand button in response to light stimuli) was used to measure psychological performance at each of five different arousal levels for 25 male subjects. When the mean scores for reaction speed were plotted against mean heart rate at each of the five work loads, the data followed an inverted-U curve illustrating performance was best at moderate levels of arousal and worst at minimum and maximum levels.

The difficulties associated with prediction based on the inverted-U curve have been pointed out by Corcoran (1965). The implication is that for a given performance (except the optimal) value, there will be two possible values of arousal. For the purpose of attaining optimal performance, it is therefore important to know whether arousal should subsequently be increased or decreased (see Figure 1). Corcoran carried out two experiments to test his hypothesis that by manipulating arousal level, it is possible to identify whether a given level of performance is associated with either the low or the high level of arousal. His assumption was that highly aroused subjects will show improvement in performance when arousal is reduced while lowly aroused subjects will decline in performance in these circumstances. Similarly, it was assumed that when arousal level is generally increased highly aroused subjects will decline and lowly aroused subjects will increase in performance. In the experiments, sleep deprivation was used to manipulate levels of arousal and highly and lowly aroused subjects were identified in terms of their scores on the introversion-extraversion scale. The experimental tasks were a five-choice serial-reaction task and a difficult tracking task. Corcoran found support for his assumptions that information could be gained concerning the level of arousal at which an individual was functioning by noting the change and direction of performance when arousal level was increased or decreased. The implications of this study are particularly important, for example, in making interpretations about the way in which various motivational procedures are related to gross physical performances. Presumably motivational procedures are applied with a view to improving performance but whether a particular form of motivation has given rise to under-arousal or over-arousal is usually not known. It would seem to be important in seeking optimal physical performances for systematic observation to be taken while motivation and arousal are manipulated so that subsequent procedures may be adapted in the right direction.

Part III Personality and physical [athletic] abilities

The assumption has long been held by physical educationists and others that an individual's physical (athletic) abilities are related to his personality structure. One explanation offered is that the environment in which physical abilities are displayed (e.g. in games and sport) constitutes an ideal setting for the development of desirable personality characteristics such as confidence, sociability, self-reliance, co-operativeness and general personal adjustment. The relationship between personality and physical abilities has also been argued by those who are concerned with advising and helping champion athletes. It has been suggested (Cofer and Johnson, 1960) that in personality champion athletes are 'a special breed' and that in the last analysis personality is the vital factor in the discriminating process which singles out the champions from amongst those who seem to have similar physical gifts. Ogilvie and Tutko (1966) claim to have identified personality dimensions which are essential to competitive success and have indicated some common personality problems of athletic 'under-achievers'. Physical educationists are also vitally interested today in the fundamental relationship between personality disposition and ability to learn motor skills required in sports, dance, recreative pursuits and in general, body management so that programmes of work may be structured to cater for individuals' personality differences.

In recent years, the interest in relating personality to physical abilities has greatly increased due, no doubt, to the improved validity of the measures available. Cattell felt able to write in 1960, 'until a generation ago neither the physical nor the psychological measures were worth a cent and findings could be construed to fit almost any view one wished to entertain.' A number of broad-based researches (e.g. Fleishman, 1964; Ismail and Gruber, 1967; and Cratty, 1967) have begun to give increasing clarity and dependability to our notions of the factors involved in gross physical ability. At the same time, procedures for assessing personality have become theoretically sounder, more meaningful and better standardized.

An increasing number of studies in this area reported in the last five or six years have used the 16 P.F. (Cattell, 1965) method of assessing personality. This has had the advantage of making some comparisons between the findings of different investigators though reviewers still find a great deal of difficulty in coming to clear-cut and generalized conclusions from the evidence now available. Interpretation is made difficult by the variety of systems used for selecting and classifying subjects, by the different analytical methods employed and essentially by the absence of either formulated hypotheses or theoretical frameworks. Nevertheless, a number of detailed reviews of the empiric research are available (e.g. Cofer and Johnson, 1960; Warburton and Kane, 1967; Ogilvie, 1968; and Husman, 1969) and from these a number of testable hypotheses may be assembled for further rigorous research. These reviews tend to give a personality description of the male athlete or physically gifted individual in terms of extravert tendencies (such as high dominance, social aggression, leadership, tough-mindedness) and general emotional control reflected in such trait measurements as low anxiety and high confidence. Women athletes are most often described as being like the men athletes on the extraversion dimension but being unlike them in showing a lower level of emotional control. There are, of course, many exceptions to these general descriptions which have been reported and no doubt both the nature of the physical activity or sport in question and the subjects' level of participation will in some way be reflected in characteristic ways of behaving. When the activity and level of participation are held constant interesting consistencies in personality have been demonstrated and evidence presented in support of the existence of certain sports 'types' for example, a 'soccer type' (Kane, 1966), or 'racing driver type' (Ogilvie, 1968) and a 'wrestlers type' (Kroll, 1967). In the search for possible sports types and more generally, in the comparison of personality group profiles, the use of discriminant function analysis has become fashionable. Many earlier studies have relied for interpretation on a simple comparison of the personality measures set out in profile form. The Cattell 16 P.F. may, for example, be conveniently set out in profile fashion showing the norm scores on the sixteen dimensions and a profile similarity coefficient (r_p) may be used to assess the level of agreement between group profile pattern. However, the simple comparison of profile dimensions taken one at a time has the disadvantage that the profile as a whole is never considered nor is the relative importance of dimensions emphasized. The discriminant function form of analysis has the particular advantage that it takes account of the variability over the entire profile range so that, in the case of the sixteen personality factors, the total personality is considered when group scores are being compared. Only when significant 'discriminant space' exists between them, may group profiles be considered to differ. The special use of discriminant function techniques in sports personality studies has been particularly well demonstrated by Kroll and Petersen (1965). In this study, the authors compared the 16 P.F. profiles of five winning and losing teams. Two functions were found which would significantly discriminate between winners and losers with the largest function emphasizing factor B (general ability), factor H (adventurousness), factor O (confidence) and factor Q3 (will-power). However, univariate tests of differences between the sixteen profile dimensions taken one at a time revealed a significant difference for factor B only thus concealing important personality factors apparently associated with successful teams.

When personality differences between the physically gifted and others are reported speculation arises as to the inferences which may be drawn. Are the personality characteristics a cause of success in physical performances or a result of long-term involvement in sport? To move from the present position where it appears that there are some links between personality traits and physical performance to a demonstration of the nature of a causal relationship would be a large step. The current evidence allows only the suggestion of a number of ways in which the association may exist. Kroll (1967) has suggested a number of alternative explanations. Firstly, it may be that a set of personality factors exist which motivate individuals to become involved in physical activities and sport. It may also be that those who possess these personality qualities in the appropriate combinations are able to persist long enough and become successful. According to this explanation, both novices and veterans will possess similar personality patterns, the only difference being in the extent to which they are present. Secondly, it could be that there is no precise 'entry' pattern but that either by modification of personality over time or by rejection of inappropriate patterns only those developing a 'suitable' pattern continue to retain their interest in physical activities and sport and progress satisfactorily. This interpretation would mean that novices would possess dissimilar patterns but veterans would possess a similar one. Thirdly, the possibility exists that there is a similar pattern for those becoming involved which in some way motivates their initial entry in physical activities and sports but participation or selective rejection results in dissimilar patterns for veterans. A fourth possibility is that both novices and veterans possess dissimilar and non-discriminant patterns.

Practically all the research so far reported in this area has been concerned with the first of these possible interpretations. Clearly longitudinal studies would be helpful. Few of these have been undertaken and even then the experimental periods have been relatively short. However, three recent researchers dealing with the possible personality effects of extended athletic involvement have reported similar findings. Werner and Gottheil (1966) investigated the effect of athletic participation over four years on West Point cadets, but found no evidence to indicate that athletic involvement affected the 16 P.F. structure of these young men. Rushall (1968) likewise could find no consistent personality change among participants in track and field, football and swimming over a three-year period. In addition, Kane (1970) could demonstrate no discriminant space between the personality profiles (16 P.F.), taken at the beginning and at the end of a three-year course, of either men or women physical education students. He concluded that involvement in physical activities and sports had no generalized personality effect on these groups of students. However, this study did clearly demonstrate that both men and women students involved in physical education (and therefore presumably in physical activities and sports) differ in personality from the general body of students. If these personality differences are in any way attributable to the 'athletic environment', then presumably the cause-and-effect reaction takes place before maturity.

Only further and more extensive longitudinal studies will reveal the extent to which personality and athletic achievement are dynamically associated. In addition, we may need, as Kroll (1969) suggests, to develop specific assessment techniques capable of accounting for behaviour in the unique athletic situation.

Multivariate correlation analyses

It is somewhat surprising to find that almost no correlational studies have been undertaken in attempting to tease out the nature of the personality/physical performance relationship. If a relationship exists at all, it would seem that appropriate correlational procedures could well demonstrate the circumstances under which it is maximized. A series of correlation analyses in this area has recently been undertaken (Kane, 1970) and these shed some light on the way in which personality is related to measures of physical performance. In these studies analyses were carried out for two groups of physical education specialist students (men and women) and for two equivalent groups of general college students so that the generality of the findings could be ascertained. Personality was measured by the 16 P.F. methods and physical performance was assessed by a variety of tests purporting to measure important and well-established aspects of gross physical ability (e.g. static strength, dynamic strength, explosive strength, endurance and power), many of which have been identified in extensive factorial investigations undertaken by Fleishman (1964). Body-type assessments were also taken. The analytic methods used based on the intercorrelation of the variables included factor analysis, with the extraction of higher order factors, multiple regression and canonical correlation. These procedures were utilized in order to describe the factors accounting for the interrelationship between the two domains and then to identify the variables and combination of variables contributing most to significant correlations obtained. The following is a generalized summary of these studies.

Factor structure

From the intercorrelation of the personality and physical variables factor structures were established for each of the four groups of subjects. The ten primary factors identified for the two groups of men subjects were very similar but did not give a clear indication of the way in which the personality and physical abilities go together. However, when these primary factors were subjected to further factoring to produce a more parsimonious solution the nature of the relationship between the two domains became more obvious. This second order solution identified four factor complexes (for both groups of men), which combines the personality and physical measures as follows:

Factor 1′ Extraversion with general athletic ability, (i.e. speed, strength and power).

Factor 2′ Stability with explosive strength.

Factor 3′ Tough-mindedness with muscularity and sports participation index (i.e. degree of sports involvement).

Factor 4′ Conservatism with endurance.

Previous studies have attempted to argue the personality/physical abilities relationship on the basis of confusing first-order correlations between simple unit measures, whereas it would seem from this second-order factor solution that the relationship has clear meaning only when a number of unit measures are ideally combined as in *extraversion* (which combines five of the 16 P.F. dimensions) and in *general athletic ability* (which combines, in this interpretation, measures of speed, strength and power).

The solution for the women subjects did not allow such a clear interpretation. However, the second-order solution showed that the association between the personality and physical measures was best defined in two factors which linked tough-mindedness with athletic ability and conservatism with endurance. There were indications, however, that differences may exist in the way in which personality and physical abilities are related among women of superior physical expertise, and those of average physical gifts.

Multiple correlation analyses

From the information gained from the factor analyses a number of multiple correlation analyses were carried out to expand the general information concerning the conditions under which the two domains are related. These analyses showed that:

1 Among women stability (i.e. the combined weighted score on 16 P.F. traits CLO, Q3 and Q4) is significantly associated with the physical abilities vector. Approximately 15 per cent of the variance in stability is accounted for by the physical ability measures.

2 Among men extraversion (i.e. 16 P.F. traits A, E, F, H, Q4) is significantly associated with the physical abilities vector. Approximately 16 per cent of the variance in extraversion is accounted for by the physical ability measures.

3 The vector of personality variables is significantly associated with an index of sports participation (i.e., degree of sport involvement) among both men and women, accounting for 20 per cent of the

variance. The most important contributing personality variables to the correlation were found to be Q2 (group dependence), E (dominance) and Q4 (low ergic tension).

While these multiple correlation analyses showed particular ways in which the two domains are related it was possible that other groupings of the variables might reveal additional information about the personality/physical correlation. For this purpose a number of canonical correlations were undertaken.

Canonical correlation analyses

The canonical correlation is the maximum correlation between the linear functions of two sets of variables and goes a stage further than regression analysis by involving both multiple criteria as well as multiple predictors. The beta weights obtained in canonical analyses indicate the relative contribution which each variable makes to the correlation between the two canonical variates (vectors) and for practical purposes ought to allow a meaningful interpretation. However, the maximizing processes involved capitalize on any chance fluctuations or variability occurring in the specific context of a particular sample of cases, so that the beta weights are usually considered to be unstable and apply only in that specific context.

It is somewhat surprising, therefore, that in general the canonical vectors for each sub-group of the subjects gave a somewhat similar picture and appeared to demonstrate high values in athletic ability, (i.e. speed, power, endurance) going with extraversion. All the canonical correlations were significant and ranged from 0·71 for the high motor performance group of one to 0·83 for the equivalent group of women. These consistent and clearly meaningful findings would seem to permit a confident interpretation of a real relationship between total personality and a broad-based array of physical abilities: the relationship by those personality traits which combine to form extraversion and those motor performances which describe general athletic ability.

These studies give some indication of the importance of correlational approaches in identifying the circumstances under which personality and physical abilities may be related. They emphasize the value of multivariate and particularly second-order factor analyses in this area of research. Further corroboration of these findings are needed, but as they stand they represent the basis for a number of testable hypotheses. The general conclusion to be drawn is that the personality and physical ability domains are demonstrably linked and that the circumstances under which they are maximally associated are best seen when simple unitary measures of personality and physical abilities are appropriately combined in factor complexes.

Bibliography

Birney, R., Burdick, H., and Teevan, R. (1969), *Fear of Failure*, Van Nostrand-Reinhold, New York.

Breen, J. (1959), 'Anxiety Factors related to Some Physical Fitness Variables', Ph.D. thesis, University of Illinois.

Brodsky, C. (1954), *A Study of Norms for Body Form-Behaviour Relationships*, Catholic University Press, Washington.

Burgess, M., and Hokansson, J. (1964), 'Effects of Increased Heart Rate on Intellectual Performance', *J. Abnorm. Psych.*, 68.

Cattell, R. (1960), 'Some Psychological Correlates of Physical Fitness and Physique', in *Exercise and Fitness*, University of Illinois.

(1965), *The Scientific Analysis of Personality*, Penguin, Baltimore.

Claridge, G. (1967), *Personality and Arousal*, Pergamon, London.

Cleveland, S. (1960), 'Body Image Changes associated with Personality Reorganization', *J. Consult. Psych.*, 24.

Cofer, C., and Johnson, W. (1960), 'Personality Dynamics in Relation to Exercise and Sports', in Johnson, W. (ed.), *Science and Medicine of Exercise and Sport*, Harper, New York.

Cogan, Max (1963), 'The Body Image in Physical Education', *66th Annual Proceedings of NCPEAM*, AAHPER, Washington.

Colquhoun, W., and Corcoran, D. (1964), 'The Effect of Time of Day and Social Isolation in Vigilance Decrement', *J. Exp. Psych.*, 68.

Corcoran, D. (1965), 'Personality and the Inverted-U Relation', *Brit. J. Psych.*, 56.

Cortes, J., and Gatti, F. (1965), 'Physique and Self-description of Temperament', *J. Consult. Psych.*, 29.

(1966), 'Physique and Motivation', *J. Consult. Psych.*, 30.

Cratty, B. (1967), *Movement Behavior and Motor Learning*, Lea & Febiger, Philadelphia.

Davies, D., and Hockey, G. (1966), 'The Effects of Noise and Doubling the Signal Frequency on Individual Differences in Visual Vigilance Performances', *Brit. J. Psych.*, 57.

Duffy, E. (1934), 'Emotion: an Example of the Need for Reorientation in Psychology', *Psych. Rev.*, 41.

(1941), 'The Conceptual Categories of Psychology: a Suggestion for Revision', *Psych. Rev.*, 48.

(1962), *Activation and Behavior*, Wiley, New York.

Eason, G., and White, C. (1961), 'Muscular Tension, Effort and Tracking Difficulty: Studies of Parameters which affect Tension Level and Performance Efficiency', *Perceptual & Motor Skills*, 12.

Eysenck, H. (1959), *Manual of the Maudsley Personality Inventory*, University of London Press, London.

(1965), *Facts and Fiction in Psychology*, Penguin.

(1967), *The Biological Basis of Personality*, Thomas, Springfield.

Fisher, S. (1963), 'A Further Appraisal of the Body Boundary Concept', *J. Consult. Psych.*, 27.

(1964), 'Sex Differences in Body Perception', *Psych. Monogr.*, 78.

(1966), 'Body Attention Patterns and Personality Defences', *Psych. Monogrs.*, 80: 9.

and Cleveland, S. E. (1958), *Body Image and Personality*, Van Nostrand, Princeton.

(1965), 'Personality, Body Perception, and Body Image Boundary', in Werner, H., and Wapner, S. (eds), *The Body Percept*, Random House, New York.

Fiske, D. (1944), 'A Study of Relationship to Somatotype', *J. Appl. Psych.*, 28.

Fleishman, E. (1964), *The Structure and Measurement of Physical Fitness*, Prentice-Hall, New Jersey.

Freud, S., in Trent, W. P. (ed.) (1961), *Sigmund Freud*, Hogarth Press, London.

Furneaux, W. D. (1962), 'The Psychologist and the University', *Univ. Q.*, 17.

Hebb, D. (1955), 'Drives and the CNS (Conceptual Nervous System)', *Psych. Rev.*, 62.

Husman, B. (1969), 'Sport and Personality Dynamics', *Proceedings of NCPEAM*, University of Minnesota.

Ismail, A. H., and Gruber, J. (1967), *Motor Aptitude and Intellectual Performance*, Merrill, Columbus, Ohio.

Johnson, L. (1956), 'Body Cathexis as a Factor in Somatic Complaints', *J. Consult. Psych.*, 20.

Jourard, S. M., and Secord, P. F. (1954), 'Body Size and Body Cathexis', *J. Consult. Psych.*, 18.

(1955), 'Body Cathexis and the Ideal Female Figure', *J. Abnorm. Soc. Psych.*, 50.

Kagan, J., and Moss, H. (1962), *Birth to Maturity*, Wiley, New York.

Kane, J. (1966), 'Personality Description of Soccer Ability', *Res. in Phys. Educ.*, Vol. 1, No. 1.

(1969), 'Body Type and Personality', *Res. in Phys. Educ.*, Vol. 1, No. 4.

(1970), 'Personality and Physical Abilities', in Kenyon, G. (ed.), *Contemporary Psychology in Sport*, Athletic Institute, Chicago.

Kiker, V., and Miller, A. (1967), 'Perceptual Judgement of Physiques as a Factor in Social Image', *Perceptual & Motor Skills*, 24.

Klein, G., Barr, H., and Wolitzky (1967), 'Personality', *Ann. Rev. Psych.*, Vol. 18.

Kreiger, J. C. (1962), 'The Influence of Figure-Ground Perception on Spatial Adjustment in Tennis', M.Sc. thesis, University of California, Los Angeles.

Kretschmer, E. (1925), *Physique and Character* (trans. Sprotte, W. J.) (1948), Harcourt Brace, New York.

Kroll, W. (1967), 'Sixteen Personality Factor Profiles of Collegiate Wrestlers', *Res. Q.*, 38.

Kroll, W. (1969), 'Current Strategies and Problems in Personality Assessment of Athletes', *Proceedings Symposium on Motor Learning*, Athletic Institute, Chicago.

and Peterson, K. (1965), 'Personality Factor Profiles of Collegiate Football Teams', *Res. Q.*, 36.

McCandless, B. (1960), 'Rate of Development, Body Build and Personality', *Psychiat. Res. Rep.*, No. 13.

McClelland, D. (1961), *The Achieving Society*, Van Nostrand, Princeton.

Malmo, R. (1957), 'Anxiety and Behavioral Arousal', *Psych. Rev.*, 64.

(1958), 'Measurement of Drive: an Unsolved Problem in Psychology', in Jones, M. (ed.), *Nebraska Symposium on Motivation*, University of Nebraska Press, Lincoln.

Miller, A., and Stewart, R. (1968), 'Perception of Female Physiques', *Perceptual & Motor Skills*, 2F.

Mira, E. (1944), *Psychiatry in War*, Chapman & Hall, London.

Moruzzi, G., and Magoun, H. (1949), 'Brainstem Recticular Formation and Activation of the E.E.G.', *Electroenceph. Clin. Neurophysiol.*, 1.

Nash, H. (1958), 'Assignment of Gender to Body Regions', *J. Genetic Psych.*, 92.

Ogilvie, B. (1968), 'Psychological Consistencies within the Personality of High Level Competitors', *J. Amer. Med. Assoc.*, Special Report.

and Tutko, T. (1966), *Problem Athletes and How to Handle Them*, Pelham, London.

Oliver, J. (1958), 'The Effects of Physical Conditioning Exercises and Activities on the Mental Characteristics of Educationally Sub-Normal Boys', *Brit. J. Educ. Psych.*, 28.

Parnell, R. (1958), *Behaviour and Physique*, Arnold, London.

Popper, J. (1957), 'Motivational and Social Factors in Children's Perception of Height', Ph.D. thesis, Stanford University.

Poulton, E. (1957), 'On Prediction in Skilled Movement', *Psych. Bull.*, 54.

Read, D. A. (1969), 'The Influence of Competitive and Non-Competitive Programs of Physical Education on Body Image and Self Concept', *Annual Proceedings of NCPEAM*, AAHPER, Washington.

Rosen, G., and Ross, A. (1968), 'Relationship of Body Image to Self Concept', *J. Consult. Psych.*, 32: 1.

Rushall, B. (1968), 'An Evaluation of the Relationship between Personality and Physical Performance Categories', *Proceedings 2nd International Congress of Sports Psychology*, Athletic Institute, Chicago.

Schneiderman, L. (1956), 'The Estimation of One's Own Bodily Traits', *J. Soc. Psych.*, 44.

Schulz, Louise, E. (1961), 'Relationships between Body Image and Physical Performance in Adolescent Girls', M.A. thesis, University of Maryland.

Schutz, W. (1967), *Joy-Expanding Human Awareness*, Grove, New York.

Secord, P. (1953), 'Objectification of Word Association Procedures by the Use of Homonyms: a Measure of Body Cathexis', *J. Pers.*, 21.

and Jourard, S. (1953), 'The Appraisal of Body-Cathexis: Body-Cathexis and the Self', *J. Consult. Psych.*, 17.

Sheldon, W. (1940), *The Varieties of Human Physique*, Harper, New York.

Sjoberg, H. (1968), 'Relations between Different Arousal Level Induced by Graded Physical Work and Psychological Efficiency', Psychology Laboratory, University of Stockholm.

Sleet, D. (1969), 'Physique and Social Image', *Perceptual & Motor Skills*, 28.

Sloan, W. W. (1963), 'A Study of the Relationship between Certain Objective Measures of Body Image and Performance on a Selected Test of Motor Abilities', M.A. thesis, University of Maryland.

Smith, H. (1949), 'Psychometric Checks on Hypotheses Derived from Sheldon's Work on Physique and Temperament', *J. Pers.*, 17.

Sugerman, A., and Haronian, F. (1964), 'Body Type and Sophistication of Body Concept', *J. Pers.*, 32.

Teplov, B. (1964), 'Problems in the Study of General Types of Higher Nervous Activity in Man and Animals', in Gray, J. (ed.), *Pavlov's Typology*, Pergamon, Oxford.

Vincent, W., and Dorsey, D. (1968), 'Body Image Phenomena and Measures of Physiological Performance', *Res. Q.*, 39.

Wapner, S., and Krus, D. (1959), 'Behavioral Effects of Lysergic Acid Diethylamide (LSD 25)', *A.M.A. Arch. Gen. Psychiat.*, 1.

Warburton, F., and Kane, J. (1967), 'Personality Related to Sport and Physical Ability', in *Readings in Physical Education*, Physical Education Association, London.

Welford, A. T. (1968), *Fundamentals of Skills*, Methuen, London.

Wells, H. (1958), 'Relationship between Physical Fitness and Psychological Variables', Ph.D. thesis, University of Illinois.

Werner, A., and Gottheil, E. (1966), 'Personality Development and Participation in College Athletics', *Res. Q.*, 37: 1.

Witkin, H. A. (1965), 'Development of the Body Concept and Psychological Differentiation', in Werner, H., and Wapner, S. (eds), *The Body Percept*, Random House, New York.

et al. (1954), *Personality through Perception*, Harper, New York.

et al. (1962), *Psychological Differentiation*, Wiley, New York.

Wooten, B. (1959), 'Spotlight on Dance: Movement Therapy in England, JOHPER, 30.

Yerkes, R., and Dodson, J. (1908), 'The Relation of Strength of Stimulus to Rapidity of Habit-Formation', *J. Comp. & Neur. Psych.*, 18.

Zion, L. (1965), 'Body Concept as it Relates to Self Concept', *Res. Q.*, 36: 4.

5

Aesthetics and the psychology of qualitative movement

Douglas Sandle

Theoretical considerations

Human movement cannot only be regarded in terms of physical efficiency and strength, but the moving body has also certain other qualities which give rise to experiences of a more aesthetic and expressive nature. Perhaps it is significant that when a sportsman is performing particularly well, an expression such as 'beautiful' is often used to describe his performance. 'Beautiful goals', 'beautiful strokes' and 'beautiful running' all abound in sports journalism. The use of such an expression may not just refer to the physical abilities of performers, but may sometimes indicate an enthusiastic approval for a style of performance which was found to be intrinsically appealing. Similarly, a cross-country runner, besides being motivated by competitive and achievement drives, may also run for the sheer exhilaration of moving freely over landscape; the football spectator may be excited not only by goals but also by the fluidity and ease present in the changing pattern of the player's movements; and generally, movement and posture, besides allowing for physical mobility, may also communicate information which may be as effective as speech in influencing our perception of others. Such aspects of human movement, pertinent to aesthetics, play, communication, dance and so on, we propose to embody within the concept of qualitative movement.

For the purposes of behavioural analysis, human movement can be differentiated into three conceptual categories: instrumental, quantitative and qualitative. These three categories are not necessarily mutually exclusive, but in each instance they meaningfully bring together related aspects of movement which requires a particular frame of reference for their further study. The three categories are defined as follows.

Instrumental movement

When the ends achieved by a movement are of a more immediate significance than the movement itself, such movement can be regarded as instrumental. Instrumental movements serve to change our relationship to other objects, where these changes are relevant to some intention, purpose or need which lie beyond the actual movement. Picking up a knife to cut bread, opening a door in order to pass from one place to another, running to catch a bus—most of our day-to-day movements are of an instrumental kind. Instrumental movements have little phenomenal significance and occur quite automatically. If we are aware of such movements then that awareness does not concern the movement itself, but rather the ends to be achieved by the movement, its immediate effects or the conditions which necessitated its occurrence. For example, in running for a bus, we may feel uncomfortable, but in an instrumental context such a feeling of unpleasantness will be experienced as a fact of our poor physical condition rather than as an intrinsic quality of the movement. Instrumental movements can be analysed in terms of geometry and evaluated in terms of their efficiency in relation to the immediate ends to which they are subservient. This concept of instrumental movement is not unlike Allport's concept of movement occurring within the context of what he calls coping behaviour, except that we would not regard such movements as in themselves phenomenally apparent to consciousness (Allport, 1961).

Quantitative movement

Quantitative movement is concerned with the physical presence of movement as force. Thus the significance of quantitative movements depends on the extent to which such movements can displace an object in time and space, irrespective of other instrumental ends this might achieve. The immediate self-referential end of quantitative movement is to change the position of an object (by which we include the body/object) by the force exerted and by the skill with which the movement is performed. Changes in the positions of objects can be measured and these measures used to evaluate the movements. Quantitative movement thus predominates in sport where such objectives as running fast, jumping high, throwing an object far or accurately are all concerned with the extent to which objects can be displayed in time and space, and where movement is assessed by measures of times, heights, distances and so on. Even in team sports, movement is directed towards displacing an object, such as a ball, towards a goal, and the success of such movement is 'measured' in terms of goals, runs and points. Awareness of movement in its quantitative aspect is one of force and effort experienced within the movement as it occurs. Quantitative movement is described within the variables of geometry and physics, while it is evaluated by measures of force and object displacement. This concept of the quantitative aspects of sport is similar to Metheny's notion of sport as an activity concerned with man's attempts to overcome inertia (Metheny, 1965, 1968). She writes:

> All forms of sports competition are structured by a personal attempt to overcome the inertia of some specific organisation of mass. The human objective is stated in terms of causing the mass to move space and time in some way determined by the person. Within this general structure, the contest may be organised in three different ways . . . the person attempts to overcome the inertia of his own body mass . . . the person attempts to overcome the interia of some external unit of mass . . . two persons, or two teams, designated as opponents, attempt to overcome the inertia in some external form of mass while opposing the efforts of the other.

Qualitative movement

When our attention and experience is directed towards the intrinsic qualities of movement as they appear to consciousness, we have an instance of qualitative movement. Qualitative movement gains its significance from how a movement experience feels irrespective of its instrumental ends and irrespective of its physical force and achievements. If strength and physical force can be qualitatively relevant, it will be for their own intrinsic qualities as experienced, rather than for their achieved effect in displacing objects in time and space. For example, a dancer may want to move faster from A to B, but her concern will be qualitative if she is not trying to achieve a greater displacement of her body through space (measured in terms of time taken), but rather is concerned with the expressive and aesthetic qualities that such a movement in its fast form and within the context of the dance, would achieve. This difference between quantitative and qualitative experience of force is between the speed of a movement, and its quality of fastness. Qualitative movement, then, is concerned with object displacement as a phenomenal event and with the feelings, moods and affective states which implicitly arise within such perceptions. Qualitative movement is especially relevant to movement expression and art forms such as dance, but has relevance also to sports and games. Such movement is most appropriately analysed not in the variables of geometry and physics, but those of perceptual and sensory experience. Qualitative movements can be evaluated in terms of their phenomenal import, that is, by their degree of potency within our perceptual awareness of ourselves and the environment.

The concept of qualitative movement enables us to focus attention on a general category of movement, which may, with varying degrees of dominance, be present in sport and other physical education activities. Our concern is now to describe different types of qualitative movement and so to further articulate the meaning of the concept. Qualitative movement can be further differentiated into five subcategories, 'ideal types', which in reality will be less strictly differentiated. These ideal types we designate as self-aware movement, form-aware movement, expressive movement, movement communication and emblematic movement.

(a) In self-aware movement the qualitative aspect concerns the process of moving where the experience of movement is itself rewarding or intentionally sustaining. We experience self-aware movement when awareness is directed towards the phenomenal realization that movement is taking place and when such a realization is of dynamic interest irrespective of instrumental or strictly quantitative ends. Self-aware movement is important in play, where for example, a child may find interest and perhaps pleasure in the process of moving and watching things being moved, for seemingly no other reason than for the facts of their movement. When a child acquires the ability to jump, it may continue to do so, just for the sensory awareness of the experience itself, and of gaining 'pleasure in being a cause'. Movement as an exploratory activity leading to a heightened awareness of one's spatial and temporal relationship to other objects is also relevant in this context. In sport and creative movement activities, the process of moving and of what Schilder (1950) described as 'loosening up one's body image' may be rewarding and intentionally experienced for its own sake. Many sportsmen enjoy the sense of space articulation provided by their sport and seek movement as a potent self-aware and self-rewarding experience.

(b) In form-aware movement the form of movement, rather than the activity as such, is the focal point of qualitative awareness. With movement, form can exist as a relationship among several moving elements, among moving and static elements, or among different phenomenal sequences of movement (such as tempo). Form gains a perceived configurational quality as these relationships become articulated within a sense of pattern. This sense of pattern is often externalized and embodied in descriptions of formal properties such as 'symmetry', 'balance', 'complexity' and so on. (In qualitative movement, however, we are not concerned so much with mathematical symmetry but with a 'sense of symmetry'.) An awareness of form can be especially potent as it imposes itself dynamically within the awareness of a spectator or performer. In a team sport, such as football, an awareness of the patterns as players move in relation to each other, may be an exhilarating experience as a sense of form, (and hence of heightened perceptual awareness) emerges. In 'abstract' dance, the dynamics of changing patterns of movement are of great importance, and the principles of composition have usually stressed the need for an articulated sense of form in a dance sequence (Turner, 1965). Dance theorists may differ as to what formal elements are appropriate but an acknowledgement of form is implicit in most dance theories. Turner (1963) summarizes several such theories of dance composition in which terms such as 'balance', 'symmetry', 'continuity', 'proportion', 'unity', 'repetition', 'contrast', are common.

(c) An awareness of the presence of form and pattern in movement can often be further experienced as an expressive quality. When we describe visual entities in terms such as 'graceful', 'sad', 'dynamic', 'angry', 'strong', we are attempting to describe what the visual forms feel like within our awareness of them. These expressive qualities, intrinsically bound up with a sense of form, can, however, predominate over a more 'classical' appreciation of form. Expressive movements then, are movements perceived in terms of their 'felt' affective qualities. These qualities appear to relate in a conceptual way to the experiences of actual emotions so that a movement which is expressively experienced as 'angry' will relate in a logical manner to the feeling of anger as experienced by an angry person (hence the common term 'angry' can be used to describe an actual emotion and a perceived quality). This relationship is a 'metaphori-

132

cal' one, for to describe an object of a movement as angry is not to imply that the perceiver is necessarily angry, nor that the object is itself in an angry mood (inanimate objects can't of course experience anger, although we often refer to them in an expressive way). The nature of this relationship between emotional states and perceived qualities is the subject of much debate among philosophers (see for example, Garvin, 1958; Hampshire, 1960; Hayner, 1961; and Hepburn, 1960). In dance, expressive qualities can be of great importance and they may be deliberately manipulated for dramatic and symbolic significance within the dance as a whole.

(d) Movement qualities within social communication have much in common with pure expressive movement, and to some extent these categories may overlap. Thus what a person communicates is often referred to as what he expresses. In social communication, movement may well be expressively perceived where, for example, we recognize a person to be angry by the angry quality of his movements. As for expressive movement, our own emotions do not have to coincide with the emotions of the perceived person and we do not have to be actually angry to experience anger in others (we may even experience a different emotion such as fear). In movement communication there is also a 'metaphorical' relationship between the expressed qualities communicative of another person's moods and the emotions felt by the perceiver. (The emotions of the perceived person may directly relate to the expressive nature of his movements, so that a person who moves angrily may actually be angry.) There is however, a fundamental difference between movement perceived expressively and movement experienced as communicatory of another person. In communication, awareness of movement and its phenomenal qualities will relate to the whole social context of the movement. Thus the qualitative significance of the movement will be partly determined by the nature of the perceiver's relationship to the other person and the actions and intended actions of each. Thus, the qualities of movement are not just centred within the movement itself, but within the perception of the total context in which it occurs. Movement and posture, however, can make a substantial contribution to this total qualitative awareness of others, as information about the person, and about our relationship towards him is communicated sometimes intentionally, sometimes incidentally, by the other person's bodily movements, postures and facial expressions. The importance that movement can have on our awareness of others is well expressed by David Wright, a poet who is deaf. He writes:

As Freud once put it: 'If a man's lips are sealed he chatters with his fingertips'. For example, as somebody waiting for a friend to finish a telephone conversation knows when it is about to end by the words said and the intonation of the voice, so does the deaf man—like a person queuing outside a glass-panelled call box—judge the movement when the goodbyes are being said or the intention formed to replace the receiver. He notices a shift of the hand cradling the instrument, a change of stance, the head drawing a fraction of a millimetre from the earphone, a slight shuffling of the feet. . . .

Cut off from auditory clues he learns to read the faintest visual evidence: the deaf man can, if he knows his friend intimately, even guess the identity of the caller at the other end of the wire. He will do this by noting his friend's expression, posture, and what his hands are doing. People turn different facets of their personality to their friends, and this orientation of personality is expressed not only by differences of tone of voice and style of conversation, but by small adjustments of the lineaments and carriage. The latter are not generally observed because most people are naturally attending to other sources for the same information. But the deaf person notes them because they are the only signals he can receive and interpret. Since few apart from professional actors, realise just how much stance and carriage of body reveal of mood and emotions even when the expression of the face is normal or disguised, it can happen that by the paradox of his deformity the deaf person is often in the position of an eavesdropper listening to what he is not intended to hear.

(e) In expressive movement and in some instance of social movement communication, the relationship between a movement, as perceived and the emotion it appears to express, is achieved by a kind of 'symbolic' process. Langer (1953) argues that visual forms can symbolically embody certain feelings by way of a common phenomenal structure between the visual form and the form of the emotion. Thus the sharpness and harshness of certain shapes and colours may 'symbolically' relate to the harshness in the form of certain emotional experiences, so that the colours can create an 'image' of the forms of emotional experience. By such a process a quality of form can relate and evoke a quality of emotion so that it becomes 'logically' possible to say that certain colours and forms are 'angry'. There has been criticism of Langer's describing such a process as symbolic and her use of the term symbolic has been modified. Reid (1965) discussed Langer's use of the words symbol and symbolic. In this category we are concerned with 'symbolic' qualities of movement, but in the sense that movement may symbolize certain beliefs and values and where this symbolic reference may influence the very qualitative nature of our perceptions of the movement. Thus a cross can symbolize Christian religion so that feelings of sacredness and devotion, basic to the beliefs of the religion, become embodied in the cross to such an extent that they seem to belong within its very appearance. In this context we prefer to write of emblematic, rather than symbolic entities, for movement which is emblematic of beliefs, attitudes and values may or may not achieve its emblematic significance by a process of symbolism as in Langer's sense of the term. The emblematic qualities of a movement may be achieved by varying degrees of arbitrariness, as follows. The most arbitrary form of emblematic movement occurs when a perceiver brings to the perception of the movement certain values which invest the movement with qualities, independent of the form of the movement and unrelated to any other qualitative aspects also present within it. For example, a movement may be a conventional gesture for love, where the form of the movement is arbitrarily chosen, and its meaning may relate to values about love in a wider context (such as love of mankind), and this in turn may affect the qualitative way in which the movement is perceived. (The relationship between the movement and the perceiver's values will be made instantaneously within his perceptions of the movement, so that the emblematic qualities will appear to belong within the movement form itself.) In some cases instrumental and quantitative movement may become qualitatively significant if they are perceived in relation to some wider context of beliefs and values.

Emblematic qualities of movement may be less arbitrary, if the form of movement is, in Langer's sense, symbolic (where for example, the gentleness and receptivity of a movement may be related to phenomenal qualities of love as emotionally experienced). Nevertheless, even here the actual emblematic qualities of the movement will still be determined by the values and beliefs of the perceiver, so that for example, if he regards love with distaste, then his reactions to the movement qualities will be modified accordingly. A more objective basis to emblematic movement can be achieved especially in dance where not only will the form of the movement be symbolic (in Langer's sense), but the dramatic and narrative context in which it appears will partly determine its evaluative significance. Thus if the movement, expressive of love, appears in the context of the hero's overthrowing destructive forces, the emblematic significance of the movement is objectively defined within the dramatic narrative of the dance. Where movement, form and dramatic context coincide, the emblematic qualities of movement are most impressive and effective. The less the emblematic arbitrariness, the more the responses of observers will become objective and less idiosyncratic.

Metheny sees the meaning of sport as symbolic, in our emblematic sense. Sport for her is emblematic of values concerning man's struggle against the forces of the universe. Thus she interprets sport where an individual performer is concerned with displacing an object in space, as follows:

> In the individual sports, as exemplified by golf and bowling, man again pits his own personal forces against the forces symbolized by a world of objects, and again and again he acts out the symbolic drama of human powers pitted against the forces of the universe. Every successful swing being more articulate, but alas, every failure clarifies his awareness of the limitations of his human powers.

The emblematic connotations of sport are for Metheny derived from the quantitative nature of movement. But clearly this quantitative aspect becomes qualitative by way of its relationship to her beliefs and values regarding 'la condition humaine'. Such connotations do have some objective basis within the force and effort of movement but the degree of 'objectivity' does depend on the extent to which the perceiver generalizes his values. Metheny sees meaning in movement dependent on symbolic (emblematic) connotation and applies this also to dance. Meanings are dependent on how the individual per- ceiver connotes movement forms and this is dependent wholly on idiosyncratic responses. She writes:

> Two or more men may reach agreement on their answers to questions about what form is and what it denotes. They may agree about the materials and how they are organized, and may agree about the name they assign to the form. But we cannot expect them to agree about the connotations they may find in a form, because each man must find his own connotations within the context of his own interests, feelings and emotions. He must also find his own meanings in the form; the form will mean to

him whatever it does mean to him, and no other person can either agree or disagree with those meanings.

However, if the forms of dance are phenomenally articulate and consistent within the dance as a whole, then it could be argued that variations in personal response would be less likely, and some degree of aesthetic objectivity might be achieved within the given presence of movements. If movement qualities are articulate, then their symbolic meanings may form the basis for any other 'logical' connotations which may be made. Metheny, unfortunately, by concentrating on symbolic connotations (in the emblematic sense) does not allow for such an objectivity in aesthetic responses to movements. Again, other qualitative aspects of movement may provide sufficient 'meaning' without the necessity of further emblematic connotation, and these in themselves might provide an objective aesthetic.

Each of these five types of qualitative movement represent ideal types which in reality may interact so that the presence of one type may be dependent on the presence of another. For example, the expressive perception of movement may be dependent upon an awareness of the dynamic qualities of a particular form of movement. Likewise an emblematic response may in part, be dependent upon the recognition of expressive feelings within the movement. Emblematic connotation may further influence social communication where, for example, a person may be experienced as 'aggressive' simply because his movement style does not conform to the expectations and values of the observer. But in all these categories of qualitative movement the emphasis is on the influence movement exerts on the qualities of perceptual awareness and experience, irrespective of instrumental and quantitative ends. The categories allow movements which have a common qualitative status to be grouped together for convenience and methodological appropriateness.

Aesthetics, sport and dance

While the various qualitative types of movement can interact and influence each other, so also can the three major types of movement— instrumental, quantitative and qualitative. For one particular movement activity there may be instrumental, quantitative and qualitative aspects all present. Thus, for example, the movements of a high jumper may be instrumental to the jumper winning a competition, breaking records and generally furthering his status as an athlete.

Quantitatively, the same jump can be regarded as effort and skill in displacing the jumper's body in time and space, and the extent of the success of the jump can be measured in terms of jumped height. Qualitatively, the jump may also be experienced as one of ease and grace as manifested in the form of the jump and the style of performance. A jumper may be quantitatively effective but may lack qualitative style, and vice versa (although in high-class performers both appear to be successfully integrated).

The degree to which quantitative and qualitative aspects of movement predominate differs with the kind of sport activity. In sports such as gymnastics, there is even a difference in emphasis between men and women performers where, for men, movement, skill and dexterity are primarily regarded in terms of the extent to which the body can be manipulated and displaced in time and space; while for women, there is more emphasis on qualities of performance, i.e. not on the extent of body displacement, but on the perceived form and style in which this is achieved. The difference in types of movement activity in sport is well summarized by Anthony (1968) who comments:

> Most sports have the straightforward, uncomplicated objective of scoring goals or points; any aesthetic element is incidental to the main aim. In some sports, however, and gymnastics, diving, and skating have been mentioned, one major aim is aesthetic— to create a 'good' or 'artistic' movement. The gymnastic judge is given official guidance to look for 'grace', 'general beauty', 'elegance', 'rhythm and precision', 'harmony' and 'perfect artistic execution'. His diving counterpart must look for 'grace'. In skating, marks are awarded for technical merit and for 'artistic impression'; among the terms used in this latter section are: 'harmonious composition of the whole'; 'conformity with music'; and 'carriage'. On the trampoline a good performer must satisfy requirements such as 'continuity and flow', 'symmetrical placing of body segments', and 'aesthetic manner', according to the 'established standards of art'.

Anthony's use of the term aesthetic is very significant, and up to now we have avoided using such a term. However, in the context of both aesthetics and art the qualitative aspects of movement are very relevant. Art and aesthetics concern qualitative experiences, and the fact that sport has a qualitative nature has led some writers to stress the link between the two. Thus, it has often been asserted that an awareness of body rhythm, patterns of movement and the expressive qualities of movement as experienced in sport and dance, will help to develop a general sensitivity to aesthetic qualities in art and the environment in general. Anthony recalls that Courbetin, the founder of the modern Olympic Games, emphasized the relationship between sport and art. Summarizing statements about the aesthetic element in sport from many writers, Anthony draws attention to a Unesco conference (1959) on 'Sport, Work and Culture' which, having defined the aesthetic attitude as 'implying enjoyment of the phenomena for its own sake because of values related to its mere existence', further maintained that 'certain phenomena could be found in sport, such as harmony, rhythm, symmetry, etc., which could be regarded as especially aesthetic'. Simpson (1967) reminds us of Plato's concern for the relationship between aesthetics and sport and she herself argues that there is an intimate relationship between the two by way of a common concern for sensory awareness and sensuous experience. Hohler (1969) regards the idea of beauty in movement as 'implicit within the physical realisation which appeals to the senses'. Elliott (1969) examines sport within the traditional concern of aesthetics for beauty (experienced as wonder and delight) and the sublime (the experience of wonder and awe). Aesthetic aspects he sees as incidental, but none the less important to sport and particularizes the aesthetic values in Association Football as follows:

If we wish to show that sport has aesthetic values comparable with those of art, then I think the qualities to be stressed, in the context of opposition, are swiftness, grace, fluency, rhythm and perceived vitality—the qualities which in various combinations constitute beauty. In soccer, beauty appears typically in a fluent and rhythmic passing movement, provided that it also possesses a sense of urgency; and when a player breasts the ball to his feet and sweeps it away as if in a single fluent movement, provided that his pass does not go astray, and when the ball is centred across the goalmouth and a player makes a running leap to head the ball into the net, minimally deflecting it and not seeming to reduce its velocity. In all these cases there is not merely skill but perceived fluency and vitality, and all possess, in addition, an aesthetically satisfying geometrical form or pattern. In the last case, for example, we are conscious of the lines of movement of the ball and player, and their resultant, the line of the ball's movement into the net.

Where movement is deliberately structured and performed to emphasize its qualitative nature, such as in dance and movement drama, then we have movement explicitly as an art form. However, it is important to realize that the relationship between art and human movement is by way of a common emphasis on qualitative modes of experience. Terms such as 'aesthetic' and 'art' have to some extent specific and perhaps limited meanings, and we are concerned to show that qualitatively modes of movement, although relevant (and indeed essential) to movement as art, can however take place in contexts which might not normally be regarded as artistic or aesthetic. An argument which we cannot extend in this paper may be proposed whereby aesthetics is seen as the *study* of qualitative experiences within all aspects of life. Art can then be regarded as an *activity* which deliberately manipulates environmental events and materials to bring about qualitative experiences. On this basis, there is little difference between qualitative experience on the football field and in an art gallery except to the extent to which the respective events have been deliberately structured and presented for qualitative ends. As one of my critical students remarked, 'there is more effective art at Elland Road (home of Leeds United) than in most so-called art galleries!' This was to imply that qualitative experiences may be more potent in a context not deliberately conceived as such.

For movement to be regarded as qualitative it must in itself have phenomenal significance and in the final analysis, movement can only be so regarded by taking into account how it appears to human consciousness. This is implicit in each of our five sub-categories outlined above. Several writers have stressed the difference between movement as an external event in geometric space (capable of being objectively plotted) and movement as a phenomenal quality whose dimensions are experiential rather than physical. Thus, Meredith (1963) comments: 'A physicist can calculate the horse-power of a ballet-dancer but cannot interpret the pattern of a dance. This pattern has a cultural geometry which has personal dimensions. We have to spell out these dimensions if this is to be more than a beguiling metaphor.' Strauss (1966) places much emphasis on the phenomenal nature of the space in which dance occurs and is experienced. He makes a distinction between visual space (in which visual stimuli are seen to occur externally located in an Euclidean geometry) and acoustical space (in which events occur within the phenomenal space of the observer). Dance, he argues occurs also within acoustical space and this is why music and movement are so intrinsically linked. A visual rhythm does not encourage human movement, yet acoustical rhythm compels us to move, and this stems from the phenomenal nature of the space in which music and dance are both experienced.

Forms of movement such as marching and dancing are possible only with music; the music founding the structure of space within which the dancing movement can occur. Optical space is the space of directed, measured and purposive movement; acoustical space is the space of dance. Purposive movement and dance cannot be understood as different combinations of the same elements. They are two entirely different basic forms of movement, related to two different modes of the spatial.

Strauss's concept of purposive movement is similar to what we have termed instrumental movement, and dance is further distinguished by Strauss from movement of a more quantitative nature as follows: 'Walking we move space from one point to another, dancing, we move within space. In walking, we leave a certain distance behind; we traverse space. The dance on the contrary, is non-directed and non-limited movement. It has no relevance to spatial measure nor to spatial and temporal limit.'

Sheets (1966) also makes a specifically phenomenological study of dance and her independent analysis has findings in common with those of Strauss. Sheets approaches dance as a phenomenally given experience and is thus concerned with dance as it appears to awareness free from any preconceptions and pre-reflective judgments. Her concern is with dance as it appears as a 'lived experience'. In her analysis, she examines the nature of spatiality and temporality in dance and discusses how the dance in its spatial and temporal form (as phenomenally experienced) achieves expressive and symbolic meaning through the creation of an illusion of force ('sheer force').

What makes each dance uniquely significant is the dynamics of the form: hence the unique interplay of qualities inherent in movement as a perpetual revelation of sheer force. . . . The dynamics of the form, are therefore created by the nature of the forces themselves, tensional qualities, and by the manner in which those forms spatialize and temporalise themselves. . . . The qualitative inter-relationships created by movement as a revelation of sheer force create the expressive character of the dance.

Thus for a particular dance, its unique spatial and temporal nature gives rise to a specific illusion of force, and this 'sheer force' enables a dance to achieve its unique expressive characteristics since the forms of force are capable of reflecting the forms of real life.

> The sheer form of dance, as pure expression, is in and of itself gloomy or joyful, agitating and soothing etc. It means that we, as audience, do not feel gloomy, joyful, or whatever. We do not interpret the dance on the stage in terms of feelings it might evoke in us and then confer upon the dance that meaning. We do not feel tension and strain and interpret these as representing a certain feeling it might evoke quality to be attributed to dance. When we look at a dance we see a form which, because of its very organization, its very dynamic flow—the way forces are released, checked, attentuated, solidified, diffused—is symbolically expressing a feeling.

Sheet's use of 'symbolic' is as used in Langer's theory of aesthetics and art, which Sheets develops within the terms of her own pheno-menological analysis of dance. Whatever the nature of the 'symbolic' process whereby movement can convey qualities of feelings it is evident from Langer's theory, and implicit in both Strauss and Sheets, that such feelings are dependent on the particular dynamic qualities present in the phenomenal form of the movement, as it appears to consciousness. In a sense the recognition of feeling qualities is but an attempt at externalizing and conceptualizing these phenomenal characteristics, and expressive terms should not detract from the phenomenal dynamics which they attempt to pinpoint. Thus if a person approaches movement in a pre-reflective manner and if movement is specifically presented within a particular narrative and dramatic context, these descriptive feelings, as an externalization of the phenomenal forms of the movement experience, should logically apply. At any rate, the dynamic quality of the movement, no matter how described, will be given, implicitly within its presentation. The theories of Sheets and Strauss, concerned with the intrinsic pheno-menal qualities of movement would not therefore lend support to Metheny's conception of idiosyncratic 'symbolic' connotations. Such connotations could be regarded as 'reflective' and hence adverse to the pre-reflective awareness which is essential for a true phenomeno-logical appreciation of movement. The degree of phenomenal validity of Metheny's movement connotations would depend on the extent to which individual connotations were related to qualitative aspects intrinsic to movement.

There is certainly a danger with Metheny's insistence on the sanctity of personal interpretations that movement may only become qualitatively meaningful within the terms of esoteric values and these may become further and further removed from the actual intrinsic qualities of movement. Qualitative meanings in sport and dance would then be wholly dependent on life philosophies and personal credos, which would deny any possibility of an objective aesthetic of sport. Her own connotations are to some extent reflections in a grand manner which appear to pass over other basic qualitative aspects of movement.

The gymnast deals almost exclusively with the action of gravitational forces on his own body. Every stunt or event in gymnastics is a metaphorical re-enactment of the drama of man using his own powers to overcome the forces that act on him. By deliberately putting himself in situations where he will be acted on by forces greater than those he encounters in his daily life, and then demonstrating his ability to overcome those forces, the gymnast makes more articulate his awareness of himself as a powerful being that can to some extent, overcome the forces that seem to structure his life.

Such emblematic conceptions seem to miss out much of importance with regard to the experimential qualities of movement. The same criticism can be made of some of Laban's writings whose theories on the expressive and symbolic qualities of movement suffered from both a sterile conception of movement in the terms of a formal geometry (hence his preoccupation with isohedronic forms and with crystalline shapes in general), and from arbitrary cosmological interpretations about the qualitative significance of such movements. Laban, failing to appreciate that dance movement takes place in a phenomenal rather than an Euclidean space, was led to impute expressive meanings into movement not qualitatively based, but by reference to a pre-conceived cosmological theory. Although Laban was a gifted teacher and had a profound effect on the historical development of creative dance, the status of his theories as revealed by a thorough analysis by Curl (1967) leaves much to be desired.

The experimental psychology of qualitative movement

The psychological nature of qualitative movement can to some extent be objectively determined by experimental analysis. For example, issues concerning the objective status of expressive qualities in movement, can be studied with experiments carefully designed to provide information of how individuals do, in fact, react to particular movement forms in terms of expressive responses. In the remaining section of this chapter, we will present some examples of psychological research which seem pertinent to qualitative movement. And, while it may be argued that qualitative experience cannot simply be reduced to psychological mechanisms, we would maintain that psychological research can greatly help to articulate such experiences, and lead to a greater understanding and sympathy for their importance to man and society in general. No psychologist can hope to completely explain qualitative movements but he can at least hope to demonstrate how they modify behaviour and how they relate to other behavioural variables. In art, and aesthetics generally, modern psychology is leading to a greater understanding of such experiences which can be regarded not as 'God-given' mysteries, but as essentially human activities which can be fostered and developed by a consideration of the behavioural variables involved (see for example, Arnheim, 1966; Gombrich, 1960; Hogg, 1969; and Munro, 1951).

With regard to qualitative movement there are many issues which may be to some extent resolved by psychological research. For example, the following questions could form the basis of research programmes: Do movements for movement's sake as found in play reflect a basic biological need for motor activity irrespective of other instrumental needs? Are there particular movement forms which are likely to be experienced as more pleasing than others? Is there an objective basis to the experience of expressive qualities in movement? To what extent does movement contribute to non-verbal communication? Are some kinds of individuals more likely to experience movement as emblematic of their beliefs and values? Up to the present time there has not been a great deal of research concerning such problems with regard to movement, while, on the other hand, there has been much research on the qualitative perception of static visual forms. Even with regard to specific areas of interest, such a dance, psychologists have shown little interest. Smith (1967) carefully scrutinized every volume of *Psychological Abstracts* over the past forty years and found little specific research on the psycho-aesthetics of dance, though there were some references to dance as psychotherapy.

(a) Self-aware movement: a psychological analysis of self-aware movement might be concerned with the motivational aspects of such movements and their relationship to other behavioural constructs such as personality, or maturation. We could ask, for example, under what psychological conditions does self-aware movement take place, and what purpose does it serve with regard to the individual performer's emotional development and well-being? Movement as a self-rewarding activity is obviously pertinent to play and while there are many facets to play activity, including social imitation and fantasy, play will now be considered with regard to self-aware movement.

Several writers have stressed play as a self-seeking and rewarding activity. Cratty (1964) for example, has described play as 'spontaneous activity motivating for its own sake'. Ewer (1968) in her analysis of animal play, notes that although play may involve enthusiastic activity, movements are not 'in earnest', and thus in fighting play, the teeth and claws may be held back so as to offer no real threat. She comments: 'one is driven to conclude that play has no biological objective other than its own performance—it is an end in itself, not a means of acquiring a full stomach, safety, cleanliness and the like.' Mussen, Conger and Kagan (1963) consider play as an aspect of 'behaviours that are not reactions to pressing environmental demands and unconcerned with realistic problems'. Miller (1968) argues that spontaneous movements in babies such as when they 'babble when no one is listening, wave their fist while staring at them, reach up to try to stand, or move from chair to chair when no one is rewarding them for doing so' are too universal and occur too easily to be explained by learning through rewards. The fact that such movements can be rewarding she relates to the concept of 'circular reactions' and neurophysiological feedback, where sensations from moving muscles can lead to further muscular action by way of a central nervous process. Manipulative play, of a more complex kind where a child's movements may bring about changes in other objects and in other people's reactions, is also regarded by her as partly self-rewarding and reinforcing.

> Children certainly exhibit signs of pleasure and glee when they produce effects upon objects or people by their own actions, quite apart from whether such results are good, bad, or indifferent in terms of getting goodies or praise. This is behaviour referred to in descriptions of play as 'pleasure in being a cause', 'mastering experiences', or 'effectance motivation'. Whether or not different mechanisms must be postulated for the perception of effects and changes produced by oneself, and

145

perception of changes and effects which do not depend upon additional information from muscle endings, still needs confirmation. But it seems reasonable to assume that some form of feedback mechanism underlies this kind of play.

That movements, such as occur in play, appear to be self-rewarding, has lead to the proposal that there is a general activity drive. Thus Morgan and King (1966) state that: 'both human beings and animals spend a good deal of time moving about for no apparent reason except that it satisfies a drive for activity.' Psychologists are often accused of simply explaining behaviour in terms of drives, and to account for play in terms of a general activity drive, does not really provide a full analysis of its dynamics. Nevertheless, there is some experimental evidence to suggest that an activity drive does have, at least, some validity. Hill (1956) for example, found that rats, confined in a space which limited opportunities for movement produced more activity on a treadwheel after confinement, than rats whose opportunity for movement was not so limited. In this context, it is worth noting that Mussen et al. (1963) suggest that in modern society the child is forced to inhibit motor activity for long periods, by having to sit still and generally 'behave', and that 'this limitation on gross motor activity appears to be frustrating to the young child, and episodes of vigorous activity appear to be necessary and gratifying.' Bodily movement, has been experimentally shown to be 'reinforcing' in the learning of a new habit or skill, and this also suggests its status as a primary drive. Kagan and Berkun (1954) had two rats perform in two treadwheels, and each was provided with a lever to pull. For the experimental rat, the lever when pressed released the brakes from both treadmills for a short period, before they were reapplied. Thus, pulling the lever lead to the opportunity for movement activity. For the control rat, however, the lever was a dummy and opportunity for movement was not controlled by lever pulling. The experimental rat acquired a habit of lever pulling, while the control rat was significantly less motivated towards pulling the dummy lever. For the experimental rat, the opportunity for movement thus acted as the reinforcer in learning to pull a lever. Harlow, Harlow and Meyer (1950) present experimental evidence to show that the opportunity for manipulative behaviour is also reinforcing.

Movement activity would therefore, seem likely to be rewarding in itself, and phenomenal states of pleasure in fulfilling such a drive are possibly an important factor in the aesthetics of sport, dance and play. If movement activity, unrelated to other more obvious instrumental ends, is to some extent a basic drive, why should this be? What biological purpose does it fulfil? While movement in play might in itself be apparently of no instrumental value, there are other secondary functions which are important for species survival. Ewer (1968) in summarizing the ethological view suggests that movement activity makes an important contribution to the experiences of a young animal as it learns to cope with its environment. What the young animal learns may be very simple, such as learning how much exertion is needed to jump accurately from A to B, or what it feels like to be pushed over backwards, but such experiences are none the less of importance to the animal's general development. A child that is active and has both the need and the opportunity for movement, will acquire a sense of its own body and learn to experience its capabilities and limitations. The child will also experience the 'rewards' of mastering self-achieved skills (standing on one's head, etc.), and develop a social awareness of others as he shares play activities. Eibl-Eibesfeldt (1967) describes play as 'an experimental dialogue with the environment, motivated by curiosity and a strong motor drive'. Such an experimental dialogue is of obvious importance to species survival for most animals could not survive without a knowledge of their environment through movement. Neurophysiological mechanisms for a general motor drive thus could have evolved to ensure that movement has reward value for its own sake and so fulfils biological requirements for a general movement need. It is not surprising, then, that the fulfilment of such a need, if it exists, would in itself be pleasurable, and that sport, dance and play are all activities which would allow such a pleasure to be achieved.

(b) Form-aware movement: psychological research with regard to qualitative aspects of form-aware movement, can be important with respect to how form is phenomenally perceived, and how such perceptions relate to aesthetic responses concerning aspects of beauty, pleasingness and so on. Gestalt psychology is especially appropriate in this context and has brought to light some of the variables which account for the way a visual form is phenomenally organized (Wertheimer, 1958; Kohler, 1958). Thus there are certain dynamic 'laws' which determine the way in which visual elements are grouped together within a sensed pattern or configuration. For example, if several dots are scattered over a blank page, then dots which are near to each other will tend to be phenomenally grouped together in relation to their degree of proximity. Similarly, if dots, triangles, squares and diamonds are scattered over a blank page, not only will proximity apply, but also similar shapes will 'strive' to be grouped together. These tendencies towards phenomenal grouping are dynamic in that a sense of 'pull' or 'force' may be qualitatively 'felt' which appears to hold the pattern elements together. Other gestalt 'laws' suggest that, in our visual awareness of shape and form, there is a tendency towards symmetry, simplicity, closure and continuation of line. These tendencies can be seen 'at work' in tests of visual memory where visual images tend to be simplified towards basic gestalt configurations, and where visual forms organized according to gestalt principles are, in some contexts, more easily remembered. In experiments with stabilized retinal images (where an image is fixated to the pupil of the eye so an effect like prolonged staring is achieved) images become distorted and even disappear in parts, as fatigue develops (Evans and Piggins, 1963; Pritchard, 1961). Often the change in shape which occurs is what would be expected if gestalt 'laws' applied, so that, for example, an asymmetrical image would tend to simplify towards symmetry. Morris (1962) gives examples of drawings and painting by chimpanzees which display a sense of form within gestalt principles. Ambiguous visual figures also show gestalt influences where the ambiguity is often resolved in favour of the visual image which is more ideally gestalt. Wohwill (1960) summarizes several experimental studies on gestalt principles with regard to the developmental aspects of perception in children.

In the perception of human movement, it can be expected that gestalt principles will also influence a sense of form, where for example, similar movements, or movements temporarily or spatially close to each other, would be grouped together within a sense of pattern. There are certainly many possibilities for experimental research in this direction. An interesting experiment would be to have movement serially reproduced (where person A performs a movement, person B tries to remember it and reproduce it for C, who then tries to reproduce it for D and so on). In serial reproduction with static visual forms, gestalt tendencies often account for the emergence of a vastly modified image, even among visually aware art students (Sandle, 1967). Important within the terms of qualitative movement, is the application of gestalt theory to aesthetics, and Arnheim (1954), for example, finds gestalt psychology pertinent to the aesthetic appreciation of good design, harmony, visual balance and so on.

With regard to such aesthetic properties, gestalt psychologists would maintain that visual stimuli with clear gestalt structures would be found pleasing, or at any rate the phenomenal axis of form as defined within gestalt terms would be a factor influencing our aesthetic appreciation of visual pattern. Experimental studies relating form with aesthetic judgments of 'pleasingness' have for many years occupied psychologists interested in art. Valentine (1962) reviews several typical studies, and Eysenck (1965) gives more recent accounts of how structural properties of form objectively relate to aesthetic preference and personality variables. Theories of what formal properties are supposed to contribute to a sense of beauty and pleasingness in dance and movement generally, could benefit by an application of the more carefully controlled techniques of psycho-aesthetics. Laban for example, makes reference to the so-called 'Golden Section' in which it is supposed that shapes and forms with certain proportions are implicit of beauty. The Golden Section of a line is achieved by dividing a line so that the ratio between the whole line and longer half is equal to the ratio of the longer half to the shorter. For example, with a rectangle, the Golden Section would be present if the longer side was to the shorter in a ratio of about eight to five. Laban's assertion that the Golden Section is 'the basis of all ratios which gives us the feeling of a beautiful and harmonious movement' (*Die Welt des Tanzens*, as cited and translated in Curl, 1967) leaves much to be desired and experimental research shows the aesthetic status of the Golden Section to be equivocal (Valentine, 1962; Stone and Collins, 1965; H. R. Schiffman, 1966).

Attempts to assess objectively the behavioural effects of form and pattern have gained in recent years with an application of information theory. Information theory is a mathematical theory originally developed within communication engineering to provide objective measures of structure in message sequences (Shannon and Weaver, 1949). It also has been applied to visual form as a measure of pattern (see for example: Attneave, 1959; Garner, 1962; Brown, 1964; Allusi, 1960). This application has revealed that an important variable in visual pattern is the amount of constraint within the individual units of a pattern. This is, the extent to which pattern units can in theory vary their positions within a given principle of patterning. This constraint can be 'operationalized' in terms of the extent to which the positions of individual units can be predicted from the positions of the other elements. The units which go to make up a bilaterally symmetrical pattern, for example, are limited in positional variation since any one half of the units determines the spatial positions of the other half. In a random pattern, however, there would be less constraint and individual elements could vary greatly within limits imposed by the size of the pattern and the number of elements used. The amount of constraint (and hence structure) in a pattern, is measured by what is known as BITS. Factors which statistically constrain pattern variation are phenomenally related to complexity, since the more variation possible, the more complex a pattern can seem to become. Information theory measures have indicated that complexity appears to be an important variable in qualitative responses to visual form. Meaningful relationships have for example, been found where:

1 visual complexity and information values relate to the amount of looking time given to visual forms by babies and infants (Cantor, Cantor and Ditrichs, 1963; Hershenson, Musinger and Kesson, 1965; Leckart, 1966).

2 visual complexity can influence visual 'preference' in animals (Dember, Earl and Paradise, 1957; Karmel, 1966; Sackett, Keith-Lee and Treat, 1963).

3 Complexity is a factor in the looking and curiosity behaviour of human subjects who have been subjected to periods of sensory deprivation (Jones, Wilkinson and Braden, 1961; Smith and Myers, 1966).

4 Visual complexity and information values are important variables in 'aesthetics' and visual preference behaviour (Berlyne and Peckham, 1966; Dorfman and McKenna, 1966; Musinger and Kesson, 1964; Paul G. Vitz, 1966).

Berlyne (1960) relates complexity to his theory of neurophysiological arousal and its role in curiosity and aesthetics. The relationship between the amount of visual structure (as measured by information theory) and aesthetic preference is itself complicated and Berlyne (1965) argues that a distinction has to be made between aesthetic preference and perceptual interest. Visual reactions to complexity are also complicated by personality factors, and there is evidence to suggest that creative individuals find visual patterns with high information content values more pleasing and interesting than low creatives (Golann, 1962).

Information theory was originally developed with regard to a sequential flow of stimulus events and as such could be most appropriately applied to the analysis of pattern structure in movement. The extent to which movement elements are predictable from other movement elements can be expected to relate to an aesthetic sense of form and one could hypothesize that, as for static visual form, creative individuals will be able to 'handle' movement sequences which are complex and contain more 'information' than uncreatives. Information theory has been applied to the aesthetics of music (Moles, 1966) and its application to dance and movement aesthetics generally would be of much interest. The nature of movement as information (in the information theory sense) is also pertinent to exploratory and curiosity behaviour and thus relevant to play and self-sustaining movement activities; and Cratty (1964) discusses Berlyne's theory with respect to movement in play.

(c) Expressive movement: psychological experiments on the expressive qualities of static visual shape and line have demonstrated that expressive responses are not wholly idiosyncratic, nor dependent on the varying subjective moods of perceivers (Dreher and Evans, 1964; Folkins and Lenrow, 1966; Valentine, 1962). Rather, it seems that expressive judgments do have a degree of objectivity, which to some extent may also be cross-culturally valid. The methods used in such experiments could be fruitfully applied to the study of expressive qualities in the perception of movement. In such studies it is not sufficient to ask a subject merely to describe how he reacts to a particular form, but there is a need to standardize procedure and to ensure that the judgment task is within the abilities of the subject tested. There is especially a need to objectify the expressive descriptions employed by subjects. One person for example, may use the word 'sad' while understanding the term to refer to a gentle kind of melancholia, while another person may use 'sad' to describe a more violent and desperate kind of feeling. While, both may thus describe a particular movement as sad, they would not necessarily be describing the same kind of phenomenal quality. The importance of defining expressive qualities within an objective 'semantic space' has been recognized with the development of the 'semantic differential' (Osgood, Suci and Tannenbaum, 1957). Experiments on the expressive value of colours are also of some relevance concerning general methodology (Wexner, 1954; Wright and Rainwater, 1962), and Ross's work on the expressive qualities of stage colours is relevant to dance drama and movement as a performing art (Ross, 1938).

The term physiognomic perception has been used by psychologists to describe perception where expressive, affective and animated qualities predominate over geometrical and instrumental characteristics. Wallach and Kogan (1966) have extensively reviewed this concept especially with regard to physiognomic sensitivity among children. In one of their own experiments which has some relevance to movement, children were required to make judgments about visual lines. Subjects were shown a series of drawn lines which they were told represented the tracks made by various persons walking through sand. These lines were presented one by one on cards and the children described the kind of person who had made each particular track (one track consisted of a straight horizontal line, another a curved line that looped itself, another an erratic 'tangle', etc.). Records were made of the number of physiognomic perceptions made where, for example, the walking person was described as 'sad', 'angry' and so on. The findings of this and other experiments carried out by Wallach and Kogan were used to analyse the relationships among sensitivity to expressive qualities, intelligence and creativity. Arnheim (1949) reports a pilot study on the expressive qualities of dance movements. Five members of a student dance group were asked to give improvizations of sadness, strength and night. The various movements were analysed according to their speed, range, shape, tension, direction and 'centre'. Arnheim found that there was some consistency between expressive qualities and the movement dimensions. For example, in all five interpretations of sadness, the speed of movements was slow; for strength all five dancers performed movement with a large sweeping range and for the interpretation of night, all movements were round in their shape. Hays (1967) has carried out a more detailed experiment in which she found that a change of movement tempo affected the expressive qualities experienced in the dance, and some tempi appeared to be appropriate for expressing certain emotions. Her experiment is a welcome attempt in the analysis of movement expression, but clearly a use of techniques such as the semantic differential would greatly benefit such studies. Theories of expressive perception such as Langer's gain some validity from studies on the phenomenon of synaesthesia. In synaesthesia information from one sense is experienced in another, so that visual images, for example, are instantaneously experienced in response to sound. The qualities of the experienced image relate in a systematic and dimensional way to the qualities of the stimulus, so that loud noises might give rise to bright visual images and so on. This suggests that more complex qualities of sensation may be meaningfully related to qualities of sensation in any one particular sensory mode, so that sadness can be related qualitatively to a dimension of visual form. It is thought that this process may have a neurophysiological basis (see McKellar, 1957; Sandle, 1967).

(d) Movement communication: Movement as change in bodily posture and gesture and as social communication is of obvious relevance to the theory and practice in the context of creative movement and dance. Jordan (1966) accordingly acknowledges the importance of movement communication with regard to children: 'It is easier to recognize the variety of childhood actions and movements than it is to understand what they express, yet, for children in their early years, movement is the only language by which they can express and communicate what they feel.' Lamb (1965) devotes a chapter to 'inter-personal communication', and while he makes some pertinent observations, he does not refer to any modern experimental studies on movement behaviour and communication. In fact, during recent years, anecdotal descriptions of the role of movement in the expression of emotion, have been greatly surpassed by the more rigorous analysis of behavioural scientists who have recognized the importance of this topic for psychiatry, social psychology and related areas of study. Allport (1938, 1961) in his own work, and that with Vernon (1933), has pioneered much of the psychologist's interest in expressive movement, and was particularly concerned with movement styles in relation to personality. He has maintained that, in everyday behaviour, movement and manipulative actions are carried out in a way which is consistent for individuals. While recognizing the importance of cultural and social habits in movement styles, he nevertheless realizes that some movement activities can be revealing of particular personalities.

Kraut (1954a, b) in his work on autistic gestures also laid the foundation of a more experimental approach. He revealed that nervous gestures, which are not intentional communicative acts but primarily serve to dissipate nervous energy, could nevertheless reveal some important consistent patterns which could be objectively related to stressful and anxiety-producing states. His technique was to present subjects with a series of provocative and conflicting questions which placed the subject in an emotionally arousing situation, and by delaying the opportunity for subjects to verbally resolve such a state, he was able to analyse the nervous movements so produced. By varying the kinds of disturbance, and relating these to the subjects' own assessment of their moods, he was able to show that certain gestures were significantly related to specific kinds of conflict and emotional disturbance. He found, for example, that fist gestures appeared during aggressive moods, that fingers on the lips related to feelings of shame and so on. He also found significant differences between typically

153

masculine and typically feminine responses. These autistic movements, not consciously produced, could therefore be used as a source of information in clinical interviews. Sainsbury (1955) objectively recorded the spontaneous movements of patients in interview and found that the frequency of movement was related to the discussion of anxiety-producing topics. He was able to relate this frequency to autonomic arousal as indicated by increased heart rate and thus demonstrated 'an association between the visceral (autonomic) and muscular manifestations of emotion'.

A controlled manipulation of interview situations has been used extensively by Eckman (1966). He controlled interviews so that interviewees were placed in a stressful situation, and then in a cathartic situation. For example, interviewees would be criticized and then badgered by interviewers for a period, and then, once reassured that this was only part of an experiment, would be interviewed in a friendly and natural manner. Subjects shown photographs of the interviewees were successfully able to indicate whether the photographs had been taken during the stressful or more pleasant interview stages. Eckman, has compared facial and head cues with bodily cues and found that even when shown the body only, subjects could make assessments of the interview situation from bodily posture and gesture. However, in general he has found that the head is more informative about the nature of an emotion, while the body is more informative about the intensity. In one of his studies (Eckman, 1964) verbal cues were related to facial and postural cues. Subjects successfully matched photographs to verbal transcripts, both taken from stress and non-stress phases of interviews. In one of the studies in this series of experiments, professional dancers were used as subjects, but unfortunately he does not compare in detail their judgments with those of other judges. Eckman and Friesen (1967) have investigated the differential role of body acts and body positions as expressive of emotional moods. Mehrabian (1968) compared the postural and facial expressions of subjects who had to imagine they were talking to other people who varied in their supposed friendliness towards the subject. In spite of the methodological limitations and difficulties in using imagined situations it was found that 'eye contact, distance, orientation of body and relaxation of body (as measured by the seated communicator's reclining angle or backward lean and by his sideways lean) are significant indices of subject's liking for the addressee.' An interesting implication of this study is that the subjects obviously had knowledge of their own body images which they could reproduce in a consistent manner while imagining specific social situations. Even if such a reproduction concerns merely stylized notions of body image, the implications for bodily gesture and movement in communication are noteworthy. Dittmann (1962) was concerned not so much with the particular form of movement gestures, but with the frequency of gesture types. The movement of a patient filmed in a clinical interview was analysed with regard to his reported moods, and Dittmann found that:

Frequency of movements differentiated these moods reliably, and an interaction effect appeared between mood and body area. The interaction means that patterns of movement differ across body areas for the different moods. During this patient's angry mood, for example, there are many head and leg movements, but few hand movements, while during the depressed mood, there are few movements of the hands and head, but many leg movements.

Reece and Whitman (1962) have investigated the effect of the interviewer's movements on the verbal responsiveness of interviewees. They have found that movements judged as warm and those judged as cold could differentially influence verbal responsiveness in a patient, to an extent that verbal reinforcement and 'encouragement' by the interviewer without such expressive movements had no significant effect on the number of words spoken by the interviewee (1961). While still photographs of bodily position represent instances of movement, there is a need for research into movement communication as a continuous process, and the use of movie film would be effective in this respect. Observations of movement communication as an ongoing process have been successfully used in the study of animal social behaviour by ethologists. Ethological methods of studying human behaviour away from the experimental laboratory may provide important information on non-verbal communication. Blurton Jones (1967) for example, has observed the role of non-verbal gestures in the social interactions of nursery school children. Grant, an ethologist interested in psychiatry (1965) has specifically, observed movements as they occur, and has isolated the importance of non-verbal communication as a source of social information. He has, for example (1967), been able to isolate movement and facial gesture patterns indicative of threat and flight behaviour which could be meaningfully related to the structure of social dominance present in the group of psychiatric patients which he observed. Gestural components of aggression and flight he isolated as follows. Indicative of aggression: a direct look, plus a sharp movement of the head towards the other person; a direct look plus a lowering and bringing together of the eyebrows; a raising of the hand; a slight opening of the mouth plus a movement of the lips. Indicative of flight were the following: a direct movement away from the other person; a sharp move of head and fore-body; movement away from the other person; closed eyes; drawing the chin into the chest; raising the shoulders and lowering the head. Richard Coss (1968, 1969) has developed ethological concepts in studying the expressive qualities of visual forms and with regard to aesthetics generally. His methods of analysing affective responses by indices such as brow movement and pupil dilation could be used to assess the expressive potency of human movements.

The experimental studies cited here are but a few examples relevant to movement as social communication. They are pertinent to dance and movement drama and are also relevant to movement as expression, for in some cases the expressive qualities of movements must relate to their role as indicative of the moods, emotions and actions of others. Facial expressions are also of importance in communication but we have limited this section to bodily movements. (For accounts of experimental research into facial expression, see Woodworth and Schlosberg, 1954; Davitz, 1964; and Warr and Knapper, 1968.) The study of movement communication and expression would greatly benefit from an interdisciplinary approach as dancers, psychologists and medical workers pooled their experiences and information. For example, a movement notation has been developed by Birdwhistell (1960) who is concerned with movement as a source of information in psychiatric diagnosis (Birdwhistell, 1963), while Dierssen, Lorenc and Spitaleri (1961) have developed a technique of recording movements in the study of nervous diseases.

In the above examples, we have tried to imply that a psychology of qualitative movement is both possible and appropriate. (We have not discussed in detail the psychology of emblematic movement, but here also research like Hastorf and Cantril's (1954) study of biased spectator reaction to a football game, may be relevant. The evaluative interest of spectators is likely to influence their qualitative awareness of the game, especially with regard to the style of the opponents' play.) There are other psychological factors which could be studied with regard to particular movement activities such as the personality and skills of dancers. For example, Hall (1953) makes some interesting comments on the particular personality difficulties likely to be encountered by professional dancers. There is also the important topic of movement therapy which is reviewed by Trevor Smith (1967) who draws attention to the work of such as Martin and Beaver (1951), Bainbridge, Duddington, Collingdon and Gardner (1953), Goldstein, Lingas and Sheafor (1965) and others. Scientific study of qualitative movement is important, not merely for the sake of academic enquiry, but also because, if qualitative movement has relevance to the development of creative and lively personalities, then it is important that its dynamics should be properly understood. Meredith (1963) asks 'Why the advocacy of the Art of Movement in education? The whole claim rests on the assumption both of permanent gains and of wider consequences. What we have to ask is— What is the meaning of the gains and what is the medium by which the consequences are to be realised?'

Such questions probably can be most effectively asked and answered within the terms of behavioural science.

Bibliography

Allport, G. W. (1938), *Personality, a Psychological Interpretation*, Constable, London.
(1961), *Pattern and Growth in Personality*, Holt, Reinhart & Winston.
and Vernon, Philip E. (1933), *Studies in Expressive Movement*, Hafner.
Allusi, E. A. (1960), 'On the Use of Information Measures in Studies of Form Perception', *Perceptual & Motor Skills*, 11: 195–203.
Anthony, D. J. (1968), 'Sport and Physical Education as a Means of Aesthetic Education', *Phys. Educ.*, 60: 1–6.
Arnheim, Rudolf (1949), 'The Gestalt Theory of Expression', *Psych. Rev.*, 56: 156–71.
(1954), *Art and Visual Perception*, Faber & Faber.
(1966), *Towards a Psychology Of Art*, Faber & Faber.
Attneave, F. (1959), *Applications of Information Theory to Psychology*, Holt, Rinehart & Winston.
Bainbridge, G., Duddington, A. E., Collingdon, M., and Gardner, C. E. (1953), 'Dance-mime. A Contribution to Treatment in Psychiatry, *J. Mental Sci.*, 99: 308–14.
Berlyne, D. E. (1960), *Conflict, Arousal and Curiosity*, McGraw-Hill.
(1965), 'Measures of Aesthetic Preference', paper read at the 1st International Colloquium on Experimental Aesthetics, Paris, reprinted in Hogg, James (ed.), *Psychology and the Visual Arts*, Penguin.
and Peckham, Sylvia (1966), 'The Semantic Differential and Other Measures of Reaction to Visual Complexity', *Can. J. Psych.*, 20: 125–35.

Birdwhistell, Ray L. (1960), 'Kinetics and Communication', in McLuhan, Marshall (ed.), *Explorations in Communication*, Beacon Press.
(1963), 'Kinesic Research in the Investigation of the Emotions', in Knapp, Peter H. (ed.), *Expression of the Emotions in Man*, International Universities Press.

Blurton Jones, N. G. (1967), 'An Ethological Study of Some Aspects of Social Behaviour of Children in Nursery School', in Morris, Desmond (ed.), *Primate Ethology*, Weidenfeld & Nicolson.

Brown, L. T. (1964), 'Quantitative Description of Visual Pattern: Some Methodological Suggestions, *Perceptual & Motor Skills*, 19: 771–4.

Cantor, G. N., Cantor, J. H., and Ditrichs, R. (1963), 'Observing Behaviour in Pre-School Children as a Function of Stimulus Complexity', *Child Dev.*, 34: 683–9.

Coss, Richard G. (1968), 'The Ethological Command in Art', *Leonardo*, 1: 273–87.
(1969), 'The Perceptual Aspects of Eyespot Patterns and their Relevance to Gaze Behaviour', in Hutt, C., and Hutt, S. J. (eds), *Behaviour Studies in Psychiatry*, Pergamon.

Cratty, Bryant J. (1964), *Movement Behaviour and Motor Learning*, Henry Kimpton.

Curl, Gordon F. (1967), *A Critical Study of Rudolf Von Laban's Theory and Practice of Movement*, M.Ed. thesis, University of Leicester.

Davitz, J. (1964) (ed.), *The Communication of Emotional Meaning*, McGraw-Hill.

Dember, W. N., Earl, R. W., and Paradise, N. (1957), 'Response by Rats to Differential Stimulus Complexity', *J. Comp. Physiol. Psych.*, 50: 514–18.

Dierssen, Guillermo, Lorenc, Mary, and Spitaleri, Marie Rose (1961), 'A New Method for Graphic Study of Human Movements', *Neurology*, 11: 610–18.

Dittmann, A. T. (1962), 'The Relationship between Body Movement and Moods in Interviews', *J. Consult. Psych.*, 26: 480.

Dorfman, Donald D., and McKenna, Helen (1966), 'Pattern Preference as a Function of Pattern Uncertainty', *Can. J. Psychol.*, 20: 143–53.

Dreher, J. J., and Evans, W. E. (1964), 'Viewer Reactions to Abstract Visual Forms', *Aerospace Medicine*, 654–7.

Eckman, Paul (1964), 'Body Position, Facial Expression and Verbal Behaviour during Interviews', *J. Abnorm. Soc. Psych.*, 68: 295–301.
(1966), 'Communication through Non-verbal Behaviour: a Source of Information about an Interpersonal Relationship', in Tomkins, Silvan S., and Izard, Caroll E. (eds), *Affect, Cognition and Personality*', Tavistock.
and Friesen, Wallace V. (1967), 'Head and Body Cues in the Judgement of Emotion: a Reformulation', *Perceptual & Motor Skills*, 24: 711–24.

Eibl-Eibesfeldt, Iranaus (1967), 'Concepts of Ethology and their Significance in the Study of Human Behaviour', in Stevenson, W., Hess, Eckman H., and Rheingold, Harriet L. (eds) *Early Behaviour*, Wiley.

Elliott, R. K. (1969), 'Aesthetics and Sport', paper delivered to Conference on Aesthetic Aspects of Sport, University of Salford.
Evans, C. R., and Piggins, D. J. (1963), 'A Comparison of Geometrical Shapes when viewed under Conditions of Steady Fixation with Apparatus for producing a Stabilised Retinal Image', *Brit. J. Optics*, 20: 1–13.
Ewer, R. F. (1968), *Ethology of Mammals*, Logos Press.
Eysenck, H. J. (1967), *Sense and Nonsense in Psychology*, Penguin.
(1965), 'Aesthetics and Personality', *Exakte Ästhetik*, 1, No. 1.
Folkins, Castyle, and Lenrow, Peter (1966), 'An Investigation of the Expressive Value of Graphenes', *Psych. Rec.*, 16: 193–200.
Garner, W. R. (1962), 'Uncertainty and Structure as Psychological Concepts', Wiley.
Garvin, Lucius (1958), 'Emotivism, Expression and Symbolic Meaning', *J. Phil.*, 55: 111–18.
Goldstein, C., Lingas, C., and Sheafor, D. (1965), 'Interpretative Movement as a Subliminal Tool in Music Therapy', *J. Music Therapy*, 2: 11–15.
Golann, Stuart E. (1962), 'The Creativity Motive', *J. Pers.*, 30: 588–600.
Gombrich, E. H. (1960), *Art and Illusion*, Pantheon.
Grant, E. C. (1965), 'The Contribution of Ethology to Child Psychiatry', in Howell (ed.), *Modern Perspectives in Child Psychiatry*, Edinburgh.
(1967), 'An Ethological Description of Some Schizophrenic Patterns of Behaviour', unpublished paper.
Hall, Fernau (1953), *An Anatomy of Ballet*, Andrew Melrose.
Hampshire, Stuart (1960), *Feeling and Expression*, Inaugural Lecture, University College, London, H. K. Lewis.
Harlow, H. F., Harlow, M. K., and Meyer, D. R. (1950), 'Learning Motivated by a Manipulation Drive', *J. Exp. Psych.*, 40: 228–34.
Hastorf, Albert H., and Cantril, Hadley (1954), 'They saw a Game: a Case Study', *J. Abnorm. Soc. Psychol.*, 49: 129–234.
Hayner, Paul C. (1961), 'Expressive Meaning in Art', *Phil. & Phenom. Res.*, 21: 543–51.
Hays, Joan C. (1967), 'Effects of Two Regulated Changes of Tempo upon Emotional Connotations in Dance', *Res. Q.*, 38: 389–97.
Hepburn, Ronald W. (1960), 'Emotions and Emotional Qualities. Some Attempt at Analysis', *Brit. J. Aesth.*, 1: 255–65.
Hershenson, M., Musinger, H., and Kesson, W. (1965), 'Preference for Shapes of Intermediate Variability in the Newborn Human', *Science*, 147: 630–1.
Hill, W. F. (1956), 'Activity as an Autonomous Drive', *J. Comp. Physiol. Psych.*, 49: 15–19.
Hogg, James (ed.) (1969), *Psychology and the Visual Arts*, Penguin.
Hohler, V. (1969), 'The Beauty of Motion', paper delivered to Conference on Aesthetics and Sport, University of Salford.
Jones, A., Wilkinson, H. J., and Braden, I. (1961), 'Information Deprivation as a Motivational Variable', *J. Exp. Psych.*, 62: 126–37.
Jordon, Diana (1966), *Childhood and Movement*, Blackwell.

Kagan, J., and Berkun, M. (1954), 'The Reward Value of Running Activity, *J. Comp. Physiol. Psych.*, 47: 108.

Karmel, Bernard Z. (1966), 'Randomness, Complexity and Visual Preference Behaviour in the Hooded Rat and Domestic Chick', *J. Comp. Physiol. Psych.*, 61: 487–9.

Kohler, Wolfgang (1958), 'Relational Determination in Perception', in Beardslee, David Cromwell, and Wertheimer, Michael (eds), *Readings in Perception*, Van Nostrand.

Kraut, Maurice H. (1954a), 'An Experimental Attempt to Produce Unconscious Symbolic Movements', *J. Genetic Psych.*, 51: 93–120.

(1954b), 'An Experimental Attempt to Determine the Significance of Unconscious Manual Symbolic Movements', *J. Genetic Psych.*, 51: 121–52.

Lamb, Warren (1965), *Posture and Gesture*, Duckworth.

Langer, Susanne K. (1953), *Feeling and Form*, Routledge & Kegan Paul.

Leckart, Bruce T. (1966), 'Looking Time. The Effects of Stimulus Complexity and Familiarity', *Percept. & Psychophys.*, 1: 142–4.

Martin, D. W., and Beaver, N. (1951), 'A Preliminary Report on the Use of Dance as an Adjuvant in the Therapy of Schizophrenics', *Psychiat. Q. Supp.*, 25: 176–90.

Mehrabian, Albert (1968), 'Relationship of Attitude to Seated Posture Orientation, and Distance', *J. Pers. Soc. Psych.*, 10: 26–30.

Meredith, Patrick (1963), 'Mind and Movement, lecture delivered to Chelsea College of Physical Education.

Metheny, Eleanor (1965), *Connotations of Movement in Sport and Dance*, William C. Brown.

(1968), *Movement and Feeling*, McGraw-Hill.

Miller, Susanna (1968), *The Psychology of Play*, Penguin.

Moles, Abraham (1966), 'Information Theory and Aesthetic Perception', University of Illinois Press.

Morgan, Clifford, and King, Richard A. (1966), *Introduction to Psychology*, McGraw-Hill.

Morris, Desmond (1962), *The Biology of Art*, Methuen.

Munro, Thomas (1951), 'Aesthetics as Science: its Development in America', *J. Aesth. Art. Crit.*, 9: 161–207.

Mussen, Paul H., Conger, John J., and Kagan, Jerome (1963), *Child Development and Personality*, Harper International.

Musinger, Harry, and Kesson, William (1964), 'Uncertainty, Structure, and Preference', *Psych. Monogr.*, 78, No. 9.

McKellar, Peter (1957), 'Imagination and Thinking', Cohen & West.

Osgood, C. E., Suci, G. J., and Tannenbaum, P. H. (1957), *The Measurement of Meaning*, University of Illinois Press.

Pritchard, Roy M. (1961), 'Stabilized Images on the Retina', *Scientific American*, June.

Reece, Michael M., and Whitman, Robert (1961), 'Warmth and Expressive Movements', *Psych. Reports*, 8: 76.

(1962), 'Expressive Movements, Warmth and Verbal Reinforcement' *J. Abnorm. Soc. Psych.*, 64: 234–6.

Reid, Louis Arnaud (1965), 'Susanne Langer and Beyond', *Brit. J. Aesth.*, 5: 357–67.

Ross, R. T. (1938), 'Studies in the Psychology of the Theatre', *Psych. Rec.*, 2: 127–90.

Sackett, G. P., Keith-Lee, P., and Treat, R. (1963), 'Food Versus Perceptual Complexity as Rewards for Rats Previously Subjected to Sensory Deprivation', *Science*, 141: 518–20.

Sainsbury, P. (1955), 'Gestural Movement during Psychiatric Interview, *Psycho-somatic Med.*, 17: 458–69.

Sandle, Douglas (1967), 'The Science of Art', *Science J.*, March.

Schiffman, H. R. (1966), 'Golden Section: Preferred Figural Orientation', *Percept. & Psychophys.*, 1: 193–4.

Schilder, Paul (1950), 'The Image and Appearance of the Human Body', International Universities Press.

Shannon, C. E., and Weaver, W. (1949), *The Mathematical Theory of Communication*, University of Illinois Press.

Sheets, Maxine (1966), *The Phenomenology of Dance*, University of Wisconsin.

Simpson, Helen M. (1967), 'Physical Education and the Arts', *Phys. Educ.*, 59: 54–61.

Smith, Trevor M. (1967), 'Psycho-aesthetic Aspects of Dance in Education', unpublished thesis submitted in part requirement for Advanced Diploma in Physical Education, University of Leeds, and Carnegie College of Physical Education, Leeds.

Smith, Seward, and Myers, Thomas I. (1966), 'Stimulation Seeking during Sensory Deprivation', *Perceptual & Motor Skills*, 23: 1151–63.

Stone, L. A., and Collins, L. G. (1965), 'The Golden Section Revisited: a Perimetric Explanation', *Amer. J. Psych.*, 78: 500–3.

Strauss, Erwin W. (1966), 'The Forms of Spatiality', in *Phenomenological Psychology*, collected papers, Tavistock Publications (see also the papers 'Lived Movement' and 'The Upright Posture').

Turner, Margery J. (1963), 'A Study of Modern Dance in relation to Communication, Choreographic Structure, and Elements of Composition', *Res. Q.*, 34: 219–27.
(1965), 'Nonliteral Modern Dance—its Nature, Forms and Means of Communication', *Res. Q.*, 36: 86–95.

Valentine, C. W. (1962), *The Experimental Psychology of Beauty*, Methuen.

Vitz, Paul C. (1966), 'Preference for Different Amounts of Visual Complexity', *Behav. Sci.*, 11: 105–14.

Wallach, Michael A., and Kogan, Nathan (1966), *Modes of Thinking in Young Children*, Holt, Rinehart & Winston.

Warr, Peter B., and Knapper, Christopher (1968), *The Perception of People and Events*, Wiley.

Wertheimer, Max (1958), 'Principles of Perceptual Organisation', in Beardslee, David Cromwell, and Wertheimer, Michael (eds), *Readings in Perception*, Van Nostrand.

Wexner, L. B. (1954), 'The Degree to which Colours are Associated with Mood Tone', *J. Appl. Psych.*, 38: 432–5.

161

Wohwill, Joachim F. (1960), 'Developmental Studies of Perception', *Psych. Bull.*, 57: 249–88.

Woodworth, R. S., and Schlosberg, H. (1954), *Experimental Psychology*, Holt.

Wright, David (1969), 'What is it Like to be Deaf?', *Daily Telegraph Magazine* No. 263.

Wright, B., and Rainwater, L. (1962), 'The Meanings of Colour', *J. Genetic Psych.* 67: 89–99.

6

The contribution of play and sports to emotional health

Emma McCloy Layman

The nature of emotional health

Since the 1908 publication of Clifford Beers' epoch-making book, *The Mind that found Itself*, various terms have been used as designations for that state of psychological well-being most frequently referred to as 'mental health'. The majority of psychologists and psychiatrists have continued to speak of mental health and mental illness, although a few have felt that the 'healthy personality' might be a less ambiguous and more descriptive term. In recent years, professional physical and health educators, as well as others interested in sport psychology, have shown an increasing preference for the terms 'emotional health' and 'emotional illness' as substitutes for the older terms. It is not proposed to defend or criticize the use of any of these terms which, imprecise as they are, can be used interchangeably by most psychologically sophisticated persons without any serious danger that the intended meaning will be misunderstood. Some persons, however, have been inclined to speak of 'emotional health *and* social adjustment', with emotional health being perceived as having an intrapersonal focus and social adjustment as having an interpersonal focus. This kind of dichotomization seems unsound, if we accept the principle of organismic unity; furthermore, the term 'emotional health' is sufficiently broad and integrative in its implications to cover what has usually been assumed to be encompassed by all the other terms in common use. There are several reasons for preferring 'emotional health' to the more familiar term, 'mental health': (a) although emotion does not lend itself to exact and succinct definition, it is possible to describe it in terms of physiological components, states of consciousness, motivational aspects and overt behavioural manifestations; (2) as a component of attitudes, emotion is closely tied in with the cognitive and interpersonal-social aspects of the personality; (3) studies of psychotic, neurotic and delinquent persons have shown the central importance of emotions in psychopathology; (4) 'emotional' does not carry the connotation of a separation of mind and body which is suggested by the adjective 'mental', so is more conducive to a holistic view of the organism.

What are the characteristics of the emotionally healthy person? Among those most frequently mentioned are peace of mind, relative freedom from tension and anxiety, the ability to direct hostile feelings into creative and constructive channels, sensitivity and responsiveness to the feelings of others, the ability to give and receive love, spontaneity of emotional expression in a form appropriate to the individual's developmental level, the ability to deal constructively with reality and adjust to change, a feeling of security, a sense of self-worth, enjoyment of human contacts, integration around values making for the good of society, flexibility, an appropriate balance between self-sufficiency and willingness to accept help, the ability to accept present frustration for future gain and the capacity to enjoy life.

The nature of play and sports

Play has been variously defined, but there is general agreement on several points, namely that play is activity; that it is of interest to the player; that the same activity may be work or play, according to the attitude taken toward it; and that an essential characteristic of play is a satisfaction in the activity for its own sake, with participation being voluntary (Mitchell and Mason, 1935). On the basis of these points of agreement, most educators and psychologists would agree with Gulick's definition of play as 'doing what we want to do, without reference primarily to any ulterior end, but simply for the joy of the process' (Mitchell and Mason, 1935). Huizinga suggests some additional characteristics of play, including the fact that it is executed within fixed limits of time and place according to rules which are freely accepted but absolutely binding in the play situation (Huizinga, 1955).

Play may involve a great deal of big-muscle activity, or very little. In early life most play does involve body movement. However, as the child grows older sedentary forms of play become more common. For our purposes here, we shall be considering only those forms of play in which there is vigorous physical activity.

Like play, 'sport' is a very broad term, covering activities ranging from teasing cats to highly organized team athletics. In the present context, however, this term will be used in a more limited sense, to include team sports such as baseball, basketball, football and cricket; individual competitive sports such as tennis, golf, track and field, and bowling; fighting sports such as boxing, wrestling and fencing; and outdoor activities such as mountaineering, skiing, fishing, hunting and sailing. It will be assumed also that we are referring to *amateur* sports. For the amateur athlete, the participation in sport should be a form of play. The 'varsity' athlete, however, is frequently under such pressure to participate and under such rigid discipline that there is no longer joy in the activity and participation becomes drudgery. Under these circumstances, engaging in the activity is not really play.

The term 'sport' as applied to physical activities usually implies the acquisition of skills, which is to a lesser degree associated also with the running and chasing games so common in children's play.

Historical background and current thinking

The idea that play and sport can contribute to man's emotional well-being goes back to antiquity, but it is only in modern times that we have attempted a scientifically-oriented approach to understanding the nature of the relationship between participation in sports or other forms of play activities and the development of emotional health. In these attempts, we have gone through four stages, which are overlapping.

The first stage was associated with the rising popularity of the 'double aspect' theory of metaphysical relationships. As the twentieth century entered its first decade, psychologists and philosophers were contending that mind and body were merely two aspects of a single functional reality. At the same time Johns Hopkins University psychiatrist, Adolf Meyer, was developing his ideas about emotional illness as an illness of the 'biosocial organism'. During this period physical educators were accepting the theory of mind–body unity as fact, and also assumed as fact that physical activity was physically beneficial. Accepting these assumptions as reality, they then went on to argue that, *because* these things were true, physical activity *must* contribute to emotional health or a healthy personality.

The second stage emerged in the 1920s and was in the ascendancy through the 1930s. At this time the theories of McDougall, Freud and Adler were applied to show how play activities and sports involve meeting man's basic needs or represent the channeling of instincts, and therefore contribute to healthy emotional development. In this stage uncontrolled observations were used as evidence to support the theories. Since the 1930s psychoanalytic writers have written extensively on the psychodynamics of play, but usually have not tied it in with emotional health. Examples of such writers are Alexander (1958), Erikson (1940), Greenacre (1959), Peller (1954), Redl (1959) and Waelder (1933). The use of play as a medium of expression in psychotherapy with children has led to some further theorizing about the values of play for the development of emotional health, but little of this has been specifically tied in with sports or other big-muscle activities.

The second stage tends to merge with the third, which extended from the 1930s through the 1950s. During these years theoretical formulations were bolstered by research in which the results of clinical case studies, surveys and questionnaire findings were analyzed and interpreted. Many of these studies related specifically to sports and other physical activities. Research of this type is still being carried out but is less common than it was a decade ago.

In the fourth stage, currently the predominant one, hypotheses are being formulated and tested, using the experimental method.

Almost no educated person any longer professes belief in a mind–body dichotomy. Nevertheless, despite protestations of commitment to the principle of organismic unity, many teachers in fields other than physical education continue to behave as if physical education and sports were irrelevant to the educational process if not actually detrimental to it. Although educational psychologists point to children's interest in play as an important resource to be used in planning learning experiences, there is a persistence of the old idea that school learning is 'work', and therefore opposed to 'play'. The idea that athletes are 'all muscle and no brain', and that physical education teachers and coaches are second-class citizens continues to persist within the academic community except in those countries where physical fitness and excellence in sports have become tied to nationalistic goals. In this climate of skepticism on the part of professional colleagues representing other disciplines, physical educators have found themselves looking for evidence of educational outcomes which would be convincing to other teachers, school administrators and taxpayers. Starting in the 1930s, general educators began putting increased emphasis on the importance of mental health as an educational objective. This provided physical educators with a long-sought opportunity, since they had long been stressing physical education as education of the 'whole person'. At the present time, most persons interested in physical education or sport psychology are convinced that participation in sports makes positive contributions to the development of emotional health. However, many of the statements commonly made by physical educators and coaches about this are statements for which the supporting evidence is either non-existent or equivocal. This is not to say that physical educators or coaches are deliberately being dishonest. When one is defending his profession against attack, however, he usually does not clearly differentiate between conclusions based on hearsay or anecdotal material and those based on replicable carefully controlled scientific experiments. He also tends to overlook or gloss over evidence which supports a position contrary to the one he has taken. Probably all of us who are ego-involved in the business of promoting greater participation in sports have been guilty of over-generalizing, in our eagerness to make a point in the face of opposition. If we took the role of devil's advocate, and looked for evidence to support the views of the opposition, we might come up with some different answers. There is now a sufficient body of sound research that it is no longer necessary to resort to arm-chair logic, to answer the important questions about the contributions of play and sports to the development of emotional health. The time has come, then, to take a hard look at our ideas about this subject, and to come up with some answers to the following questions: What do we know to be true? What ideas are still untested hypotheses? In what areas is the evidence still equivocal? What types of new research are needed?

Let us look at some of the statements frequently made by physical educators and see how they stand up in the face of careful scrutiny. We shall state these as six propositions.

Proposition 1 *Engaging in sports promotes physical fitness: fitness is associated with good emotional health and a lack of fitness with poor emotional health.*

In these days virtually nobody disputes the idea of psychosomatic unity. This concept is supported by experimental work on the electrophysiology of mental activities, psychopharmacological studies showing the concomitant physical and psychological effects of drugs and physiological research on the physiological and psychological effects of hormones. It is also supported by clinical evidence from psychosomatic medicine showing that, not only may physical symptoms be at least in part expressive of emotional conflicts, but disease processes usually considered somatic in nature may result in symptoms of emotional disturbance such as anxiety, depression, poor emotional control and social maladjustment.

A number of research studies have investigated the relation between physical fitness and various aspects of emotional health. Of seventeen such studies, thirteen reported a negative relation between fitness and symptoms of emotional disturbance, together with a positive relation between fitness and emotional health. The results of one study were inconsistent. Wells (1958) and Breen (1959) found physical fitness to be negatively related to characteristics such as anxiety, tension, emotionality and withdrawal in college men, and Weber (1953) reported a positive relation between physical fitness and academic achievement in college men, although he found no relation between physical fitness and emotional health as indicated by scores on the Minnesota Multiphasic Personality Inventory. Hart and Shuey (1964) reported a positive relation between physical fitness and academic achievement in college women, and Harris (1963) found a negative relation between fitness and anxiety. Schulz (1961) found significant superiority in the body image (self-concept) in high-school girls of high physical fitness as compared with girls of low fitness. Cureton (1963) found that a program of physical conditioning helped adult men to make more friends, and resulted in the disappearance of tension as well as appearance of greater mental and physical energy. McFarland and Huddleston (1936) found mental patients to have lower fitness than normals or athletes; Rosenberg and Rice (1964) reported schizophrenic patients to be lower in fitness than neurotics or non-patient groups. Among the more impressive studies reporting a positive relation between fitness and emotional health are those by Johnson and his co-workers at the Children's Physical Developmental Clinic at the University of Maryland (1966), where they have found improvement in fitness to be associated with improvement in various aspects of emotional health, although improvement in motor control and the relation between child and therapist were also factors related to improvement.

Most studies of the physically handicapped show that, on the average, their educational achievement is below that of children without such handicaps, and they tend to be less well adjusted than unhandicapped children (Brockway, 1939; Burt, 1933; Cornell, 1908;

Heider, 1948; Pintner, Eisenson and Stanton, 1941; Stedman, 1934). However, some studies indicate that this is not always true (Barbour, 1935; Brown, 1938; Hinrichs, 1941; Kammerer, 1940). Hardy (1937) found the incidence of physical disease in poorly adjusted elementary school children to be lower than for the well-adjusted or those of average adjustment, although vigorous health and absence of physical defects tended to be associated with good adjustment. Doscher (1947) found the adjustment of physically handicapped college students to be neither oustandingly good nor poor.

The preponderance of the evidence seems rather convincingly to support the hypothesis of a positive relation between physical fitness and emotional health, although some studies have not shown a clear-cut relationship and a few have seemed to indicate no relationship. Those studies which do not show a relationship between physical fitness and emotional health may fail to do so either because the instruments used to assess emotional health are measuring different characteristics or because the criteria of fitness vary in different studies.

Lest we get carried away with the possibilities of sports for the development of emotional health by means of promoting physical fitness, there are several points which should be kept in mind.

(1) Different sports as well as different positions played in team sports are by no means uniform in the extent to which they contribute toward the development of physical fitness. In fact, it seems likely that some types of sports participation do not contribute to fitness at all, except indirectly through the physical conditioning program planned for sports participants. For example, it would seem improbable that serving as goal-keeper on a field hockey team would contribute significantly to physical fitness unless playing on the team were contingent on participating in a conditioning program.

(2) The causes of poor emotional health are many, and even an individual with a sound physique can become emotionally ill if one or more of these other factors is operative.

(3) The picture is confused by the fact that different studies use different criteria to assess physical fitness. Sometimes strength tests are used, sometimes cardiovascular tests and sometimes tests of motor skill. Again in some studies physical fitness is judged on the basis of the individual's having participated in a physical conditioning program, with no actual assessment of physical fitness having been made but with evaluations of emotional health being made on a before and after basis.

(4) It should be pointed out that many studies assessing the relation between physical status and emotional health have been made in connection with programs in which a therapist or clinician has had a relationship with students or patients in a program designed to improve fitness. This, of course, makes it impossible to say to what extent improved emotional health is the result of improved fitness and to what extent it stems from the student-teacher or therapist-patient relationship.

Proposition 2 *The acquisition of motor skills involved in sports contributes toward meeting the basic needs of safety and esteem in young children of both sexes and in boys and young men from the early grades through the college years.*

The importance of acceptance by the social group as a condition necessary for emotional health has been repeatedly stressed by mental hygienists. Studies made by psychologists as well as by physical educators have been consistent in showing that, in boys and men from kindergarten through the university, athletic skill is related to status and prestige in the peer group, and makes other positive contributions to emotional health. Representative of the many studies showing this are ones by McGraw and Tolbert (1953), Rarick and McKee (1949), Clarke and Greene (1964), Cowell and Ismail (1962), Smith and Hurst (1961), Jones (1946) and Biddulph (1954). There seems also to be a positive relation between motor skill and status for girls in the elementary school, but as puberty approaches the athletic girl tends frequently to be identified with the 'masculine' girl, and athletic skill contributes less to social status. This is shown in studies by Bell (1955) and Flemming (1934). Relatively few studies have used adolescent girls as subjects but most of those that have involved adolescent girls have shown that athletic skills in adolescent girls tend to be related to team-mate status but not to friendship status or more general social acceptance (see Breck, 1950).

A propos of the findings with respect to sports for women as being associated with masculinity, two comments should be made. First, it should be noted that the studies reviewed by the writer were all done in the United States, and there undoubtedly is a cultural variable operating here. It would be interesting to do some cross-cultural comparisons in this area, to note the degree to which there are likenesses and differences in different societies with reference to the extent to which athletic skills in girls and women contribute to social acceptance and status in the peer group. Second, it is a fact that some kinds of sports are considered less masculine than others. For example, boxing, rugby and American football would be considered quite masculine and dancing more feminine, with tennis, gymnastics and archery being in-between. This was shown in a study by Layman (1968).

An important point to note about athletic skills in relation to emotional health is that, for those with little aptitude for the development of motor skills, experiences with sports may result in increased feelings of inferiority and insecurity unless the teacher or coach makes adaptations in the program which will enable even the most inept to attain success and prestige in the group. Sometimes this must be in conjunction with a program in psychotherapy.

Proposition 3 *Participation in play and sports presents potentialities for promoting emotional health and preventing delinquency.*

Much has been written on the values of play and sports for promoting the development of emotional health and encouraging the acquisition of attitudes, values and habits implied in the concept of good 'character'. For example, Slavson (1946) points out the value of active recreation for developing a feeling of self-worth. Bower (1952) calls attention to the potentialities of physical education, recreation and sports for developing qualities such as 'personal and group integrity, loyalty, cooperation, courtesy, respect for the body, fairness, and that galaxy of traits known as sportsmanship' (p. 80). McKinney(1939) states the values of play as follows: (1) it increases social poise and spontaneity; (2) it develops independence; (3) it releases tensions; (4) it forms the basis for friendship, popularity and leadership (pp. 194–5). Summarizing the research findings in this area, most studies show that active participation in play or recreational activities tends to be associated with emotional health and socially acceptable behaviour patterns. Examples of such studies are those by McKinney (1937), Cowell (1949) and Blanchard (1946). Although the results of such studies are fairly consistent, in the case of studies involving *athletic* activities, it frequently is difficult to tell whether the relevant independent variable is *participation* or *skill* in sports. Also, although the potential character education values of sports have been demonstrated, there are indications that in a situation where the importance of winning is stressed and takes precedence over all else, these values will not accrue. There also is no evidence that values such as 'sportsmanship', 'fair play' and 'team work' automatically transfer to other situations.

One of the major arguments advanced for the establishment and support of boys' clubs, community recreation centers, recreational centers for teenagers and organized sports programs of various sorts is the value of such programs for the prevention of delinquency. Several studies have shown that delinquency rates often are high in areas where recreational facilities are scarce (Witmer and Tufts, 1954), and various studies have shown a diminution of delinquent acts following establishment of programs in supervised play (Cole, 1936; Harris, 1943; Horwitz, 1939; Oakland Survey, 1946; Witmer and Tufts, 1954). However, despite the findings showing the reduction of juvenile delinquency in some communities following the establishment of supervised recreation programs, studies such as those by Thurstone (1918), Powers and Witmer (1951), Shanas and Dunning (1942), Fine (1955), Reinhardt and Harper (1931), Kvaraceus (1945) and the Gluecks (1952) show that, even when recreational facilities and supervised programs are available, delinquents seldom participate in these programs and, in fact, do not want supervision of any kind. Looking at all of the findings objectively, it is apparent that having a supervised recreation program available is not enough in itself to prevent delinquency, whether or not delinquency is associated with poor emotional health. Many delinquents find their delinquent activities far more exciting and interesting than anything which is offered in the recreation program, and many use the playground or gymnasium as a gathering place for the delinquent gang, performing their delinquent acts on the way home. Some studies show that delinquents are better than non-delinquents in motor skills, although they may not know the rules of the game as well as do non-delinquents (Glueck and Glueck, 1934; Glueck and Glueck, 1952; Healy and Bronner, 1926; Murray, 1931). Supervised recreation as a part of a larger delinquency-prevention program can make an important contribution, but only if the following conditions are met: (1) if the program is broad enough to appeal to varied interests; (2) if the adult leaders are well selected; and (3) if the leaders proceed on the basis of meeting not only group needs but the unique, personalized needs of individual members of the group and small sub-groups.

Supervised recreation programs in the United States of America have most frequently been established in large metropolitan areas, where numerous public and private agencies have concerned themselves with providing supervised leisure-time activities for children, adolescents and adults. Here we have programs planned and supervised by park commissions, city recreation departments, public schools, police departments, settlement houses, Y.M.C.A.s, Y.W.C.A.s, churches and a variety of other agencies with overlapping functions. The areas in which these programs are established also are those where known delinquency rates are the highest. Indications are, however, that delinquency is increasing more rapidly in the small towns than in the large cities, and it is in the small towns that attempts at organizing recreation programs have been spotty and sporadic. (In the United Kingdom it appears that organization of comprehensive recreation programs in small town and semi-rural areas is more systematic than in the United States.) In the small towns of the United States it has frequently been observed that a marked change has taken place in the recreational patterns of young people in the last generation. As recently as thirty years ago—and even more recently in some localities—it was common practice in villages and small towns for spontaneous play groups to organize themselves after school and in the early evening hours, with vacant lots, back yards, and small parks being used for games in which frequently children and adolescents representing a wide age range played together. Most vacant lots have disappeared and the running and chasing games which in years gone by had such a universal appeal have been displaced by television programs, drive-in theaters and road houses. Sandlot baseball which was so appealing to the American youth of yesteryear has been replaced by the more highly organized, competitive and exclusive Little League and Middle League baseball. It may be that in the small towns the cause of emotional health would be better served by a development of backyard playground facilities and a return to the spontaneous play spirit of a generation ago than by a development of more adult-supervised, highly organized recreational programs.

Proposition 4 *Clinical evidence from play therapy, group therapy and the use of physical exercise as a psychiatric adjunct in the treatment of emotionally ill patients indicates that when play, recreational and athletic activities are planned with individual needs in mind, they may be very valuable means of improving emotional health.*

It has frequently been pointed out that several characteristics of play make it ideal as a substitute for the verbal interview in psychotherapy with children. Among these characteristics are the following: (1)

it is a medium of self-expression and the 'language' of the young child; (2) it is a 'projection' of the child's personality; (3) it is in a social context; (4) it involves vigorous activity. Play therapy has become the standard approach to the treatment of emotionally disturbed children. However, it should be noted that play itself is not therapeutic—sometimes may even be harmful—and that the relationship between the child and the therapist is of crucial importance in determining the effectiveness of play therapy.

'Activity group therapy', as described by Slavson (1947), also utilizes sports and other play activities in its program, but here again the role of the therapist is important and so is the structure of the group.

In mental hospitals the prescription of physical exercise for the treatment of emotionally disturbed patients is a common practice as a supplement to other forms of therapy. The program for each patient is based on an understanding of that patient's needs and on an understanding of the psychodynamics of different kinds of physical activity. Special attention is given to sports and other physical activities which have potentialities for encouraging self-expression, promoting communication, developing socialized habits and attitudes, increasing the range of interests, improving self-confidence, motivating the patient to return to reality, gratifying narcissistic needs, expiating feelings of guilt and facilitating relaxation. Where used, physical exercise therapy is one of the adjunctive therapies employed in a multi-faceted program to rehabilitate the psychiatric patient, with the program including such varied approaches as psychotherapy, chemotherapy, shock therapy, bibliotherapy, occupational therapy, physiotherapy, educational therapy and others. Included in physical activity therapy are frequently activities such as weight lifting, swimming, boxing, dancing and different team sports.

The clinical and research literature is full of glowing reports of the effectiveness of individually prescribed exercise in promoting improvement of hospitalized psychiatric patients—particularly schizophrenic patients who have been hospitalized for long periods and have not responded to other therapies. There seems no doubt that it *does* promote improvement. However, most of the reports are not based on controlled studies, but on 'before and after' observations made by persons who, in some instances, probably were not too objective in their evaluations. Some of the studies showing significant changes taking place in patients after participation in a program of sports or some other type of physical activity are such as to make it impossible to rule out the chance that these changes might have resulted from some other kind of therapy, or from the overall program. A few studies have utilized control groups and a research design such as to make the conclusions scientifically tenable. Among these are studies by Meyer (1955) (recreation therapy), Van Fleet (1950) (physical education therapy), Timmerman (1954) (swimming), and Kramer and Bauer (1955) (swimming). Although the findings of Kramer and Bauer are somewhat equivocal, the studies as a whole point to the beneficial effects of physical exercise in improving the adjustment of hospitalized psychiatric patients.

We should say again that, whether we are speaking of play therapy, group therapy, recreational therapy or corrective therapy, none of the studies make it possible for us to tell the extent to which the therapy program is successful because of the activities, and the extent to which it is successful because of the relationship between the patient and the therapist.

Proposition 5 *Play and sports supply outlets for the expression of emotion, and outward expression of emotion in approved activities in approved activities is conducive to the development and maintenance of emotional health.*

Anyone who has seen children participating in an exciting competitive game could not doubt that emotion was being expressed, and it has often been suggested that competitive sports represent a valuable means of sublimating aggressive impulses.

When we speak of aggression we mean the initiation of an attack. At this time psychologists are not in agreement concerning whether aggressive behaviour is instinctive, is a reaction to frustration or is learned behaviour acquired by means of conditioning. The near-universality of instigation to aggression is recognized, however, as are the problems this creates from the standpoint of the amount of destructive violence on the international scene and the high incidence of emotional illness centering on problems related to aggression.

It is generally recognized that, among human beings there are two major types of aggression: *reactive* aggression and *instrumental* aggression. Reactive aggression involves a goal-response which is the injury of the group or person perceived as the 'enemy' who has been the agent of frustration, the source of some noxious stimulus or the originator of a threat of unpleasantness or frustration of some kind. Both perception of an enemy and the emotion of anger are involved in reactive aggression.

Instrumental aggression is attack in which the primary goal is not injury to the enemy, but attainment of a reward. Instrumental aggression does not involve anger, and it is not a response to frustration or noxious stimuli.

For reactive aggression, the major reinforcer is the stimulus of the victim suffering injury or being in pain; for instrumental aggression, the major reinforcer is an extrinsic reward.

Probably for many athletes, competitive sports involve principally instrumental aggression. That is, the athlete attempts to defeat his rival because of the satisfaction he will experience from proving his own competence, and because of the praise and approval he will receive, but he does not really feel anger toward his opponent. On the other hand, because winning in a sports contest always involves doing injury to another either physically or psychologically, there are some athletes who cannot force themselves to win unless they can perceive the opponent as the enemy and can experience anger toward him. Otherwise, their expression of aggression would generate too much of a feeling of guilt. Sometimes coaches try to cause the team members to become angry with the opponents, so that they will make a greater effort to win.

The contention that expression of aggression through play and sports contributes to the development of emotional health is based on the catharsis hypothesis. According to this hypothesis, the performance of an aggressive act releases pent-up aggressive energy, reduces tension, decreases the remaining instigation to aggression and makes the individual feel better. Presumably it would therefore contribute to emotional health.

Controlled studies indicate that when aggression occurs in the presence of anger there *is* a decrease in the level of anger and a decrease in the tendency to aggress for a short period. Also, unless the individual has feelings of guilt because of the aggressive act, there will be a reduction of tension and improved feeling of well-being. However when aggression occurs in the absence of anger, there is an *increase* in the tendency to aggress, unless the tendency to aggress is weakened by feelings of guilt or anxiety. Thus reactive aggression in general supports the catharsis hypothesis but instrumental aggression does not.

What is the relevance of this for play and sports? Some psychiatrists express doubt that athletics are really an outlet for aggressive impulses because the controls involved in game rules make it impossible for the participant to really express himself freely. Also, we might note that the unwritten rules of sportsmanship call on the individual to shake hands with his opponent and to congratulate the winner. Yet at the same time athletes are told by the coach to 'get out there and fight' and the cheering fans shout, 'Kill him', 'Murder them', 'Tear into them', 'Fight, fight, fight'. Probably in the beginning of a sports competition most of the players are not angry, so any aggression they might express would be instrumental aggression. If they play vigorously there will be a discharge of energy through activity and at the end of the game the players should be fatigued and therefore not eager to repeat the performance immediately. But if the aggression has brought the reward of winning the game and the desired social approval for fighting hard, after a short rest the players will be ready for a more aggressive attack the next time. If the result of the aggressive behaviour has been one of failure to win and failure to receive approval, there will be no reinforcement of the aggression and the team members will perhaps not fight as hard the next time, unless they become angry.

But it is not as simple as this. As pointed out by Beisser (1967), many athletes are not able to be aggressive and make themselves win unless they can look on the opponent as an enemy, and can be angry at him. Probably others respond to the suggestions of the coach and fans, and work up at least mildly angry feelings. Some will be angry because of a tongue-lashing by the coach or for some other reason, and can readily displace their anger on to the opponent. Still others will become angry when fouled against, hit by an opponent or out-played in the game. In the average athletic contest there are many frustrations, and the most usual reactions to frustration are anger and aggression. Thus, for many players there will be opportunities for discharge of angry aggression even with the restrictions imposed by the rules, although this would probably be more possible in some sports than in others.

Despite the reservations of some psychiatrists about the applicability of the catharsis theory in the field of sports, and the apparent complexity of the situation, other psychoanalytically oriented psychiatrists contend that competitive sports do provide a social outlet for the aggressive drive.

Several studies have attempted to test the catharsis hypothesis in a sports situation. Stone (1950) studied fantasy aggression as revealed by the Thematic Apperception Test, before and after football scrimmage as well as before and after the competitive season. Scrimmage had no effect on fantasy aggression but there was a reduction in fantasy aggression at the end of the season. Johnson and Hutton (1955) studied aggression in wrestlers, using the House-Tree-Person test for measuring aggression. They reported increased aggressive feelings immediately before an intercollegiate match and less aggression after the match, with the aggression before the match being of an intrapunitive sort. In a study by Husman (1955), the Rosenzweig Picture-Frustration Study, several TAT cards, and a sentence completion test were administered at intervals in the competitive season to four groups: 9 boxers, 8 wrestlers, 9 cross-country runners and 7 control subjects. The TAT showed the boxers to have significantly less fantasy aggression than the other groups, and the P.-F. Study showed that the boxers' aggression tended to be more intrapunitive than was true for the other groups, with the cross-country runners being more extrapunitive. This difference was especially pronounced in tests given less than two days after a boxing match.

Any research performed in 'real-life' situations is likely to be difficult to interpret, because of the impossibility of avoiding contamination. In these studies there is the likelihood that both instrumental and reactive aggression entered into the picture, and that some of the reduction in aggression was related to guilt and anxiety rather than representing a 'draining-off' of pent-up energy. There seems to be little support, then, for the idea that sports provide a catharsis, and so reduce the instigation to aggression. We tend to agree with Berkowitz, who says (1962), 'Most nondisturbed persons do *not* seem to have either (a) weaker aggressive inclinations or (b) less concern about their hostile tendencies after engaging in socially sanctioned aggressive sports. If hostile behaviors are less apparent following such competitive activities, . . . these actions may have been inhibited by game-induced guilt or anxiety' (*Aggression: A Social-Psychological Analysis*, p. 207).

In play therapy with children who have problems centering on aggression, it has been a common practice for the therapist to be quite permissive about the expression of aggression, and even to encourage it. Since this amounts to instrumental aggression, we would not expect such expression, in and of itself, to result in a prolonged reduction of hostile tendencies. What it does do is bring the child's feelings into the open where the therapist can help him with the problems of accepting and understanding them. But without the intervention of the therapist, the permissiveness results in increasing aggressiveness on the part of the child. This is consistent with the finding of Sears and his co-workers (1953) who reported that aggressive behavior toward the mother was high when aggression was punished and when it was permitted, but low when the mother was firm in not permitting such behavior and used the threat of withdrawal of love in coping with it.

In summary, then, we do not have any very convincing evidence that either sports or non-athletic play support the catharsis hypothesis as being generally applicable.

By definition, the ability to express feelings outwardly is a manifestation of emotional health, but psychotherapists indicate that expression of *negative* feelings is therapeutic only in a context where it does not increase feelings of guilt, and when it can lead to self-acceptance, self-understanding and freer communication. The value of expression of *positive* feelings through games and sports is self-evident, but clinical evidence suggests that expression of aggression through sports may be either helpful or harmful from the standpoint of emotional health, depending on the nature of the individual's problems with aggression. The creative dance is an activity through which the individual may express his feelings, acquire some self-understanding and communicate with others. However, for the dance to be of value as a means of expression it must be used in ways that permit spontaneity.

Proposition 6 *Competitive sports, if properly used, may enhance emotional health and the acquisition of desirable personality traits.*

Social scientists and educators have been concerned about the highly competitive nature of our twentieth-century society. Because competition involves self-devaluation for those who are defeated, but enhances feelings of self-worth for those who are successful, it appears to have potentialities for either improving emotional health or being detrimental to it.

A number of studies have been concerned specifically with sports competition and its relation to emotional health. These studies are of three types, as follows: (1) studies of the attitudes and opinions of various persons with reference to the effects of sports competition on participants of different ages; (2) comparisons of personality traits and adjustment patterns for participants and non-participants in competitive sports; (3) evaluations of emotional status of individuals before and after their participation in important sports contests. These studies show that most persons have positive attitudes toward important sports contests, at all age levels and for both sexes (McGee,

1954; Scott, 1953; Skubic, 1956; Stalnaker, 1933); that competitive sports tend to favor the maintenance of emotional health, although not to an overwhelming degree (Bell, 1955; Seymour, 1956; Skubic, 1955, 1956); that intensive 'high pressure' competition produces only transitory emotional changes in high school and college males, although its effect on females is not entirely clear.

Despite the fact that most studies point to the value of competitive sports, it is probably unwise to generalize about this because of the many variables that determine the effects of competition—variables such as age, sex, whether or not the individual or group has a reasonable chance of winning, the degree to which the importance of winning is stressed, whether or not losing a game results in blame and rejection, the extent to which competition is divorced from community pressure or hysteria, and individual differences in drive to win as well as in stress tolerance. It should be noted that most, if not all, of the emotional health benefits of competitive sports may be realized in a good intramural program.

Discussion and conclusions

What, then, can we conclude about the contribution of play and sports to emotional health? I think it is clear that play and sports do have potentialities for contributing positively to the attainment of emotional health. On the other hand, there are indications that, under some circumstances, with some groups, and for certain individuals, sports activities seem unrelated to the development of emotional health or may be detrimental to it. Sports are conducive to emotional health if they promote physical fitness, but not all sports promote physical fitness. They encourage healthy emotional development if the participant has enough skill to merit the approval and admiration of his peers, and enough so that he can have a feeling of success, but not all participants will have such skills. They encourage healthy emotional development if the participant can use them for spontaneous expression of positive feelings and discharge of aggressive tensions, but not all participants have emotional experiences of this type.

There are still many gaps in our knowledge, and much of the research relating to the contributions of sports to emotional health has defects in the research design. We know very little about the relation between early play history and the adjustments of individuals in later childhood or adolescence. We know only a little about the contribution of play and sports to the development of emotional health in adolescent girls. And we know little about the relationship between sports participation in school and emotional health in adulthood, or about the relation between emotional health and continued participation in sports in adulthood.

In order to fill in the gaps and to clarify the role of play and sports in developing emotional health, we need to do more studies using girls and women as subjects, more experiments with individually prescribed sports programs to meet the emotional needs of specific children and adults, more cross-cultural research and more inter-disciplinary research. In connection with the latter, there is a great need for longitudinal developmental studies which will include detailed information about play interests and activities at each stage of development, so that these may be related to other personality variables.

Many of the studies on sports in relation to emotional health are defective in the sense that there is contamination in the design. That is, not all of the relevant independent variables are controlled, so it is not possible to tell whether variations in emotional health are due to sports participation, sports skill or some other variable. Also, some of the 'before and after' studies reflect bias in that clinicians involved in the exercise program have frequently done some of the evaluation of results. The use of control groups and 'blind' evaluations would improve these studies. Of course, in any experiments done in 'real-life' settings, rigid controls are always difficult and sometimes impossible. Nevertheless, with more conscientious efforts at designing experiments that pay careful attention to controls, with avoidance of contamination and bias, we should be able to plan research that would provide us with definitive answers to some of the as yet unanswered questions.

Bibliography

Alexander, F. (1958), 'A Contribution to the Theory of Play', *Psychoanal. Q.*, 27: 185–93.
American Association for Health, Physical Education and Recreation (1952), *Desirable Athletic Competition for Children*, AAHPER, Washington.
Barbour, E. H. (1935), 'Adjustment during Four Years of Patients Handicapped by Poliomyelitis', *New England J. Med.*, 213: 563–5.
Beisser, A. (1967), *The Madness of Sport*, Appleton-Century-Crofts, New York.

181

Emma McCloy Layman

Bell, Mary M. (1955), 'Measurement of Selected Outcomes of Participation in Girls' High School Interscholastic Basketball', *Dissertation
Abstracts*, 15: 1544.

Berkowitz, L. (1962), *Aggression: A Social-Psychological Analysis*,
McGraw-Hill, New York.

Biddulph, L. G. (1954), 'Athletic Achievement and the Personal and
Social Adjustment of High School Boys', *Res. Q.*, 25: 1–7.

Blanchard, B. E. (1946), 'A Comparative Analysis of Secondary School
Boys' and Girls' Character and Personality Traits in Physical
Education Classes', *Res. Q.*, 17: 33–9.

Bower, W. C. (1952), *Moral and Spiritual Values in Education*,
University of Kentucky Press, Lexington.

Breck, Sabina J. (1950), 'A Sociometric Measurement of Status in
Physical Education Classes', *Res. Q.*, 21: 75–82.

Breen, J. L. (1959), *Anxiety Factors Related to Physical Fitness
Variables*, doctoral dissertation, University of Illinois, Urbana.

Brockway, A. (1939), 'The Problem of the Spastic Child', *J. Amer. Med.
Assoc.*, 106: 1635–9.

Brown, P. A. (1938), 'Responses of Blind and Seeing Adolescents to an
Introversion-Extroversion Questionnaire', *J. Psych.*, 6: 137–47.

Burt, C. L. (1933), *The Young Delinquent*, Appleton-Century-Crofts,
New York.

Christie, A. (1934), 'Physical Defects in Delinquent Boys', *J. Juvenile
Res.*, 18: 13–22.

Clarke, H. H., and Greene, W. H. (1964), 'Relationships between
Personal-Social Measures Applied to 10-Year-Old Boys', *Res. Q.*,
34: 288–98.

Cole, E. W. (1936), 'Organized Recreation as a Preventive Agency',
Indiana Bull. of Character Correction, No. 222: 166–70.

Cornell, W. S. (1908), 'The Relation of Physical to Mental Defect in
School Children', *Psychological Clinic*, 1: 231–4.

Cowell, C. C. (1949), 'Mental Hygiene Functions and Possibilities of
Play and Physical Education', *Elementary School J.*, 50: 196–203.
and Ismail, A. H. (1962), 'Relationships between Selected Social and
Physical Factors', *Res. Q.*, 33: 40–3.

Cureton, T. K. (1963), 'Improvement of Psychological States by Means
of Exercise-Fitness Programs', *J. Assoc. for Phys. & Mental Rehab.*,
17: 14–17, 25.

Doscher, N. (1947), 'Adjustment of the Physically Handicapped College
Student', *Mental Hygiene*, 31: 576–81.

Erikson, E. H. (1940), 'Studies in the Interpretation of Play', *Genetic
Psych. Monogrs.*, 12: 563–4.

Fine, B. (1955), *1,000,000 Delinquents*, World Publishing, Cleveland and
New York.

Flemming, E. G. (1934), 'Personality and the Athletic Girl', *School &
Society*, 39: 166–9.

Fraleigh, W. P. (1956), 'The Influence of Play upon Social and
Emotional Adjustment with Implications for Physical Education',
Dissertation Abstracts, 16: 495.

Glueck, S., and Glueck, Eleanor T. (1934), *One Thousand Juvenile Delinquents*, Harvard University Press, Cambridge, Massachusetts. (1952), *Delinquents in the Making: Paths to Prevention*, Harper, New York.

Greenacre, Phyllis (1959), 'Play in Relation to Creative Imagination', *Psychoanal. Stud. Child*, 14: 61–80.

Hardy, Martha C. (1937), 'Some Evidence of an Inverse Relation between Health History and Behavior Adjustment during Childhood', *J. Abnorm. & Soc. Psych.*, 31: 406–17.

Harris, D. B. (1943), 'Relationships among Play Interests and Delinquency in Boys', *Amer. J. Orthopsychiatry*, 13: 631–8.

Harris, D. V. (1963), 'Comparison of Physical Performance and Psychological Traits of College Women with High and Low Fitness Indices', *Perceptual & Motor Skills*, 17: 293–4.

Hart, Marcia E., and Shuey, C. T. (1964), 'Relationship between Physical Fitness and Academic Success', *Res. Q.*, 35: 443–5.

Hazelton, H. W., and Piper, J. A. (1940), 'A Study of the Social Values of a Team Game and of Two Individual Sports as Judged by the Attitudes of Freshman College Women', *Res. Q.*, 11: 54–9.

Healy, W., and Bronner, Augusta F. (1926), *Delinquents and Criminals, their Making and Unmaking: Studies in Two American Cities*, Judge Baker Foundation Publication No. 3, Macmillan, New York.

Heider, G. M. (1948), 'Adjustment Problems of the Deaf Child', *Nervous Child*, 7: 38–44.

Hinrichs, M. A. (1941), 'Some Correlations between Health, Intelligence Quotient, Extracurricular Activities, and Scholastic Record', *Res. Q.*, 12: 228–41.

Horwitz, A. B. (1939), *Recorded Juvenile Delinquency in Duluth, Minnesota, 1928–1936*, Duluth City Planning Department.

Huizinga, J. (1955), *Homo Ludens: a Study of the Play Element in Culture*, Beacon, Boston (German edition published in Switzerland, 1944).

Husman, B. (1955), 'An Analysis of Aggression of Boxers and Wrestlers as Measured by Projective Techniques', *Res. Q.* 26: 421–5.

Johnson, W. R. (1949), 'A Study of Emotion Revealed in Two Types of Athletic Sports Contests', *Res. Q.*, 20: 72–9.
(1951), 'Psychogalvanic and Word Association Studies of Athletes', *Res. Q.*, 22: 427–33.
(1962), 'Some Psychological Aspects of Physical Rehabilitation: toward an Organismic Theory', *J. Assoc. for Phys. & Mental Rehab.*, 16: 165–8.
(1965–6), 'Children's Physical Developmental Clinic', *Challenge*, December 1965, March and May 1966.
and Hutton, D. C. (1955), 'Effects of a Combative Sport upon Personality Dynamics as Measured by a Projective Test', *Res. Q.*, 26: 49–53.

Hutton, D. C., and Johnson, G. B., Jr (1954), 'Personality Traits of Some Champion Athletes as Measured by Two Projective Tests: Rorschach and House-Tree-Person', *Res. Q.*, 25: 484–5.

183

Jones, H. E. (1946), 'Physical Ability as a Factor in Social Adjustment in Adolescence', *J. Educ. Res.*, 40: 287–301.

Kammerer, R. C. (1940), 'An Exploratory Psychological Study of Crippled Children', *Psych. Rec.*, 4: 47–100.

Kramer, R., and Bauer, R. (1955), 'Behavioral Effects of Hydrogymnastics', *J. Assoc. for Phys. & Mental Rehab.*, 9: 10–12.

Kvaraceus, W. C. (1945), *Juvenile Delinquency and the School*, World Books, Yonkers.

Layman, Emma McCloy (1968), 'Attitudes toward Sports for Girls and Women in Relation to Masculinity-Femininity Stereotypes of Women Athletes', paper read at the 135th meeting of the American Association for the Advancement of Science, 27 December (mimeographed).

McFarland, J. F., and Huddleston, J. N. (1936), 'Neurocirculatory Reactions in the Psychoneuroses Studied by the Schneider Method', *Amer. J. Psychiatry*, 93: 567–72.

McGee, Rosemary (1954), 'Comparison of Attitudes toward Intensive Competition for High School Girls', *Dissertation Abstracts*, 14: 1612.

McGraw, L. W., and Tolbert, J. W. (1953), 'Sociometric Status and Athletic Ability of Junior High School Boys', *Res. Q.*, 24: 72–80.

McKinney, F. (1937), 'Concomitants of Adjustment and Maladjustment among College Students', *J. Abnorm. & Soc. Psych.*, 31: 435–7.

(1939), 'Personality Adjustment of College Students as Related to Factors in Personal History', *J. Appl. Psych.*, 23: 660–8.

Meyer, M. W. (1955), 'The Influence of Recreation Participation upon the Behavior of Schizophrenic Patients', unpublished doctoral dissertation, New York University.

Mitchell, D., and Mason, B. S. (1935), *The Theory of Play*, Barnes, New York.

Murray, V. (1931), 'A Comparative Study of Play Information and Athletic Achievement in Delinquents and Non-delinquents', *J. Juvenile Res.* 15: 111–20.

Oakland Community Chest Survey (1946), *Studies in Population and Juvenile Delinquency—1944–1945*, Community Chest, Oakland.

Oberteuffer, D. (1955), 'Interscholastic Athletics for the Elementary Years?', *Proceedings, 23rd Annual Convention, Southern District, AAHPER*, 20–2.

Peller, L. (1954), 'Libidinal Phases, Ego Development and Play', *Psychoanal. Stud. Child*, 91: 178–98.

Pintner, R., Eisenson, J., and Stanton, M. (1941), *The Psychology of the Physically Handicapped*, Crofts, New York.

Powers, E., and Witmer, Helen (1951), *Prevention of Delinquency*, Columbia University Press, New York.

Rarick, G. L., and McKee, R. (1949), 'A Study of 20 Third-Grade Children Exhibiting Extreme Levels of Achievement on Tests of Motor Proficiency', *Res. Q.*, 20: 142–51.

Redl, F. (1959), 'The Impact of Game Ingredients on Children's Play Behavior', in Schaffner (ed.), *Group Processes*, Transactions of Fourth Conference, Josiah Macy Foundation, pp. 38–81.

The contribution of play and sports to emotional health

Reinhardt, J. M., and Harper, F. M. (1931), 'Comparison of Environmental Factors of Delinquent and Non-delinquent Boys', *J. Juvenile Res.*, 15: 271–7.

Rogers, G. G., and Thomas, L. C. (1938), 'Emotional Adjustment of the Spastic Child', *Crippled Child*, 16: 6–24, 91–3.

Rosenberg, D., and Rice, D. C. (1964), 'Physical Fitness and Psychiatric Diagnosis', *J. Assoc. for Phys. & Mental Rehab.*, 18: 73–84.

Schulz, Louise E. (1961), 'Relationships between Body Image and Physical Performance in Adolescent Girls', M.A. thesis, College Park, University of Maryland.

Scott, Phebe M. (1953), 'Attitudes toward Athletic Competition in Elementary Schools', *Res. Q.*, 24: 352–61.

Sears, R. R., Whiting, J. W. M., Nowlis, V., and Sears, Pauline S. (1953), 'Some Child-Rearing Antecedents of Aggression and Dependency in Young Children', *Genetic Psych. Monogr.*, 47: 135–234.

Seymour, E. W. (1956), 'Comparative Study of Certain Behavior Characteristics of Participant and Non-participant Boys in Little League Baseball', *Res. Q.*, 27: 338–46.

Shanas, Ethel, and Dunning, Catherine E. (1942), *Recreation and Delinquency*, Chicago Recreation Commission, Chicago.

Skubic, Elvera (1955), 'Emotional Responses of Boys to Little League and Middle League Baseball', *Res. Q.*, 26: 342–52.
    (1956), 'Studies of Little League and Middle League Baseball', *Res. Q.*, 27: 97–110.

Slavson, S. R. (1946), *Recreation and the Total Personality*, Association Press, New York.
    (1947), *The Practice of Group Therapy*, International Universities Press, New York.

Smith, Judith R., and Hurst, J. G. (1961), 'The Relationship of Motor Abilities and Peer Acceptance of Mentally Retarded Children', *Amer. J. of Mental Deficiency*, 66: 81–5.

Stalnaker, J. (1933), 'Attitudes toward Intercollegiate Athletics', *School & Society*, 37: 409–504.

Stedman, M. B. (1934), 'The Influence of Health upon Intelligence and School Grades of High School Pupils', *J. Appl. Psych.*, 18: 799–809.

Stone, A. (1950), 'The Cathartic Theory of Aggression', *Laboratory Bull.*, Laboratory of Social Relations, 2: 9–13.

Thurstone, H. W. (1918), *Delinquency and Spare Time*, Cleveland Recreation Survey, Vol. I. Cleveland Foundation, Cleveland.

Timmerman, J. (1954), 'Effectiveness of Hydrogymnastic Therapy in Treating the Acutely Disturbed Psychotic', *J. Assoc. for Phys. & Mental Rehab.*, 8: 192–4.

Van Fleet, Phyllis P. (1950), *Some Effects of Physical Education Therapy on the Personality Characteristics of Schizophrenic Patients*, doctoral thesis, University of California, Berkeley.

Waelder, R. (1933), 'The Psychoanalytic Theory of Play', *Psychoanal. Q.*, 2: 208–24.

Weber, J. R. (1953), 'Relationship of Physical Fitness to Success in College and to Personality, *Res. Q.*, 24: 471–4.

Emma McCloy Layman

Wells, H. P. (1958), 'Relationship between Physical Fitness and Psychological Variables', doctoral dissertation, University of Illinois, Urbana.

Witmer, Helen L., and Tufts, E. (1954), *The Effectiveness of Delinquency Prevention Programs*, U.S. Government Printing Office, Washington, D.C.

7

Physical activity and the psychological development of the handicapped

James N Oliver

The main theme of this chapter is the understanding and interpretation of the effects of physical activity on the general growth and development of handicapped children. It is concerned with the effects of physical activity on mental as well as physical health. In this context it is essential to define health as something more than freedom from disease and to regard it as a condition of efficiency both physically, mentally, emotionally and socially so that life can be lived to the full.

Total growth must be regarded as a composite of growing and growing up. The former can be measured accurately in pounds and inches and is concerned with the physical characteristics of the body. The latter consists of developing and functioning often in conjunction with other people and as such is concerned with all aspects of growth—with the physical, the mental, the emotional and social growth of the individual. These aspects of growth are intimately related to each other, each is affected by the others and in turn affects the others.

Too often in the past the physical and mental have been treated as though they were mutually exclusive and this has resulted in some of the benefits which accrue from physical activity being lost. Because of the intimate relationship of the functioning of all aspects of growth an individual cannot be divided into two parts, therefore, we do not believe that one type of experience trains the body and that another type of experience educates the mind. We believe rather that the whole child reacts to the total situation, in other words, we believe that each individual reacts to each experience in his own unique way and this may leave him slightly changed. This change we call education.

In passing it is as well to remind ourselves that not all changes made in this respect are necessarily for the good of the individual. Indeed, many may be harmful and do considerable damage to the individual's personality or his outlook, or even his mode of living. In the choice of experiences for the handicapped it would be wise to seek for those which are good and to avoid those which might do harm.

Education then, as described here, means change. It is not an end-product but a process. It is something that is going on all the time. Since it is concerned with the modification of the individual resulting from his experiences, it follows that physical activity has a part to play in the process. It may be that as far as handicapped children are concerned it has a greater part to play than any other source of experience.

Physical growth

Physical activity is essential to aid physical growth. Unfortunately there are many people who, whilst recognizing the needs of children for physical activity, imagine that these needs can be adequately catered for by the free activity of children during school breaks or after school hours. This is not necessarily so. By leaving things to chance there are likely to be gaps and deficiencies in a child's experiences. If a child is to achieve his maximum growth potential all his physical activity needs have to be met and this cannot be done by leaving a child to his own devices. Before a child can take part in many of the experiences and situations that are so important for his growth he needs to have the necessary tools; he needs the physical where-withal to take part. He needs such qualities as strength, mobility, endurance and skill ability. He needs general physical fitness or physical vitality.

There is abundant evidence in the literature which suggests that handicapped children are lacking in these physical qualities. On the whole handicapped children tend to be smaller than their more normal counterparts, many of them are weak and susceptible to fatigue. They lack physical strength and fitness is below par. There is a fairly high incidence of obesity, especially after puberty. In particular, many of the severely mentally handicapped, the visually handicapped and the physically handicapped present a picture of muscular debility and lowered vitality. These deficiencies may be due partly to the handicap, but there are many other limitations which prevent the handicapped child from reaching his physical potential and achieving the full psychological benefits of physical activity.

Blind children are delayed in reaching their physical potential from the very earliest days. When normal children are crawling around and exploring their surroundings the visually handicapped children often remain relatively immobile. They are not motivated to crawl and examine objects in their environment, merely because they do not see them and curiosity is not aroused. Nor are visually handicapped children likely to take part in free crawling to the same extent as sighted children. Hurtful experiences against obstacles in their path tend to inhibit exploration of the surroundings. They seem to have more difficulty in learning physical skills at all stages of growth. Normal children are able to profit from the imitation of the skills of others at each stage, but not so the blind. Since these children see nothing they have nothing to imitate and most motor activities are learned more easily when assisted by sight. As visually handicapped children grow up they are unable to take part in the vigorous activities of normal children, they are unable to keep up with their more normal counterparts in the rough and tumble of free play and are, therefore, precluded from the many spontaneous activities which are so necessary for general development. As well as being deprived of appropriate new experiences they never catch up on the physical qualities. Buell (1950) showed that blind children fall below the level of normal children in the performance of stunt-type activities and in track and field athletics. Corlett (1967) found them to be deficient in speed, agility, co-ordination and body control, and Siegel (1966) notes their lack of both dynamic and static posture.

There is a tendency for the mentally handicapped to play less than normal children. Walker (1950) points out that many of the severely handicapped never learn to play and this at one time was regarded as normal behaviour. However, if the optimum conditions for play can be established, the mentally handicapped play in a manner similar to normal children of the same mental age. Salvin (1958) after using many play activities in a camping programme with severely mentally handicapped children came to the conclusion that such children need to be taught to play. Hollis (1965) studied the play activities of retarded children when given the opportunity to play. One salient feature that emerged from his investigation was that for the profoundly retarded there was almost absolute lack of activity that could be defined as play. The author points out that physical interaction between the children was stopped by those who were looking after them, and the environment was bare of suitable objects for manipulation and exploration; it was probable, therefore, that the arousal level for play was never reached by the children. Capobianco and Cole (1960) in an investigation into the social behaviour of mentally retarded children found that the educable retarded showed a lower degree of participation in free play than did normal children, but a higher degree of participation than trainable mental retardates. Contrary to the finding of Walker, these investigators did not find that it was mental age that influenced the pattern of social participation so much as the I.Q. It is plausible to suggest here that the more often retarded children take part in play the greater will be their physical experience and their general physical ability and this in itself would be likely to influence the pattern of the play which would eventually approximate to the play of normal children of similar intelligence. This might be regarded as an example of the effects of physical activity on the intellectual development of handicapped children.

There is some evidence (G. O. Johnson, 1950) that as mentally handicapped children grow up they tend to be rejected in free play by normal children, not because of limited intelligence or even limited physical ability, but rather because of behaviour including such things as bullying, fighting, not playing to the rules and so on. Behaviour of this description may be compensation for lack of playing ability but it leads to rejection and a further loss of physical power and skill ability. Frances and Rarick (1960) found that on tests of physical achievement the standards of the retarded are lower than those of normal children, both by sex and by age. They found there to be a lag of anything up to three or four years with educable retarded children and an even greater retardation in such activities as running, hitting and throwing with trainable children.

The physically handicapped and delicate children often lack the physical power to take part in, or to continue in, the strenuous activities of normal children and this leads to further deficiencies in physical ability. Brown (1968) has pointed out that there is a tendency for the cerebral palsied child to deteriorate in physical efficiency unless he is engaged in some form of systematic physical activity. He emphasizes the need for improved physical condition in order that the child shall be able to take part in the physical experiences of normal children and thereby obtain the benefits that stem from physical activity.

Maladjusted children are constantly under-achieving and failing to reach their potential in aspects of physical growth for other reasons. They tend to be anxious and tense and there is evidence that it is more difficult to learn under such conditions, hence we find them lagging in skill ability. Lack of skill in the basic activities of throwing, running, jumping, climbing and so on does not encourage them to take part in these activities with normal children, especially at the age of adolescence. If they withdraw from the group they do not have to attempt the activities, with no attempt there can be no failure and with no failure there is no humiliation; unfortunately, there is no practice of the skills either and the children soon lag further and further in the skills. This eventually leads to rejection in normal play including group and co-operative play with the resultant loss of social experiences.

Handicapped children, for various reasons then, are deprived of physical activity. Some are unable to withstand the rigours of strenuous play activities of normal children, some find the activities too dangerous, some are rejected by the other participants and some tend to withdraw from play situations. Because of this, the physical characteristics of the children tend to deteriorate instead of improving. Now it is generally understood that because of their disability the handicapped cannot afford to miss any opportunity which will contribute to their total development. Physical activity with its many worthwhile 'by-products' has much to contribute to this total development, yet the low levels of fitness that are found amongst the handicapped prevent many of them achieving the desirable goals of an educational nature that stem from physical situations. There appears to be an urgent need for systematic physical activity, either in the form of carefully structured programmes of physical education or in the form of spontaneous play and recreation, for all handicapped children.

Intellectual growth

The relationships between physical activity, intellectual growth, emotional growth and social development are so close that in practice it is impossible to separate them; however, for ease of discussion and presentation of the data, broad artificial divisions will be attempted.

Perception, learning and thinking are aspects of the intellectual growth of the individual. Forgus (1966) describes perception as the process by which an organism receives, or extracts, certain information about the environment, learning he regards as the process by

191

which the information is acquired through experience and becomes part of the organism's storage of facts. The need for a rich perceptual stimulation is emphasized by Hebb (1949). He suggests that learning probably occurs as cell-assemblies, or networks of cells which function as one unit, are formed in the nervous system. The cell-assemblies combine and interact within systems of such assemblies to give more complex patterns of learning.

Physical activity it would seem plays a very important part in providing many of the stimuli which are so necessary for these patterns of learning described by Hebb. This is stressed by others. Sherrington (1951), for example, talks of motor activity starting the mind on its road to recognizability; he claims that as motor integration proceeds the mind proceeds with it. Gesell (1940) regards mental growth as a process of behaviour patterning, he says that even before the child is born it is beginning to make 'characteristic movements' and these are but patterns of behaviour. Buhler (1960) found that the apparently purposeless movements of the young child are eventually replaced by investigating activity with materials, and this in turn gives way to creative activity with materials. Wright (1967) reports that an enriched environment for very young children is likely to produce accelerated development in some of this investigating activity. Piaget (1950) has described the stages through which children pass as their thinking develops. The first of these is the sensory-motor stage which lasts from birth up to about 20 months. This is the period when the child is gathering impressions from the world around him, learning to pattern it and to act in a variety of ways in relation to his experiences. The next stages are those of pre-concepts and intuitive thought. Here the child is making his first attempts at conceptual thinking but his thinking is not rational and he is led astray by irrelevant factors in what he perceives. The next stage is that of concrete operations when the child begins to reason in relation to things, and finally there is the stage of formal operations when the child can think and reason in the abstract. For Piaget this cumulative development of the intellect is derived from the child's activity acting in internalized thought (or mental operation). He constructs schemes of thought which enable him to organize his experiences of his environment.

For the normal baby in the cradle everything around him is a new experience. He waves his arms, clenches his first, lifts his leg, catches his toes and allows them to drop and the more often he does these things the better he does them. By these acts he begins to amass knowledge of objects and things around him. As he grows older he is able to explore the space around him in his early crawling activities. Not only is he now exploring and developing his physical powers by this means but he is gaining experience of objects and things in his environment. He picks things up, feels them, throws them away and so on and in the various manipulations with the objects he learns about the properties and qualities of things. He profits from his past experiences and he attempts to initiate new ones; as skills are learned he repeats them with other objects and in different ways. He watches others around him and attempts to repeat some of the things he sees them performing. Through physical activity the child extends his knowledge, develops his intellect and reinforces his physical powers.

Each stage in the child's development leads quite naturally to the next and crawling gives way to walking. This gives greater mobility and range and leads to increased experiences. As the time passes his exploration of things is considerably assisted by verbal means. He begins to ask questions about objects, he wants to know how they are made, what makes them go or where they come from, thus language is developed. As stage follows stage more and more difficult tasks are attempted and more complex situations are encountered. Greater mobility and improved physical ability leads eventually to play with others and it is here that the child learns to adjust to other children and to social situations. Play is important because it is the natural medium for the provision of many of the experiences that children need; it is the natural medium of expression and creativity, but it is more than that, it is also an acceptable and satisfying means of improving the physical qualities of strength, endurance, skill ability and the like which enable the children to take part in the more complicated and difficult physical situations.

Various authors indicate that the basic needs of the handicapped are the same as those of normal children. We have seen that one of these is for new experiences in order to help both intellectual and physical development. Since new experiences are acquired through the senses it is plain that if one sense is lacking it becomes all the more important for the remaining ones to be used effectively. Physical activity has its own unique contribution to make towards the provision of new experiences, it can, therefore, be of valuable assistance to the handicapped.

Little rigorous research seems to have been conducted which attempts to evaluate the contribution of physical activity to the intellectual development of handicapped children. Most authors who have studied children do agree that physical activity is of the utmost importance in the general development of such children. Speaking of the mentally handicapped Pietrowics (1956) says that since mental retardation encompasses the total personality special training should focus on manual skills, that is, on a hand-eye method rather than an auditory approach, and on areas of motor expression. Benoit (1955) emphasizes the need for play for mentally handicapped children because it is in play that they obtain the beneficial stimulation that is required for development. He suggests that the more sluggish nervous systems of the retarded are stimulated through the senses, therefore more growth is likely to be recorded, moreover, the earlier in life that such stimulation occurs the greater will be its effect. Applying Hebb's theory of the organization of behaviour to the education of retarded children Benoit (1957) suggests that the training of such children should concentrate on tasks in which large objects and gross muscle systems are involved. Their initial training should be 'thing-oriented'; if in the early stages 'thing-percepts' can be well established then it may be easier to link them with words at a later stage.

Leland et al. (1959) spread 90 hours of free play over one month to retarded boys aged from 4 to 8 years. The teachers joined in the games and activities with the children. There was no claim to have improved the I.Q. of the children but some interesting trends were observed. It seemed that the activity had been able to tap some intellectual potential which could not be tapped before the experiment began. Similar findings were reported by Groves (1967) who gave a series of 'movement' lessons to 14- to 15-year-old educationally subnormal girls. She found that the girls were able to express their ideas and feelings, not only in movement, but in written work which had previously been limited to recording facts. This would confirm the findings of Oliver (1957) who used log exercises as part of a physical conditioning programme for educationally subnormal boys aged 13 to 15 years. The log activities were good fun for the boys, they gave scope for self-expression and creative ability, they also gave a feeling of achievement and success. When asked to write about their log activities at the end of the experimental period the boys tackled the writing with confidence and enthusiasm and showed powers of expression far ahead of anything they had ever done before. Oliver attributed this to improved confidence and morale due to the feeling of achievement and success obtained with the physical activities. Weiner (1954) replaced formal instruction for a group of mentally handicapped boys by a prolonged pre-academic programme in which the emphasis was on socialization, language and concept development, play and recreative skills. Two years later when the boys were compared with a comparable group who had remained in the normal programme the difference in reading and arithmetic was significant. It is interesting to note that after four years the difference between the two groups in these subjects was found to be negligible.

The value of early training of physical manipulation skills for blind children is indicated by Gomulicki (1961). In an experimental investigation into the efficiency with which blind children exercise non-visual skills he found that blind children at the age of 5 were at a decided disadvantage as compared with sighted children in manipulation skills such as tying shoelaces, fastening buttons and so on. Progress of the sighted children from 5 years onwards is in general slower than that of blind children who more or less manage to draw level over a period of four to ten years. The author concludes that deliberate training in the perceptual skills available to blind children would be of decided advantage to them. In discussing play therapy with blind children Rothschild (1966) notes that it is assumed that play is an area where the normal child is expected to react spontaneously, naturally and in an unguarded manner; that in play the child will develop interests quickly. These assumptions, however, are not so evident with blind children who are unable to see danger. Indeed, play may be an anxiety-laden experience for many of them. Ireland (1958), on the other hand, considers that a carefully arranged recreative programme which takes into account the interests and aptitudes of the individual can do much to help the blind. It offers opportunities for fulfilment of creative urges and gives release from emotional and physical tensions that are likely to build up due to restriction on mobility of most blind people. The important point that Ireland makes here is that the activities should suit the interests and aptitudes of the children. This is emphasized by Salvin (1958) in his description of programmes for severely mentally handicapped children. He says that the activities and equipment should meet the needs of the children. Strang (1962) points out that in the learning of physical skills, as in any other type of learning, both mental and physical maturation are important. The stages of growth are sequential and there seems to be a 'right time' for the introduction of new skills to each individual if those skills are to be learned efficiently. If the skills are introduced too early the children are not ready for them and they are only learned with difficulty. According to Fait and Kupferer

(1956) this may give rise to strong emotional tension and reduced learning in the case of mentally handicapped children. On the other hand, if the skill has been missed at the 'best time' for learning that skill may be more difficult to learn at a later stage. What is more, as was shown by Oliver and Keogh (1967) in their work with clumsy children, when a skill has been missed at an early stage it is then not available to assist in the learning of more complex skills at a later stage.

Pearson (1965) points out that a lack of spatial orientation is one of the factors contributing to the difficulties of the blind and he suggests that movement training can help to counter this. Perception and learning we have seen is based on an individual's past experiences; since the blind lack vision they find themselves more dependent on auditory and kinesthetic cues and this would emphasize the importance of movement training. Pearson goes on to suggest that improvement in gross motor ability has a positive effect on a blind child's ability to improve in other areas directly related to his education. The work of Cratty (1969) with blind children in Los Angeles tends to confirm the findings of Pearson. According to Kelmer Pringle (1965) physically handicapped children may fail to acquire adequate experience of space and movement because of their lack of experience in this area and this is likely to disturb their concepts of distance and dimensions. She queries whether this may not even affect concepts of number also. Jakeman (1968) describes a programme to help a spastic boy in the development of perceptual abilities. He lacked hand–eye co-ordination and had difficulty with cutting and drawing and similar activities so he was given gross motor activities in the physical education lessons. He had faulty perception of his own position in space so he was given exercises to develop body awareness and directionality. The author claims that through these exercises and activities the boy is learning to conquer space and there has been improvement in body awareness, body concept, directionality and co-ordination.

Kephart (1960) believes that we cannot separate perceptual activities from motor activities but we must think of the entire process as perceptual-motor. He considers that the concepts of laterality, directionality and spatial orientation are essential in the development of eye–hand co-ordination. Children who have been prevented from exploring and manipulating a variety of objects are lacking in basic perceptual-motor skills. Kephart has devised a developmental programme which includes many eye–hand co-ordination activities and which is intended to improve the perceptual-motor skills. Giles (1969) used a physical education programme on the lines of Kephart's suggestions with educationally subnormal boys who were experiencing reading difficulties. He found that the training programme contributed significantly to the development of laterality, directionality and body image, thereby confirming the beliefs of Kephart. His conclusion was that lateral confusion of a perceptual nature can be remedied by specific physical training. This was also the conclusion of Painter (1966) who gave a special physical programme to kindergarten children in which the emphasis was on such qualities as spatial awareness, body awareness, rhythmical activities and unilateral and bilateral movement. The children showed improved ability to draw a man, perceptual-motor spatial ability and body-image concept.

In 1958 Oliver conducted an experiment with educationally subnormal boys aged 13 to 15 years. He replaced everything but English and arithmetic in the school programme with strenuous physical activity. The aim in this conditioning programme was physical fitness, physical achievement and a feeling of success. At the end of ten weeks when the boys in the experimental group were compared with a control group which had followed the normal programme there was significant improvement in most aspects of growth. The most startling result was probably in the significant increase in I.Q. for the experimental group. This improvement, Oliver claims, was due, not so much to the physical activity per se, but to increased confidence that the boys had acquired through achievement and success in the physical activities that were included in the training programme. Oliver's findings were confirmed by Corder (1966) and Lowe (1966). Solomon and Pangle (1967), in a replication of the Oliver study were unable to confirm the improvement in the mental characteristics. Since the timing of the post testing in this investigation was inappropriate and the testing conditions on the part of the boys poor, the results of the mental test are open to question. Rarick and Broadhead (1968) sought to assess the role of physical education activity programmes on the motor, intellectual, emotional and social behaviour of some 481 mentally handicapped children in Texas. They found that well-designed programmes of physical education produced greater changes on the above characteristics than did the normal programme. When the physical education programme was oriented toward the individual rather than the group, greater changes were found in the intellectual and social behaviour of the children.

Considerably much more controlled experimental work has been carried out with the mentally handicapped than with other forms of handicap. Despite the paucity of such studies in relation to the effect of physical activity on the intellectual growth of handicapped children there seems to be general agreement that physical activity, in whatever form it is presented, whether it be a highly structured physical education lesson in school hours, as 'organized' free play or as the spontaneous play of children, has a great contribution to make. Many handicapped children are deprived of physical activity and their general growth is apt to suffer thereby; there is a wealth of subjective evidence which emphasizes the necessity of physical activity for them.

Emotional and social development

In the course of growing up a child learns, not only about people and objects in the world around him, but about himself. This self aware-ness is a growth process which begins in childhood and develops through his interaction with people and his total environment. It changes as he compares himself with his peers in competition, it changes as he develops confidence and courage and it changes according to his successes and failures. Success enhances a child's self-concept and he is therefore likely to seek areas where this can be found and to avoid areas where failure is likely. If a child anticipates that he will not do well and not gain acceptance he tends to give up easily, whereas, if he thinks he will do well he tends to persist. There is general acceptance that children and adults with poor self-concept are more anxious and tense, and less well-adjusted than those with good self-concept. They are generally less effective and popular in groups. Growing up then, as has already been mentioned, consists of developing and functioning, often in conjunction with other people. It is concerned with such qualities as co-operation, tolerance, patience, perseverance, self-control, the ability to give and take and many other things concerned with interpersonal relationships. It is concerned with self-adjustment and adjustment to others.

There is plenty of evidence that the handicapped are not as well-adjusted as normal children. According to Telford and Sawrey (1967) they show variously a higher degree of emotional instability and social maladjustment and a higher incidence of behavioural disorders. Mangus (1950) found a preponderance of adjustment problems amongst children who were seriously retarded in their school work; it appeared that failure led to maladjustment. The mentally handicapped who are constantly experiencing failure tend to develop emotional and adjustment problems. Cromwell (1961) found that these personality and behaviour patterns that develop in many of the retarded because of failure experiences tend to lower their social and intellectual efficiency below what would be expected on their impairment. G. O. Johnson (1950) was able to show that mentally handicapped children in the regular grades were less socially competent than normal children, they were less accepted and more rejected because of anti-social behaviour. Lapp (1957) suggests that they were not sought but were 'tolerated'; they appeared to have no particular personality trait which made them disliked, but were neglected because they had no special abilities to contribute to the group. Force (1954) using a sociometric technique compared handicapped children with normal children in integrated classes in schools and was able to show much the same results for the visually handicapped that Johnson had shown with the mentally retarded. The visually handicapped were definitely not as well accepted as normal children, they received significantly lower numbers of choices on all criteria used in the investigation. Davis (1964) points out that it is more difficult and a much slower process for a blind child to develop a mental image of his body and a satisfactory concept of himself. He needs others against whom he can compare himself, and it is through play and school experiences that ample opportunities may be found for this. If, as Force showed, these children are not being accepted in school they will be deprived of one of the effective methods of developing satisfactory concepts about themselves.

According to Garrison and Force (1965) partially sighted children are frequently socially and emotionally immature when compared with other children; they note that some visually handicapped children have personality problems but these they say are relatively small. Elser (1959) found that children who are hard of hearing tend to be less well accepted than their more normal class mates and according to Kirk (1938) such children show greater behaviour problems than normally hearing children. Barker et al. (1946) in their survey on adjustment to physical handicap conclude that there is some evidence that withdrawn, timid and self-conscious behaviour is more frequent in the physically handicapped than in normal people and they more frequently exhibit behaviour which is termed maladjusted. Richardson et al. (1964) found that when physically handicapped children were required to describe themselves they showed an awareness of their inability to live up to the expectations that stem from the high values placed on physical activities. They recognized their own deprivation of social experiences and the limitation in involvement in the social world. Donofrio (1951) came to the conclusion in his investigation of children suffering from a wide range of physical handicap that emotional adjustment fell within a normal range. There was a tendency for maladjustment to decrease with increasing chronological age and there was some indication that the less severely handicapped showed less maladjustment. With a group of junior and high school physically handicapped children Cruickshank (1956) concluded that there was a definite tendency for many of the children to withdraw from social contacts and social relations. The investigation by Force (1954) into the social relations in a school where handicapped and normal children were educated together in the same class indicated that the physically handicapped were chosen as playmates, friends and workmates a less number of times than normal children. Dewey (1956) using sociometric techniques showed that physical disability tended to magnify difficulties of a child achieving social acceptance from normal peers. He claimed that few physically handicapped children have enough positive assets to offset completely the negative effect of being labelled handicapped. The problem of acceptance is evident in those as young as 6 years.

Rawls (1957) points out that the basic social process is interaction, that is, the influence that individuals and groups have on one another. Interaction is a continuous process and it is basic to socialization. Since handicapped children are less accepted than normal children they are deprived of interaction and this results in diminished social and emotional competence. It is in this area that physical activity can make a great contribution to the social and emotional growth of such children because it can engineer for them many opportunities for interaction with others. Activities such as games, social dancing, the outdoor pursuits and play-like activities provide situations where the traits of co-operation, unselfishness, loyalty, fair play and the like are required. It is in play and the play-like activities that children first learn to adjust to other children and to social situations; in this respect physical education, with its bias toward play, becomes a powerful tool in the hands of those responsible for dealing with the emotional and social growth of the handicapped. It must be recognized, of course, that taking part in these situations will not automatically give social qualities, or even emotional adjustment. There is no automatic transfer from one situation to another; the aims have to be sought deligently by the teacher, the relationships have to be pointed out and correct attitudes fostered. As Kirkland (1962) so rightly points out in his discussion on integrated group work and recreation for the blind, play is not sufficient unless it has purpose, focus, initiative and new learning experiences. Part of the new learning experiences should be the learning of correct attitudes to the play and to the others taking part in it.

Many investigations have been carried out to discover the effect of physical education and play therapy on the handicapped, unfortunately the majority of these only give the subjective observations of the investigators but as with the relationship between physical activity and the growth of the intellect, there is general agreement amongst the investigators. Tither (1965) introduced rather free and loosely structured physical education, consisting mainly of activity on climbing apparatus and free activities on the floor, to a group of cerebral palsied children. Physically the children were challenged, many overcame fear and achieved success in the activities with resulting satisfaction and enjoyment. Ringness (1960) suggests that mentally handicapped children have less realistic self-concepts than normal children and tend to overestimate success in their activities. Overestimation of success leads to persistent failure, to frustration and eventually to withdrawal from the activity situation. Gardner (1966) found that retarded children were less strongly influenced by failure than normal children, they did not show the typical reaction of facilitation of performance following failure. Bailey and Cromwell (1965) on the other hand, report that moderate failure with a group of educable mentally retarded children can have a motivating effect. Physical activity lends itself to manipulation of failure or success situations for the participants and thereby presents great opportunities for helping the handicapped. Oliver (1958) in a highly structured programme of strengthening activities which were so organized that the mentally handicapped boys in the programme continually challenged themselves and were able to see progress, observed considerable improvement in such qualities as perseverance, co-operation, tolerance and adjustment to others. Tofte (1950) instituted a broad scheme of recreative activities, with considerable emphasis on physical activity, to defectives in a mental institution. There was no attempt at objective evaluation but the general impression of all who worked with the participants was that there was improved morale and a reduction in those serious behaviour problems that stem from inactivity. Oliver (1968) reports similar findings at a hospital for mentally handicapped patients in England. The patients were involved in a recreation programme in which the emphasis was on physical activities and dancing. Since the inception of this programme there has been improved social relationships between the patients, improved relations with the staff, less damage to clothes and to hospital property and a reduction in drug bills. Maisner (1950) studied a group of 8- to 13-year-old educable retarded children who had been referred because of disturbing behaviour; they were unable to relate to adults, there was conflict and anxiety and general social maladjustment. The children were placed in a room with toys with which they could play freely and then observed in this play therapy situation. There was no controlled evaluation but subjective assessment indicated that all the children showed some improvement in adjustment. Salvin (1958) describes a scouting programme for severely mentally handicapped children in which the usual scouting activities and games figured prominently. He found that the activities helped the children to respect the rights of others, to take defeat and victory in their stride and generally to enter into the daily life of the camp. In other words, he found improvement in both social and emotional competence.

Jackson (1957) suggests that it is through play that a blind child shows others what he thinks about himself. It is here that he can express emotions in a healthy form. The child who can experience achievement and success and social acceptance has a chance to correct the image that he holds about himself. The child who is denied play and recreation, however, often retreats into fantasy and fails to develop skills which make him socially acceptable to his friends. According to Clunk (1950) sighted children learn a great deal about fair play, team work and co-operation from their companions in the ordinary sports and play of children. In life it is essential to be a good loser as well as a good winner and principles such as these are most easily taught through competitive games. If these are taught and applied properly they can do much to eliminate jealousy, bitterness and ill will. Blind children are at some disadvantage in this respect yet Furst (1966) when trying to improve the physical characteristics of a group of multiply handicapped blind children was able to report that by means of competitive activities the interest of the children was stimulated, co-operation was improved and there was an increased desire to win. He noted that the members of the group began to interact and to express greater interest in each other.

Ireland (1958) emphasizes the importance of recreation for the blind and claims that it can do much to build morale and to give feeling of belonging and self-respect. This is the opinion of others. Glass (1959) for example incorporated a number of sightless children into a day camp for sighted children in which the main emphasis was on games and physical activities. There was noticeable improvement in the physical characteristics of the blind children; they showed greater integration with the other children and came to grips with new situations. Cohen (1966) in a case study on the development of a blind spastic child also reports that a good programme of physical activity with emphasis on play activities resulted in the child making good progress, intellectual potential was realized and social and emotional growth were much improved.

Play if often synonymous with games and it is worth noting that there is still a large body of opinion which claims that games and sports comprise the most effective medium for the socialization of the individual. Be that so, or not, there is evidence that those children who do not play are handicapped in their social development. Guttman (1969) commenting on the world-wide problem of sports for the disabled suggests that for youth, play and sport, and in particular competitive team games, represent a natural outlet for energy and in some individuals it helps character building by preventing misfired energy resulting in anti-social activities. For the physically handicapped sport has proved invaluable for physical and psychological adjustment to, and victory over, their disability as well as social integration into society.

Less obvious than the organized activities for improving a child's self-concept and helping socialization are the many little spontaneous physical acts in which children achieve success in their daily interactions. Even the improvement of physical characteristics such as strength has its part to play, for boys the mere possession of strength often gives a feeling of importance and prestige. We have seen that success is a fundamental need of all children; a lack of it may lead to a lack of motivation in all aspects of life. The very nature of physical skills offers possibilities for success for most handicapped children and the problems of motivation become less acute. Typical of this type of success, reported by Cooper (1967), is the improved communication of autistic children through loosely organized physical activity on the trampoline and the trampette.

Considerably more experimental work seems to have been carried out in relation to the effects of physical activity on the social and emotional characteristics of handicapped children than on their intellectual development. Most of these studies indicate quite clearly that physical activity, whether it be in the form of structured programmes or as spontaneous play, has a very important contribution to make towards the emotional and social growth of the handicapped.

Conclusion

Physical activity has its own unique contribution to make to the physical, mental, emotional and social growth of children. If this contribution is important for normal children it is even more important for the handicapped. Since learning is acquired through the senses it is plain that if one sense is lacking it becomes imperative for the remainder to be used effectively. Often the very nature of the handicap prevents children from taking part in those spontaneous plays and activities that contribute to physical development, and the low levels of fitness that are then found amongst them prevent many of them from taking part in the physical situations from which so many of the desirable goals of an educational nature stem.

Systematic physical activity, therefore, is essential for handicapped children. Whether this is in the form of spontaneous free play, organized play therapy or highly structured physical education lessons is of no moment providing the activity suits the needs, interests and aptitudes of the children. In any case, much of what we call physical education consists of play and play-like activities. It would seem that unless we are prepared to offer opportunities for the handicapped to profit from physical activity their handicap may be much greater than their specific disability.

Bibliography

Bailey, I., and Cromwell, R. L. (1965), 'Failure as Motivation with Mentally Retarded Children', *Amer. J. Mental Deficiency*, 69: 680–4.

Barker, R. G., Wright, B. A., and Gonick, M. R. (1946), *Adjustment to Physical Handicap and Illness. A Survey of the Social Psychology of Physique and Disease*, Bulletin 55, New York, Social Science Research Council.

Benoit, E. P. (1955), 'The Play Problem of Retarded Children, *Amer. J. Mental Deficiency*, 60: 41–55.

(1957), 'Relevance of Hebb's Theory of the Organisation of Behaviour to Educational Research on the Mentally Retarded', *Amer. J. Mental Deficiency*, 61: 497–507.

Physical activity and the psychological development of the handicapped

Brown, A. (1968), 'Physical Education for Cerebral Palsied Children', *Phys. Educ.*, 60: 179, 16–20.

Buell, C. (1950), 'Motor Performance of Visually Handicapped Children', *Exceptional Children*, 17: 69–72.

Buhler, C. (1960), *From Birth to Maturity. An Outline of the Psychological Development of the Child*, Routledge & Kegan Paul, London.

Capobianco, R. J., and Cole, D. A. (1960), 'Social Behaviour of Mentally Retarded Children', *Amer. J. Mental Deficiency*, 64: 638–51.

Clunk, J. F. (1950), 'Adequacy of Secondary Schools in the Preparation of Blind Youngsters for Adult Life, *New Outlook for the Blind*, 44: 245–50.

Cohen, J. (1966), 'Development of a Blind Spastic Child. A Case Study', *Exceptional Children*, 32: 291–4.

Cooper, D. F. (1967), personal communication, St Mary's College, Strawberry Hill, Twickenham, Middlesex.

Corder, W. O. (1966), 'Effects of Physical Education on the Intellectual, Physical and Social Development of Educable Mentally Retarded Boys', *Exceptional Children*, 32: 357–64.

Corlett, G. (1967), 'Physical Performance of Blind Boys. A Pilot Study', unpublished dissertation for the Diploma in Education, University of Birmingham.

Cratty, B. J. (1969), *Perceptual-Motor Behaviour and Educational Processes*, Thomas, Springfield, Illinois.

Cromwell, R. L. (1961), 'Selected Aspects of Personality Development in Mentally Retarded Children', *Exceptional Children*, 28: 44–51.

Cruickshank, W. M. (1956), 'Psychological Considerations with Crippled Children', in Cruickshank, W. M. (ed.), *Psychology of Exceptional Children and Youth*, 284–344, Staples, London.

Davis, C. J. (1964), 'Development of the Self Concept', *New Outlook for the Blind*, 58: 49–51.

Dewey, G. F. (1956), 'Social Status of Physically Handicapped Children', *Exceptional Children*, 23: 104–7 and 132–3.

Donofrio, A. F. (1951), 'A Study of Crippled Children in an Orthopedic Hospital School', *Exceptional Children*, 18: 33–8.

Elser, R. P. (1959), 'The Social Position of Hearing Handicapped Children in the Regular Grades', *Exceptional Children*, 25: 305–9.

Fait, H. F. and Kupferer, H. J. (1956), 'A Study of Two Motor Achievement Tests and its Implication in Planning Physical Education Activities for the Mentally Retarded', *Amer. J. Mental Deficiency*, 60: 729–32.

Force, D. G., Jr (1954), 'A Comparison of Physically Handicapped Children and Normal Children in the Same Elementary School Classes with Reference to Social Status and Self-perceived Status". Unpublished doctor's thesis reported in Garrison, K. C., and Force, D. G., Jr (1965), *The Psychology of Exceptional Children*, Ronald Press.

Forgus, R. H. (1966), *Perception*, McGraw-Hill.

Frances, R. J., and Rarick, G. L. (1960), *Motor Characteristics of the Mentally Retarded*, U.S. Dept of Health, Education and Welfare, Cooperative Research Monograph, No. 1.

205

James N. Oliver

Furst, R. T. (1966), 'An Approach to Multiply Handicapped Blind Persons through Physical Recreation', *New Outlook for the Blind*, 60: 218–21.

Gardner, W. I. (1966), 'The Effects of Failure on Intellectually Retarded and Normal Boys', *Amer. J. Mental Deficiency*, 70: 899–902.

Garrison, K. C., and Force, D. G., Jr (1965), *The Psychology of Exceptional Children*, Ronald Press.

Gesell, A. (1940), *The First Five Years of Life*, Harper Bros, London.

Giles, A. M. (1969), 'A Training Programme for the Development of Laterality, Directionality and Body Image—an Experimental Study', unpublished dissertation for the Diploma of Special Education, University of Birmingham.

Glass, R. (1959), 'Report on an Integrated Day Camp Program', *New Outlook for the Blind*, 53: 55–7.

Gomulicki, B. R. (1961), *The Development of Perception and Learning in Blind Children*, Psychology Laboratory, Cambridge University.

Groves, L. (1967), 'Music, Movement and Mime', *Spec. Educ.*, 56: 9–11.

Guttman, L. (1969), 'Sports for Disabled as a World Problem', *Rehabilitation*, 68: 29–43.

Hebb, D. O. (1949), *The Organisation of Behaviour*, Wiley, New York.

Hollis, J. H. (1965), 'The Effect of Social and Non-social Stimuli on the Behaviour of Profoundly Retarded Children', *Amer. J. Mental Deficiency*, 69: Pt I, 755–71, Pt II, 772–89.

Ireland, R. R. (1958), 'Recreation's Role in Rehabilitating Blind People', *New Outlook for the Blind*, 52: 134–8.

Jackson, C. L. (1957), 'Recreation and the Blind Child', *New Outlook for the Blind*, 51: 402–6.

Jakeman, D. (1968), 'Using a Frostig Programme', *Spec. Educ.*, 57: 25–8.

Johnson, G. O. (1950), 'A Study of the Social Position of Mentally Handicapped Children in the Regular Grades', *Amer. J. Mental Deficiency*, 55: 60–89.

Kelmer Pringle, M. L. (1965), 'The Psychological Needs of Handicapped Children', in Loring, James (ed.), *Teaching the Cerebral Palsied Child*, Proceedings of a study group at Grey College, Durham.

Kephart, N. C. (1960), *The Slow Learner in the Classroom*, Merrill.

Kirk, S. A. (1938), 'Behaviour Problem Tendencies in Deaf and Hard of Hearing Children', *Amer. Annals of the Deaf*, 83: 131–7.

Kirkland, J. A. (1962), 'Integrated Group Work and Recreation', *New Outlook for the Blind*, 56: 166–8.

Lapp, E. R. (1957), 'A Study of the Social Adjustment of Slow Learning Children who were assigned Part Time to Regular Classes', *Amer. J. Mental Deficiency*, 62: 254–62.

Leland, H., Walker, J., and Taboada, A. N. (1959), 'Group Play Therapy with a Group of Post Nursery Male Retardates', *Amer. J. Mental Deficiency*, 63: 848–51.

Lowe, B. J. (1966), 'The Effects of Physical Conditioning on the Cognitive Functioning of Educationally Sub-normal boys', unpublished dissertation, Department of Psychology, University of Birmingham.

Maisner, E. A. (1950), 'Contribution of Play Therapy Techniques to Total Rehabilitative Design in an Institution for High Grade Mentally Deficient and Borderline Children', *Amer. J. Mental Deficiency*, 55: 235–50.

Mangus, A. R. (1950), 'Effect of Mental and Educational Retardation on Personality Development of Children', *Amer. J. Mental Deficiency*, 55: 208–12.

Oliver, J. N. (1957), 'Motivation of Educationally Sub-normal Boys through Physical Activities', *Slow Learning Child*, 4: 1, 27–35.

(1958), 'The Effects of Physical Conditioning Exercises and Activities on the Mental Characteristics of Educationally Sub-normal Boys', *Brit. J. Educ. Psych.*, 28: 155–65.

(1960), 'The Effects of Physical Conditioning on the Sociometric Status of Educationally Sub-normal Boys', *Phys. Educ.*, 52: 156, 38–46.

(1968), 'Recreation for the Severely Mentally Handicapped', in *Expanding Concepts in Mental Retardation*, Proceedings of Third Scientific Symposium of the Joseph P. Kennedy, Jr Foundation, Boston.

and Keogh, J. F. (1967), 'Helping the Physically Awkward', *Spec. Educ.*, 56: 1, 22–5.

Painter, G. (1966), 'The Effect of a Rhythmic and Sensory Motor Activity Program on Perceptual Motor Spatial Abilities of Kindergarten Children', *Exceptional Children*, 33: 113–16.

Pearson, K. (1965), 'Taking a New Look at Physical Education', *New Outlook for the Blind*, 59: 315–17.

Piaget, J. (1950), *The Psychology of Intelligence*, Routledge & Kegan Paul, London.

Pietrowics, B. (1956), 'Psychologie des Entwicklungsgeheimnis Kindes und Methoden seiner Erziehung', *Prax. Kinderpsychol. Kinderpsychiat.*, No. 5, 55–7.

Rarick, G. L., and Broadhead, G. D. (1968), *The Effects of Individualized versus Group Oriented Physical Education Programs on Selected Parameters of the Development of Educable Mentally Retarded, and Minimally Brain Injured Children*, Department of Physical Education, University of Wisconsin, Madison. U.S. Office of Education, Department of Health, Education and Welfare (Contract OEG-0-8-071097-1760) and the Joseph P. Kennedy, Jr Foundation.

Rawls, H. D. (1957), 'Social Factors in Disability', *New Outlook for the Blind*, 51: 6, 231–6.

Richardson, S. A., Hastorf, A. H., and Dornbusch, S. M. (1964), 'Effects of Physical Disability on a Child's Description of Himself', *Child Dev.*, 35: 893–907.

Ringness, T. A. (1960), 'Self Concept of Children of Low, Average and High Intelligence', *Amer. J. Mental Deficiency*, 65: 453–61.

Rothschild, J. (1966), 'Play Therapy with Blind Children', *New Outlook for the Blind*, 54: 329–33.

Salvin, S. T. (1958), 'Programs for Severely Mentally Retarded Pupils', *Amer. J. Mental Deficiency*, 63: 274–81.

James N. Oliver

Sherrington, C. (1951), *Man on his Nature*, Cambridge University Press.
Siegel, I. M. (1966), 'Selected Athletics in a Posture Training Program for the Blind', *New Outlook for the Blind*, 60: 248–9.
Solomon, A. H., and Pangle, R. (1967), 'The Effects of a Structured Physical Education Program on Physical, Intellectual, and Self-concept Development of Educable Retarded Boys', *Behav. Sci. Monogr.* No. 4, George Peabody College, Nashville, Tennessee.
Strang, R. (1962), *An Introduction to Child Study*, Macmillan, New York.
Telford, C. W., and Sawrey, J. M. (1967), *The Exceptional Individual*, Prentice-Hall.
Tither, A. (1965), 'An Experiment in Physical Education', in Loring, James (ed.), *Teaching the Cerebral Palsied Child*, Proceedings of a study group at Grey College, Durham.
Tofte, D. F. (1950), 'Initiating and Developing a Recreational Program for Institutional Mental Defectives', *Amer. J. Mental Deficiency*, 55: 341–4.
Walker, G. H. (1950), 'Social and Emotional Problems of the Mentally Retarded Child', *Amer. J. Mental Deficiency*, 55: 132–8.
Weiner, B. B. (1954), 'A Report on the Final Academic Achievement of 37 Mentally Handicapped Boys who had been enrolled in a Prolonged Pre-academic Program, *Amer. J. Mental Deficiency*, 59: 210–19.
Wright, B. L. (1967), 'An Experimental Approach to the Effects of Experience in Early Human Behaviour, in Hill, J. P. (ed.), *Minnesota Symposia on Child Psychology*, Vol. 1, pp. 201–26, University of Minnesota Press.

8

Motivation and psychometric approach in coaching

Bruce C Ogilvie and Thomas Tutko

The direction and content of this chapter is much more than an appeal for the refinement of the skilled use of psychological testing in the area of athletic competition. Therefore, it seems appropriate to present once again the introduction of the paper which was published in 1964 (Ogilvie). This paper was a statement of our goals and philosophy prior to our extensive research efforts which since 1963 have broadened to include all major sports.

> The role of psychology as a contributor to track and field has received but passing interest by behavioral scientists during the past quarter of a century. There is little disagreement among coaches that the more successful coach is the one who is versed in the application of psychological insights about his team members. Where there is considerable disagreement is in the concern about what is valid in terms of coaching insight. Or, 'When is a coach actually observing a true picture of his athlete and using it as a basis for intelligent teaching and coaching?' In our studies of athletic motivation one of the most fascinating findings deals with the biases in selection of team members. It seems that for various sports there are coaches who select their teams for reasons that are entirely unknown to them consciously. For these dedicated men have systematically looked for traits or characteristics which to them are habitually associated with what should be success in track and field. There is no question that most coaches are quite reliable in identifying the physical components that contribute to athletic success, but when it

comes to psychological components we find that intuitions are often considerably limited.

This would be an area in which the psychologist could make an invaluable contribution. Although he is totally unable to evaluate physical potential, it is possible for him to determine what are the motivational factors for each athlete. In our investigation of psychological motivation of basketball and football as well as track athletes, we have found a number of common factors that are consistent for most athletes. We are also able to state that although there are common motives no two athletes are actually alike. Each is remarkably different from every other. This means that those coaches who continue to see and handle their team members as if they were all quite similar will never motivate more than a small number according to the athletes' individual needs. The rest will have to struggle along as best they can, using whatever the coach offers that accidentally meets their needs.

During the past six years our data have increased from hundreds of subjects to many thousands and have contributed to increased confidence in the foregoing statements. The mass of data collected for males and the limited data for female competitors at every level of competition have led to a reinforcement of the general statement which is best stated as follows: 'Each athlete, though he or she share some common traits, does remain psychologically unique and must be understood more in terms of this uniqueness than in terms of common traits.'

The psychometric approach in the area of athletic motivation

It is not the purpose of this chapter to present a critical review of the uses and abuses of psychological inventories. A bibliography has been included for those who might wish a more extended background in the use of tests and measurements in psychology. Research finding based upon the use of psychological instruments that have been utilized most consistently since 1960 makes it imperative that certain warnings be communicated to those physical educators or behavioral scientists who wish to experiment with this approach (Ogilvie, 1965; Ogilvie and Johnsgard, 1967). Psychological trait measurement has a broad basis and a long history in the United States. It is estimated that 50 per cent of the large companies invest in testing programs. The primary goal of testing has been an emphasis on screening or selection of employees. Extensive research has led to increased doubt about the potential value of personality measurement in terms of its relationship to actual job performance. This does not preclude the possibility that trait measurement could provide psychological insights about individual differences which can sharpen or objectify perception of coaches. In order that psychological instruments take on an increased reliability, we have found it necessary to take into consideration all of the following facts. There is a need to remain constantly vigilant as to the possibility of norm differences which are used to relate the individual scores to some general population. In particular, the most appropriate educational, socio-economic, and in some cases even area norms, must be used as a basis for trait identification. Recently published studies have indicated that sports' specific psychological patterns have received considerable empirical support and must therefore receive studied consideration. We have found very significant differences between university and state college athletes within the state of California. In those institutions where the selection procedure varies or the criteria for acceptance differs, such as when the subjects have been exposed to more restrictive admission requirements, there have also been highly predictive trait differences. Few investigators have been able to control for the socio-economic factors as they may have contributed to the observed difference in the athletic samples. It must be assumed that when subjects are selected on the basis of athletic qualification, trait homogeneity will increase for certain specific traits under examination. Some of these observed differences are consistent with social class and personality trait reinforcement. In order to document the need for caution, four of these differences are worth reviewing at this time. University athletes were found to be significantly higher in their need for achievement and autonomy, but were significantly lower in self-abasement and deference than were state college athletes. These findings would be consistent with the expectancies if one were to compare upper-middle class/lower-upper class individuals with another sample which was a combination of lower-middle class/upper-lower class subjects. The state college athletes appear to receive much greater social reward for the development of traits associated with self-abasement and deferentialness, while the university athletes seem to receive more positive reinforcement for achievement and independence. The investigation of the personality structure of Air Force cadets greatly reinforces the reliability of the foregoing statement. These findings seem perfectly consistent with the expectancies when upper class individuals are compared with lower-middle class/upper-lower class subjects (Ogilvie and Tutko, 1965). At this particular point in our knowledge sports specificity in terms of personality structure seems highly probable. Careful investigations must be conducted across sports while controlling at the same time for the level of participation. An excellent opportunity for this important research would be to study the entire Olympic team, which provides the only opportunity for a legitimate control of ability. Unfortunately, our attempts to elicit support from the Olympic authorities has been met with a dismal failure. We have found that profile differences exist between basketball and American football athletes who are competing at the same intercollegiate level. It was found that basketball players measures significantly higher in both aggression and self-abasement. These findings remain consistent even when we are able to control for the level of academic selection. These two differences are presented simply as a reminder that caution is demanded when any individual is compared with his normative group. The growing empirical evidence that individual and team sports personality will differ significantly adds another distracting variable that must receive critical consideration when one uses psychological measurement in order to objectify perception with regard to individual differences among athletes.

Critical application of psychometric approach

The area of our work which has received the most critical responses has been the use of the psychometrics approach as a valid measure or predictor of athletic behavior. Our typical defense when challenged on these grounds has been our insistence that we have not made dogmatic statements nor attempted to affirm personality characteristics in some absolute form. The emphasis upon trait measurement has always been directed toward the enhancement of coaching perception. We have been strongly antagonistic toward labeling behavior. We can never emphasize too often that our basic goal has been that of expanding the perception of teachers and coaches in relation to the individuals under their charge. One of the important reasons that our work has received such general support from the participators themselves is that they have come to recognize that this information would only be used in order to increase their potential as human beings. It has been our experience that this philosophy has been violated by extremely few individuals with whom we have consulted during the past twelve years. As with every other sensitive form of human interaction, you will find a small minority of individuals who are ill-equipped by personality to handle psychological insights in a sensitive and constructive manner. An example of such behavior would be that of the coach who, during a moment of anguish or frustration in relation to an individual's performance, chooses to use one single aspect of his psychological profile as a punitive weapon. Take, for instance, the coach who has been informed that his young athlete is sensitive and inclined toward being tender-minded. The coach, in his moment of frustration, might say, 'Those psychologists told me that you didn't have any guts and that you couldn't take it when the goin' gets rough. We knew that about you all along.' This is not only an example of the worst form of coaching, but it also represents totally unethical professional behavior. Not only does the athlete come to distrust those of us who seek to be of service to him, but what is the young man to think when he finds he has been violated and betrayed by information which he has volunteered out of trust and faith in professional people? There can be no justification for such behavior, as I have related. There should be no room in physical education nor the teaching profession for individuals with so little integrity and self-control.

An important responsibility of those professional people who seek to use the psychometric approach toward understanding athletes must be their responsibility to educate those physical educators who seek to include this technique within their total coaching repertoire. We have found during the past three or four years that presentations at coaching clinics and the offering of special courses in the psychology of coaching have established a growing need based on an increased awareness as to the potential value of this approach in the area of coaching. We have come a long way since our first introduction at the N.C.A.A. National Coaches Clinic held at the University of California. At this national meeting upon the announcement of our names and the topics to be covered we experienced a mass exodus of the 200 or so coaches who were in attendance. The audience was eventually reduced to approximately 19 to 20 individuals. You can imagine our chagrin after hours of preparation to experience this form of rejection from the mass of leading coaches in the track and field area. We were to find early during our first attempts to make a contribution to the coaching profession that our offering was treated as an intrusion into an area in which we had no valid right. We are most grateful to coaches of the calibre of Payton Jordon at Stanford and Bud Winter at San Jose State who were able to open the door to serious study and permit the gathering of data which was to become the basis for much that we have been able to learn about the motivation, personality and character make-up of young men who seek to compete in intercollegiate athletics. Since that gray day in Berkeley, we have consulted with the staffs of many professional teams and have been consultants to over 100 colleges and high school coaches. These consultation experiences have been the basis for much more effective communication and led to the refinement of our clinical skills in terms of understanding athletic motivation.

We have extended our knowledge by attempting to use the psychological profile of the team as well as that of the individual in order to provide a basis for more critical thinking in relation to team performance. This has become an exciting innovation and offers promise for further research into the understanding of team as well as individual motivation. The use of team profile for the determination of handling or coaching techniques appears at this moment in the development of our knowledge of team dynamics to be more suited to the so-called team sports, such as basketball, football and water polo, as compared with the traditional individual sports, such as swimming and track and field. This is not to imply that team profile analysis does not have applicability, but the basis for our present insights has developed mainly from our consultation in the so-called team sports.

In our attempt to establish a battery of tests which would identify the specific traits that have the greatest relevance in terms of athletic competition, we have attempted to standardize a wide range of representative tests using mainly paper and pencil tests which can be administered in group situations. The psychological instruments that have been included in our investigations over the past years have included the following instruments: (1) the Minnesota Multiphasic Inventory (Hathaway, 1951), (2) the Rotter Sentence Completion Test (Rotter, 1957), (3) the Edwards Personal Preference Inventory (Edwards, 1954), (4) Jackson Research Inventory (Jackson, 1965), (5) Cattell 16 P.F. (Cattell, 1957), (6) Family Constellation Scale, (7) a semantic differential scale designed specifically for athletics, and (8) we have also used the Cattell C.P.Q. and H.S.P.Q. for our investigation of youth athletic programs. It will be a number of years before sufficient studies have been published in the literature to allow for a more critical selection of the most significant traits of personality as they contribute to athletic success. An extensive review

214

of the literature led us to the same conclusion as that of Warren Johnson in his chapter dealing with the psychology of sport that was that there were less than twenty studies that would provide the basis for deeper insight into the motivational characteristics of successful high-level competitors. The data that we have collected over the past six years does not permit a highly reliable predictive statement to be made about the hierarchical form that human motives might take in the personality of successful athletes. We are at least provided with much more intelligent speculations about the form that they might eventually be shown to take. Which of the personality traits takes precedence over the other seems to be an extremely important question and certainly is asked at every coaching clinic in which we have ever participated. We are continually being asked, 'What is the most important quality in the personality make-up of one who becomes a champion?' Is it coachability? Is it this capacity to remain open to instruction and yet retain one's own critical powers? Is it this ability to allow for the integration of the new, the different, the innovative that contributes to exceptional development and performance? Is it the ability to be free to express aggression appropriate to the sport without the burden of conscious or unconscious guilt? Is it the magical quality of self-confidence—this general positive orientation toward one's self and the ability to see one's self in a positive light? What about the ability to endure pressure, to remain calm under all circumstances, not getting easily upset by the unexpected—the remarkable quality of adaptability to stress? Certainly we must include the personality trait emotional stability which determines an individual's capacity to handle feelings in a mature and adult manner and not retreat to childish or immature solutions for immediate conflicts. How about ambition, desire for success, need to be on top, a personality dimension that is found so generally to be highly developed in those individuals who succeed in any area of life? These are people who say about themselves that they must be winners, they must be front runners. Will this general trait of ambition be found to be the most significant in relation to athletic performance? The list of primary motives must include psychological endurance, which is the ability to stay with things, the ability to repeatedly return to an unfinished task, the old-fashioned form of 'stickability'. Where are we to put this in our hierarchical list? How important is the internalization of guilt accompanied by a deep sense of personal responsibility for one's behavior? Included in this trait would be the willingness to accept blame, see one's own errors and to feel a deep sense of responsibility to the team and the coach. Where does tough-mindedness lie along this continuum, this trait which includes the ability to bounce back after failure, to see reality clearly and not have the need to cloud mistakes over with personal idiosyncratic preoccupations? Certainly to face life or competition realistically must be an important contribution to future success. A review of the literature published through the year 1967 (Ogilvie and Johnsgard) established that for the investigations based upon English-speaking subjects eight personality traits did emerge as being most consistent of high-level competitors. One of these traits, extroversion, because of its extremely stable nature, would have limited relevance in terms of the problem of psychological handling. To understand that the athlete is outgoing, warm-hearted and enjoys participating with other individuals is an interesting bit of information but does not have as much to contribute to our dealing with problem athletes as would certain other of these traits. We have found that test information as to the degree of introversion has provided numerous coaches with sensitivity about individual differences and has greatly improved communication. This has been true particularly when the coach has felt threatened by the degree of reserve and coolness exhibited by certain specific athletes. When the coach could understand that this person is distant by nature and not being defensive and shutting him out as a communicator or teacher, we have found a very significant improvement in the communication setting. It is very easy for the teacher to feel that the reserved person is acting 'stand-offish' or rebellious or even acting disinterested in what the coach is attempting to communicate. We have observed remarkable shifts in relationships once this information has been shared. The other seven most general traits exhibited in the personality of these competitors were emotional stability, a basic trusting nature, highly developed conscience, capacity to trust others, high-self-control, tough mindedness and low levels of resting anxiety. It was not possible to order these in any hierarchical form. Whether tough-mindedness contributes more than emotional stability, or a basic trusting nature contributes more than low levels of resting anxiety remains to be answered by future research. Even to expect that one might find all eight of these plus the other ten traits in the personality of any one given successful athlete is highly problematic. We do consistently find a select number of athletes from every sport who possess every one of these traits to a very high degree. This number has never been calculated accurately, but we can assure you that the number is extremely small. The few studies that we have completed dealing with the personality structure of men in the coaching profession strongly supports the notion that these traits do in fact make an important contribution to athletic participation.

These complex human motives are often unconscious—that is, repressed from conscious awareness. Yet, these driving forces must be identified and investigated in the hope that they can be used as constructive forces in the training and conditioning of our young people who show athletic potential. Much of our research has been seriously limited by one important contaminating feature—and that has been out inability to develop athletic behaviour rating scales that can be used as reliable measures of performance. In five separate studies using our player rating inventory we have found that the unreliability of coaches' ratings has made it impossible to relate our psychological data to performance or athletic behavior. We have found that independent coaches' ratings of the same individual will be highly reliable in terms of the best five to ten players on any particular team or the lowest six to seven players on any individual team. The player rating judgments for the middle 80 per cent of competitors is so unreliable that no meaningful correlations are permissible. This is an area of investigation that holds much fascination but commitment to on-going research and consultation has been a limiting factor. The foregoing criticism holds true for all levels of competition from the highest-level professional right on through high school team participants. Until such time as it is possible to relate psychological traits to level of performance, it seems unwise that any generalization as to the hierarchical ordering or personality traits as they contribute to athletic performance be seriously considered.

When is trait difference meaningful?

The following examples of individual differences are presented as a reminder that caution is demanded when any individual is found to differ from test norms. The most restrictive requirement is that psychological information has validity only when the trait difference reaches the 5 per cent level of significance. This would imply that no difference could be considered as real until this difference reached that portion of the probability curve that it can be equated with statistical significance. Sophisticated psychometricians could not help but fail to appreciate this recommendation as an ideal. Reality forces the practitioner in the testing field into a position of using a far lower degree of confidence. There is a need for extreme caution when one interprets the psychological profile of an individual in terms of deviation from the norm. This can be well documented by the past years of consulting experience. We have been particularly wary of the exaggerated use of any single trait deviation because of the tendency to respond in an exaggerated way and over-generalize with regard to the personality make-up of a given individual. There has been a tendency for a significant number of physical educators with whom we have consulted to overreact to specific high or low traits without due consideration for the total psychological picture. It has been necessary to constantly admonish those who were so inclined by the repeated statement 'Never take a single trait nor a combination of a small number of traits as a basis for handling or teaching.' 'You must study the interaction of the various measure traits as they contribute to the overall personality structure.' The personality gestalt must take precedence over isolated trait variance. An example might be a footballer who measures in the highest 5 per cent of his population for the trait 'exhibitionism'. Would this allow a clinician or coach to make a prediction or to anticipate actual behavior patterns during training or competition? (Note: because our consultation is independent of observation and based only upon the paper and pencil test information, the psychological model for training which we develop must take a broad hypothetical form.) Whether or not exhibitionism will be overtly expressed or remain submerged and masked by other more influential traits of personality must be determined. There will be both suppressor and enhansor traits, a few of which can be highlighted at this time. Compare, in Figure 1, the two following young men, both of whom share a high need for exhibitionism, both at the 5 per cent level with regard to this trait, which means that 95 per cent of the other subjects upon whom this trait was standardized fall below them with regard to this need.

Subject A: exhibitionism—5 per cent; subject B—5 per cent. For conscience development: subject A—in the upper 20 per cent; subject B—in the lower 10 per cent. Impulsiveness: subject A—at the 50th percentile; subject B—in the lower 15 per cent. Order: Subject A—the upper 30 per cent; subject B—in the lower 40 per cent. Introversion: subject A—upper 10 per cent; subject B—lower 10 per cent. Self-control: subject A—in the upper 30 per cent; subject B—in the lower 30 per cent. As we increase the trait evidence for these two young men, the more complex will become the handling model that will evolve from a serious study of their psychological profiles. The recommendations during a consulting session with the coach of either or both of these young men will be remarkably different. Just utilizing six traits out of the typical 60, which we have included in our consulting, greatly reduces the probability of exaggerated dependency upon isolated personality trends. These two young athletes, as described above, can be expected to respond quite differently to their need for the spotlight and acclaim. The coach or trainer of athlete A will probably be critical of the test instrument because it might be so much at variance with his own personal perception of the young man's behavior. Athlete B, by his very nature, can be expected to telegraph his personal needs by his overt behavior. These two young college men happen to be swimmers who had outstanding records but required remarkably different attention from their coach, George

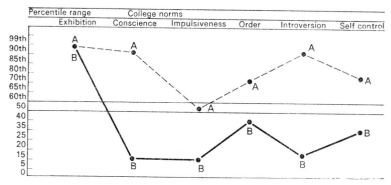

Figure 1 Profiles of two athletes.

Haines of the Santa Clara Swim Club. The coaching model that would provide the most effective environment for the teacher-learner relationship must be based upon hypothetical differences in terms of each athlete's expected behavior during training. It is essential that an important qualification be reinforced before further comment or speculation is offered with regard to these two cases. We must insist that actual practice behavior have higher validity in terms of personal observation and must always take precedence over psychometric interpretations. How the human being actually relates to his coach, sport and team-mates must be taken at face value independent of the psychological profile of this athlete. Psychological test information should be referred to when there seems to be no obvious explanation for failure or non-achievement of either the goals of the athlete or the coach.

Bruce C. Ogilvie and Thomas Tutko

The exposed differences between these two young men in terms of personality measurement may seem almost too extreme to be examples of the personality structure of former national-level competitors. Based upon the data collected on the highly successful swimmers that represented the United States in the 1964 Olympic Games, athlete B varies considerably from this criterion group in a number of important ways. Independent of these differences, athlete B is willing to meet the requirements of the rigid training schedule that coach Haines has programmed for his national level competitors. This young man must meet a 2-hour training session morning and evening during the pre-season portion of the year and three-a-day training schedules immediately prior to national competition. In the light of this information, the important consideration would now become, 'How does one develop an explanatory model that can be used to provide an environment that will offer him the highest probability that his swimming skill will be enhanced?' Whatever the complex interaction of motives within this young man, one aspect of his behavior should receive primary consideration. And that, of course, was his willingness to spend from 4 to 6 hours a day perfecting his skill. This type of commitment demands our respect as teachers and should call forth the best of our talent and lead us to offer him every chance for success, based upon his own personal needs. Subject A, with the highly developed conscience and a deep commitment to ethical standards, would suggest that he makes a much more ready adjustment to the requirements of others. He is not particularly impulsive, exhibits the capacity for orderliness, organization and thoughtful planning ahead. He is basically introverted by nature, which suggests that he is on the shy, reserved side and would prefer probably training alone rather than with large numbers of others. He has very good self-control, which suggests that he would have his emotions during stress well within his own personal limits. Knowing only these six traits in relation to the personality development of subject B, we would expect that rules and regulations are very difficult for him and that he acts on impulse rather than on forethought. He's not too badly organized, but his self-control appears to be one of the important problems for him. These traits in a young man who is obviously an outgoing, extroverted young man, suggest very strongly that these differences will be projected outward and there will be many manifestations in his overt behaviour of these particular trends in his personality. It is quite evident, even from just this amount of information, that these two young men will respond

220

to different styles of coaching. In a very real sense, each young athlete brings his own particular internal environment to the training session. It seems highly probable that the exhibitionistic needs of the shy, withdrawn, introverted young man will remain covert, but we must be reminded that the potentiality for motivated behavior in terms of this exhibitionistic need will be manifest in some form in the behavior of even the shy athlete. It may be the quiet joy that he receives from applause or acclaim, although his posture and manner might not telegraph that satisfaction is being derived from such forms of recognition or acclaim.

A legitimate question that might be posed in relation to the foregoing two examples would be 'Does this information have any real utility in terms of changing athletic behavior?' The most difficult aspect of our work has been to provide the sort of documentary support that would justify this approach. In most cases, our use of this information in order to develop a program for handling has been in a setting where privileged communication has been a guarantee. There have been a few cases where we have sought a formal release in order to present the information as a training aid, such as the publication that our Olympic hammer thrower in Tokyo, Burk, permitted some four years ago. The great professional athletes and national or Olympic stars have never been approached with respect to seeking release for publication of selected information from their psychological profiles. One means of substantiating that trait identification does have utility not only for the coach but for the individuals involved would be our attempts to be of service to individual athletes. During the past four years we have reviewed the personality data with some 600-plus professional athletes. Our aim was to establish the degree of validity in terms of the individual's personal perception of his personality as compared with the measured personality as described by the pencil and paper tests. We have shared the entire psychological profile, defining and describing each trait in terms of the manual and in terms of expected behavior in order to gain some degree of the consistency between subjective evaluation of personality and measured personality. The most characteristic response on the part of professional athletes when one describes an aspect of personality that is inconsistent with that of other athletes participating at the same level and in the same sport has been, 'What can I do to develop that trait in my personality, or, is there some way that I can eradicate the negative influence of this trait in my personality?' There seems to be a universal need to apply

221

the information gained for modification or restructuring of personality along the lines that are most consistent with future success. As our data has continually borne out, athletes in general are non-defensive personalities and seem to be more open and more accepting with regard to the critical aspects of their personality. We have attempted follow-up interviews in order to determine the extent to which this information could be used in order to modify potential negative aspects of personality. The feedback has been extremely positive, particularly from the professional race driving fraternity. We have no way of determining the degree to which the affirmative response has been a function of 'the halo effect'. This is an area of investigation that has the potential to make the most important contribution but will require extremely innovative research design.

The use of psychological profile for individual case study

Reference to individual profile or team profile is always based upon the required need as expressed by the coach. During the initial review of test data, the coach typically takes long-hand notes with regard to specific aspects of the personality of each individual athlete. Each coach responds in a selective manner, depending upon his own personality and experience or insight into the personality of each of his athletes. Special attention is always given to those personality traits that deviate consistently from the overall profile of the team under investigation. The frame of reference that the individual coach brings to bear during any single consultation will be found to differ from coach to coach and also vary, depending upon the particular mood of the coach with whom we are consulting at that moment in time. As consultants, we have typically three unique frames of reference: (1) the norms for the sport under investigation; (2) the individual profile, which is a statement that the athlete has made about himself; and (3) knowledge of the personality structure of the coach with whom we are attempting to communicate. In those few cases where we do not have test data as to the personality structure of the coach, we typically utilize as a point of reference the norms from our studies of approximately 300 coaches. There is no question that we would greatly increase the validity of our interpretation if we were able to relate the individual athlete's personality to that of the man responsible for teaching him. The three studies we have completed to date on the personality profiles of coaches at high school, college and professional level are so similar that it becomes difficult not to stereotype men in this profession.

Independent of the trait uniqueness of the individual coach, and caution with regard to norms, it is possible to subsume all statements of inquiry under a single definition. The single most important goal will be to improve or re-establish effective communication between teacher and student. For example, the following statements of inquiry on the part of the coach all reflect this goal. Imagine yourself attempting to relate the following questions to the individual profile of one of your athletes. (1): 'I have found it very difficult to encourage this athlete to eliminate old habits and adjust to new techniques. What is it about his personality that makes him so resistent to change?' (2) 'I find it almost impossible to communicate with this athlete. He seems to shut off all of my attempts to relate my knowledge and experience to him.' (3) 'What is it about this athlete that makes him so passive in the face of failure? He seems never to get excited or never to get upset and never seems to be able to be critical of his own performance.' (4) 'Why does this athlete continually seem to lack motivation and find it difficult to get to practice on time, even missing certain important practice sessions?' (5) 'I don't understand this athlete. His personal appearance is at variance with my requirements as a member of my team—his hair, his dress, his beard, his mustache. Why won't he conform—why can't he conform to the standards of my team?' (6) 'I can't seem to make this athlete ever become angry or ever assert himself to express agression. What is it about him that he should be so lacking in this quality?' (7) 'This very fine athlete could become a champion. He has all the ability, all the tools to work with, but he just doesn't seem to have any desire. What is missing in him? What buttons can I push to get this man to drive himself and express his true potential?' (8) 'I have a great need to find a leader for my team. There don't seem to be any natural leaders. Is there anyone on this team that seems best suited by personality to take over this role?' (9) 'This athlete's performances vary so greatly from practice to practice and meet to meet that I find it very difficult to understand and coach him. He is so disappointing to me because he could be outstanding, but I have found no way to reduce the variability of his performance.' (10) 'I have this athlete who just doesn't seem to want to train with the team. He keeps requesting to train alone, and he would like to come at odd hours and select his own practice times. This would be all right, but it concerns me as far as the rest of the team is concerned. Could it create a problem of team morale if I set different standards for him?' (11) 'I don't understand this team; it exhibits behavior that I have never experienced before from a team. All of my past experience doesn't seem to help me understand what is going on in this team. Could it be something about me that is affecting them this way?' (12) 'I'm interested in learning if I must behave differently when handling minority athletes. I have not had a great deal of experience with minority athletes in the past; I wonder if there isn't something I could learn that would make me more effective with them. I'm not sure that I am communicating with them as well as I might.'

It is evident that the inquiry can take a hundred different forms, but each of these is an attempt to gain insight that will make teaching and learning more effective. When the coach must face his own test profile, the question becomes how does one change negative influence of this trait in my personality? There has been a consistent response in the direction of inquiring about how one changes. There seems to be a universal need to apply the information gained for modification or restructuring of personality along the lines that are most consistent with future coaching success. One of the great advantages of having the complete profile available during a consultation experience is that it can be used to temper interpretation and sometimes reduce an over-reaction on the part of the coach. When he has some way of objectifying his personality in relation to individual team members or the team as a whole, it provides him with a new frame of reference and greatly increases problem-solving possibilities. An examination of the disparity between the statements the coach would make about himself with regard to a particular trait and the statements that a particular athlete might make on the basis of his estimate of his personality structure with regard to the same trait has been an effective way to modify coaching perception. This similarity-disparity examination does provide the opportunity for the coach to begin to re-examine the way he relates to particular individuals. It will also telegraph some of the expectancies in terms of his perception of what constitutes the emotional make-up of a competitor. Examine with us now the actual personality profile of a coach who is described as being one of the most successful college coaches in America. It has been possible with the permission of this coach, Don Coryell, of San Diego College to use certain aspects of his personality in order to provide a model example of the use of psychological data. Describing his personality in terms of percentiles and that of one of his young athletes offers an opportunity for increased insight about the probable learning environment and coaching environment in which the coach and student dialogue will occur.

Comparing athlete and coach on a number of important personality traits we find that coach Coryell falls above the 99 percentile with regard to his achievement needs; his athlete falls slightly below the 40th. Coach in terms of orderliness and organization falls at the 74th percentile; his athlete falls at the 33rd percentile. Coach achieved a score at the 70th percentile in terms of his need for autonomy while his athlete falls at the 80th percentile in terms of his need for autonomy. The coach's need for self-abasement places him at the 20th percentile while his athlete falls at the 90th percentile. The coach's need for endurance places him at the 95th, while the athlete's falls at the 70th percentile. The coach's need for aggression places him at the 85th percentile; the athlete's places him at the 60th. The coach falls in the upper 5 per cent of the population with regard to abstract ability; the athlete falls in the lower 40 per cent. In terms of ego strength, the coach falls in the upper 25 per cent of the population, while the athlete falls in the lower 30 per cent of the population. The coach is at the 75th percentile in terms of conscience development; the athlete falls at the 40th percentile. For the trait of self-confidence, the coach falls at the 65th percentile, while his athlete falls at the 30th percentile. Trait comparisons for these twelve possible differences afford us much evidence that we are comparing two remarkably different human beings in terms of their needs and their motivational characteristics. Using just this much profile information, we can now focus on the three different frames of reference that will allow us to provide a handling program that will maximize coaching insight. It is axiomatic in psychology that needs dictate perception. It has proven to be a valid assumption that in men with personality structures such as coach Coryell's there will be a strong tendency to project trait expectancies on to others that would be more consistent with their own highly developed personalities. Take, for example, the disparity between this young athlete's ambition and that of his team as well as his coach. We have determined from past research that college athletes in general are significantly above the average in terms of need achievement. In this case, we find an athlete who falls in the lowest 10 per cent of the team with regard to this trait. He is 25 percentile points below the team and 65 percentile points below his coach. He is like his coach in that he tends to be independent, naturally aggressive, self-assertive and has the ability to apply himself to things over a sustained period of time. He is playing under a man who

225

is bright and taken an abstract approach to life while he has a very concrete approach, and in a sense, relates to the world in a very direct, non-abstract manner. While his coach is an extremely stable mature person, this young athlete has considerable distance to grow emotionally. He seems to have a very serious problem with rules and regulations while playing under a man who has a very highly developed sense of right and wrong. This athlete is a tender-minded person who will probably overrespond to failure; possibly, he may even become self-punishing while relating to a coach who is average with regard to this trait.

When coach Coryell stated this young man's problem in terms of practice behavior, it became evident that we were dealing with a problem athlete who is extremely complex and who would require extremely sensitive handling if he were to continue as a participant in intercollegiate athletics. He was described as being moody and inclined to become depressed. There was much evidence that he would punish himself severely, even resorting to physical attacks upon his own person at times, when he failed an assignment or missed one of his cues. He was subject to emotional outbursts that approached a hostile rage which would be followed by periods of deep remorse. This highly talented athlete had actually approached coach Coryell and told him that he was going to turn in his uniform and quit the team. He projected an attitude of abject failure in spite of all the evidence that his performance had been exceptional, and in many ways he was the most self-sacrificing man on the team. It would be sheer folly to suggest that the substantial evidence that we have on the personality structure of this young man would enable us to bring about a miraculous modification of his personality. Although this might be a long-range goal, the total focus at this time would be upon using the data to enlighten the coach as to behavioural expectancies associated with the high-level stress of athletic competition. Simply for the coach to be aware of the extent to which this athlete differs from his own characteristic way of responding to stress would be an extremely valuable bit of information. The coach is now prepared for behaviour that might fall out of his range of expectancies, and he can remain constantly in tune with the unique needs that might be expressed by this young man.

As we have seen from our past experience, there have been many examples of abusive treatment of young men who demonstrate similar neurotic trends in their personality. This is particularly in evidence when the athlete is truly gifted. It should not be necessary to continually remind the coaching fraternity that neuromuscular giftedness is simply one aspect of the total personality of any given athlete. The past years of consulting experience have led us to reinforce this reality with constant monotonous regularity at each coaching clinic. The question is continually being raised as to the advisability of sharing psychological information with coaches in general. The questioning takes a number of forms, such as how many coaches, by personality, are able to handle information of this kind in a sensitive and constructive manner. The question takes this form, 'Are coaches trained in the area of psychology and motivation to a sufficient level of sophistication that would permit them to use psychological information in a reliable way?' An estimated 30 to 40 hours of consulting time was necessary in order to communicate the psychological information for coach Coryell's team of 54 players. The information was shared with his five coaching assistants, each of whom was responsible for one sub-team within the total team. For instance, one coach would be responsible for defensive backfield; another would be responsible for offensive backfield. Each of these coaches was given a studied description of the individuals under his charge as well as some psychological expectancies with respect to his individual sub-group. As would be expected for any group of 50 to 60 individuals, there was evidence that ten to twelve of them would require very special understanding. It was evident once again that the great bulk of the team would not require special attention or special handling. Once the staff became aware of individual differences, they described themselves as feeling more confident about their method of communication with their individual players. The general attitude of the players has been an extremely positive one, most expressing the feeling that the coaches must be very interested in them to expend the money and time for such a sophisticated study of them as an individual. It has been through these consulting experiences that we have been able to reinforce the potential value of restructuring in an important way the training of physical educators. On the basis of our years of study, we strongly recommend that all coaches receive training in both sociology and psychology.

Team profile as a method of communication

The empirical validation for the experimental use of psychological data based on team profile will necessitate some qualifications. The use of team profile as a predictor of team variability will be an extremely difficult technique to validate. The research design necessary for the investigation of team trait differences would require match control teams who would not be offered any consulting help. The competitive necessity of intercollegiate athletics has made coaches reluctant to sacrifice the time required for such a study. The emphasis on winning and its relation to professional survival support this reluctance. The possibility of dividing a league of eight teams into four which receive consulting help and four which do not seems highly unlikely at this time.

This aspect of our work must remain more of an art than a science until experimental validation becomes possible. In way of introducing this experimental technique, it is possible to share our most recent experiment with San Jose State freshman basketball team. This example will be offered simply as an introduction as to the possible worth of this approach.

This example is offered with the permission of head coach Daniel Glines and assistant coach, freshman coach, Stanley Morrison. Just prior to the opening of the training season, coach Morrison subjected his entire freshman team to psychological testing. Upon completion of testing, coach Morrison was presented with his team profile. This presentation occurred early in the practice season immediately after individual profiles had been shared with each individual player. The authors reviewed these data with each team member in a private interview session. During the consulting session with coach Morrison, he was able to report a number of early concerns about this young team without specifying which of these concerns was causing him the most confusion. (1) He reported that practice sessions were almost totally without verbal exchange between the players. There was an absence of kidding or baiting one another or the typical verbal interactions that one usually experiences in team sports. (2) There was a serious lack of cohesiveness. He felt it was much like coaching a group of individuals rather than a team. (3) He reported a serious lack of self-assertiveness and reported that rarely did a player resort to a physical confrontation, even those which would have been well within the regulations that prevail in the sport of basketball. (4) There seems to be a complete lack of leadership potential. At no time did any player individually exhibit spontaneous leadership, even during practice sessions. (5) The general demeanor of the 16 athletes was one of shyness and basically retiring in nature. There were other concerns, but these five will suffice for the example presented here. Limiting outselves to ten traits as an experimental model for exploring team dynamics, the following profile represents the team. The team fell at the 64th percentile for achievement, 70th percentile for deference, 40th percentile for dominance, 75th percentile for abasement, 65th percentile for endurance, 40th percentile for aggression, 40th percentile for self-confidence, 90th percentile guilt proneness, 30th percentile for self-assertion and 65th percentile for order. This much evidence suggested a number of psychological models upon which a theory of observed team behaviour could be developed. The first clinical interpretation focused upon the consistency between coaches' observations and test data. During the consulting session, it was determined that our program of team modification would be made by a concentration upon the team's low tendency towards aggression. The normative data for college and professional basketball indicated that, with respect to this trait, the team was 30 percentage points below the norm. It was decided to await the results of coaching emphasis in this area, but remain constantly aware of the need for change in terms of dominance and self-confidence. The justification for concentration on this aspect of team personality followed from the conclusion that coach Morrison could integrate most effectively drills designed to modify this trait. It was possible to introduce a series of aggression release drills, which had a profound effect upon the total team behaviour. These changes were so dramatic that coach Morrison has agreed to collaborate on an article which will detail the experiment and the observed modification of team behavior during the season.

Summary recommendations

When any given individual subjects himself to the requirements of paper and pencil personality tests, we can only assume that he is presenting the most reliable subjective picture of himself. He will project this subjective image in terms of the way he either affirms or denies the questions included in the inventory. Typically, he is being asked to affirm or deny twenty to thirty statements which have been selected to correlate with a specific trait. Obviously, when an individual affirms a very high or a very low percentage of questions, we have greater security that this individual will differ on this trait. It will always be possible to fake good or bad by developing a particular mental set while taking any psychological test. Those instruments that have reliability scales included in their construction, such as the Minnesota Multiphasic Inventory and the Edwards Personal

Bruce C. Ogilvie and Thomas Tutko

Preference Schedule, have consistently established high reliability for our athletic samples. It is estimated that unreliability of test-taking behavior would approximate only 1 per cent of the total number tested.

Those who seek to experiment with this approach to coaching will have a number of extremely important responsibilities. The team or athlete must have absolute confidence that you are not using his self-exposure for any judgmental purposes. Should it be used as a screening device for excluding participants or to gain evidence which can be used for some selfish manipulative purpose, it will greatly reduce test reliability. Your athletes must have implicit faith in your integrity as well as your statement of purpose for the use of psychological testing. The following recommendations will greatly increase the reliability of the information gained from testing. (1) Offer absolute assurance that the test information will be used only as a means to aid the individual in achieving his athletic goals. (2) Share complete data with each athlete in a private communication setting. (3) Allow athletes to contest certain aspects of their profile which they feel are inconsistent with their true personality. (4) Give the athlete the opportunity to return to the test data for deeper or continued exploration of the meanings of the traits. (5) Whenever possible, provide each athlete with written description of personality areas in which future development may be possible. (6) Should you be a non-defensive person, share openly the ways in which you might differ in personality from your athletes. The extent to which you can honor the six foregoing recommendations will determine the degree to which this approach will contribute meaningfully to your coaching success.

Bibliography

Cattell, R. B. (1957), *Handbook. Sixteen Personality Factors Questionnaire*, Institute for Personality and Ability Testing, Champaigne, Illinois.
Edwards, A. L. (1954), *Edwards Personal Preference Schedule* (Manual), Psychological Corporation, New York.
Hathaway, S. R., and McKinley, J. E. (1951), *Minnesota Multiphasic Personality Inventory* (Manual), Psychological Corporation, New York.
Jackson, D. N. (1965), *Personality Research Form (A-B)*, Research Psychologists Press, Goshen, New York.

Ogilvie, B. C. (1964), 'Future Contribution of Motivational Research in Track and Field', *Track Techniques*, Vol. 13.

(1965), 'Field Application of Psychological Information', *Track Techniques*, Vol. 10.

and Johnsgard, K. W. (1967), *The Personality of the Male Athlete*, paper, American Academy of Physical Education, Las Vegas, Nevada, April.

and Tutko, T. A. (1965), 'Comparison Athletes—Non-Athletes: Air Force Cadets', unpublished study.

Rotter, J. B., and Rafferty, J. E. (1957), *The Rotter Incomplete Sentence Blank*, Psychological Corporation, New York.

Index

The names of authors whose works are mentioned in the bibliographies following each chapter are not indexed.

233